Felicia Dorothea Browne Hemans

The Select Poetical Works

Felicia Dorothea Browne Hemans

The Select Poetical Works

ISBN/EAN: 9783742808424

Manufactured in Europe, USA, Canada, Australia, Japa

Cover: Foto ©Andreas Hilbeck / pixelio.de

Manufactured and distributed by brebook publishing software (www.brebook.com)

Felicia Dorothea Browne Hemans

The Select Poetical Works

COLLECTION
OF
BRITISH AUTHORS.
VOL. 763.

THE SELECT POETICAL WORKS
OF
FELICIA HEMANS.

IN ONE VOLUME.

THE SELECT
POETICAL WORKS

OF

FELICIA HEMANS.

COPYRIGHT EDITION.

LEIPZIG
BERNHARD TAUCHNITZ
1865.

CONTENTS.

	Page
The Forest Sanctuary	1

TALES AND HISTORIC SCENES.

The Last Constantine	67
The Widow of Crescentius	107
Alaric in Italy	131
The Last Banquet of Antony and Cleopatra	139
Heliodorus in the Temple	144
The Maremma	148

RECORDS OF WOMAN.

Arabella Stuart	157
The Switzer's Wife	167
Properzia Rossi	172
Pauline	177
Joana	180
The Grave of a Poetess	184

LAYS OF MANY LANDS.

The Bird's Release	187
The Cavern of the Three Tells; a Swiss Tradition	189
Swiss Song, on the Anniversary of an Ancient Battle	191
The Messenger Bird	193

CONTENTS.

	Page
Cœur de Lion at the Bier of his Father	195
The Wild Huntsman	199
The Shade of Theseus	201
Ancient Greek Song of Exile	203
The Suliote Mother	204
The Farewell to the Dead	206

SONGS OF THE AFFECTIONS.

A Spirit's Return	208
The Coronation of Inez de Castro	217
The Vaudois Wife	220
The Guerilla Leader's Vow	224
Bernardo del Carpio	226
The Dreaming Child	229
The Charmed Picture	231
The Message to the Dead	233
The Deserted House	235
The Stranger's Heart	237
The Fountain of Oblivion	239

SCENES AND HYMNS OF LIFE.

Prayer of the Lonely Student	241
Easter-Day in a Mountain Churchyard	245
A Poet's Dying Hymn	249
Hymn of the Vaudois Mountaineers in Times of Persecution	253
Prayer at Sea after Victory	255

MISCELLANEOUS POEMS.

The Voice of Spring	257
The Treasures of the Deep	260
The Homes of England	261
The Graves of a Household	263

CONTENTS.

	Page
Casabianca	264
The Landing of the Pilgrim Fathers in New England	266
The Child's First Grief	267
The Hour of Death	269
Books and Flowers	270
The World in the Open Air	272
The Dial of Flowers	274
The Dreamer	276
The Streams	277
The Child's Return from the Woodlands	280
The Wreck	282
Elysium	284
England's Dead	288
The Graves of Martyrs	290
The Lyre's Lament	292
The Lyre and Flower	293
The Ruin	294
A Song of the Rose	297
The Sunbeam	299
Triumphant Music	301
The Cross in the Wilderness	303
Our Daily Paths	306
Last Rites	308

SONGS FOR SUMMER HOURS.

And I too in Arcadia	310
The Wandering Wind	312
Ye are not miss'd, fair Flowers!	313
The Willow Song	313
Leave me not yet	314
The Orange Bough	315
The Stream set Free	315

CONTENTS.

	Page
The Summer's Call	317
Oh! Skylark, for thy Wing!	318

MISCELLANEOUS POEMS.

The Two Monuments	320
A Thought of Paradise	323
Communings with Thought	325
To the Blue Anemone	327

SONNETS.

The Return to Poetry	330
Design and Performance	330
Memorial of a Conversation	331
Thought at Sunset	332
Happy Hour	332
A Prayer	333
Prayer Continued	334
Hope of Communion with Nature	335

Despondency and Aspiration 336

THE FOREST SANCTUARY.

> "Long time against oppression have I fought,
> And for the native liberty of faith
> Have bled and suffer'd bonds."
>
> *Remorse; a Tragedy.*

[The following poem is intended to describe the mental conflicts, as well as outward sufferings, of a Spaniard, who, flying from the religious persecutions of his own country, in the sixteenth century, takes refuge, with his child, in a North American forest. The story is supposed to be related by himself, amidst the wilderness which has afforded him an asylum.]

I.

The voices of my home! — I hear them still!
They have been with me through the dreamy night —
The blessed household voices, wont to fill
My heart's clear depths with unalloy'd delight!
I hear them still, unchanged: though some from earth
Are music parted, and the tones of mirth —
Wild, silvery tones, that rang through days more bright —
Have died in others; yet to me they come
Singing of boyhood back — the voices of my home!

Mrs. Hemans.

II.

They call me through this hush of woods reposing
In the gray stillness of the summer morn;
They wander by when heavy flowers are closing,
And thoughts grow deep, and winds and stars are born.
Even as a fount's remember'd gushings burst
On the parch'd traveller in his hour of thirst,
E'en thus they haunt me with sweet sounds, till worn
By quenchless longings, to my soul I say —
Oh! for the dove's swift wings, that I might flee away,

III.

And find mine ark! Yet whither? I must bear
A yearning heart within me to the grave.
I am of those o'er whom a breath of air —
Just darkening in its course the lake's bright wave,
And sighing through the feathery canes — hath power
To call up shadows, in the silent hour,
From the dim past, as from a wizard's cave!
So must it be! These skies above me spread:
Are they my own soft skies? — Ye rest not here, my dead!

IV.

Ye far amidst the southern flowers lie sleeping,
Your graves all smiling in the sunshine clear;
Save one! a blue, lone, distant main is sweeping
High o'er *one* gentle head. Ye rest not here! —
'Tis not the olive, with a whisper swaying,
Not thy low ripplings, glassy water, playing
Through my own chestnut groves which fill mine ear;
But the faint echoes in my breast that dwell,
And for their birthplace moan, as moans the ocean-shell.

V.

Peace! — I will dash these fond regrets to earth,
Even as an eagle shakes the cumbering rain
From his strong pinion. Thou that gavest me birth,
And lineage, and once home, — my native Spain!
My own bright land — my fathers' land -- my child's!
What hath thy son brought from thee to the wilds?
He hath brought marks of torture and the chain —
Traces of things which pass not as a breeze;
A blighted name, dark thoughts, wrath, woe — thy gifts are these!

VI.

A blighted name! I hear the winds of morn —
Their sounds are not of this! I hear the shiver
Of the green reeds, and all the rustlings, borne
From the high forest, when the light leaves quiver:
Their sounds are not of this! — the cedars, waving,
Lend it no tone: His wide savannahs laving,
It is not murmur'd by the joyous river!
What part hath mortal name, where God alone
Speaks to the mighty waste, and through its heart is known?

VII.

Is it not much that I may worship Him
With naught my spirit's breathings to control,
And feel His presence in the vast, and dim,
And whispery woods, where dying thunders roll
From the far cataracts? Shall I not rejoice
That I have learn'd at last to know *His* voice
From man's? I will rejoice! — my soaring soul
Now hath redeem'd her birthright of the day,
And won, through clouds, to Him her own unfetter'd way!

VIII.

And thou, my boy! that silent at my knee
Dost lift to mine thy soft, dark, earnest eyes,
Fill'd with the love of childhood, which I see
Pure through its depths, a thing without disguise;
Thou that hast breathed in slumber on my breast,
When I have check'd its throbs to give thee rest,
Mine own! whose young thoughts fresh before me rise!
Is it not much that I may guide thy prayer,
And circle thy glad soul with free and healthful air?

IX.

Why should I weep on thy bright head, my boy?
Within thy fathers' halls thou wilt not dwell,
Nor lift their banner, with a warrior's joy,
Amidst the sons of mountain chiefs, who fell
For Spain of old. Yet what if rolling waves
Have borne us far from our ancestral graves?
Thou shalt not feel thy bursting heart rebel,
As mine hath done; nor bear what I have borne,
Casting in falsehood's mould th' indignant brow of scorn.

X.

This shall not be thy lot, my blessed child!
I have not sorrow'd, struggled, lived in vain.
Hear me! magnificent and ancient wild;
And mighty rivers, ye that meet the main,
As deep meets deep; and forests, whose dim shade
The flood's voice, and the wind's, by swells pervade;
Hear me! 'Tis well to die, and not complain;
Yet there are hours when the charged heart must speak,
E'en in the desert's ear to pour itself, or break!

XI.

I see an oak before me:* it hath been
The crown'd one of the woods; and might have flung
Its hundred arms to heaven, still freshly green;
But a wild vine around the stem hath clung,
From branch to branch close wreaths of bondage throw-
  ing,
Till the proud tree, before no tempest bowing,
Hath shrunk and died those serpent folds among.
Alas! alas! what is it that I see?
An image of man's mind, land of my sires, with thee!

XII.

Yet art thou lovely! Song is on thy hills:
O sweet and mournful melodies of Spain,
That lull'd my boyhood, how your memory thrills
The exile's heart with sudden-wakening pain!
Your sounds are on the rocks: — that I might hear
Once more the music of the mountaineer!
And from the sunny vales the shepherd's strain
Floats out, and fills the solitary place
With the old tuneful names of Spain's heroic race.

---

* "I recollect hearing a traveller, of poetical temperament, expressing the kind of horror which he felt on beholding, on the banks of the Missouri, an oak of prodigious size, which had been in a manner overpowered by an enormous wild-grape vine. The vine had clasped its huge folds round the trunk, and from thence had wound about every branch and twig, until the mighty tree had withered in its embrace. It seemed like Laocoon struggling ineffectually in the hideous coils of the monster Python." — *Bracebridge Hall*. Chapter on Forest-Trees.

XIII.

But there was silence one bright, golden day,
T'hrough my own pine-hung mountains. Clear, yet lone
In the rich autumn light the vineyards lay,
And from the fields the peasant's voice was gone;
And the red grapes untrodden strew'd the ground;
And the free flocks, untended, roam'd around.
Where was the pastor? — where the pipe's wild tone?
Music and mirth were hush'd the hills among,
While to the city's gates each hamlet pour'd its throng.

XIV.

Silence upon the mountains! But within
The city's gate a rush, a press, a swell
Of multitudes, their torrent-way to win;
And heavy boomings of a dull deep bell,
A dead pause following each — like that which parts
The dash of billows, holding breathless hearts
Fast in the hush of fear — knell after knell;
And sounds of thickening steps, like thunder-rain
That plashes on the roof of some vast echoing fane!

XV.

What pageant's hour approach'd? The sullen gate
Of a strong ancient prison-house was thrown
Back to the day. And who, in mournful state,
Came forth, led slowly o'er its threshold-stone?
They that had learn'd, in cells of secret gloom,
How sunshine is forgotten! They to whom
The very features of mankind were grown
Things that bewilder'd! O'er that dazzled sight
They lifted their wan hands, and cower'd before the light!

XVI.

To this, man brings his brother! Some were there,
Who, with their desolation, had entwined
Fierce strength, and girt the sternness of despair
Fast round their bosoms, even as warriors bind
The breastplate on for fight; but brow and cheek
Seem'd *theirs* a torturing panoply to speak!
And there were some, from whom the very mind
Had been wrung out; they smiled — oh, startling smile,
Whence man's high soul is fled! Where doth it sleep the
    while?

XVII.

But onward moved the melancholy train,
For their false creeds in fiery pangs to die.
This was the solemn sacrifice of Spain —
Heaven's offering from the land of chivalry!
Through thousands, thousands of their race they moved —
Oh, how unlike all others! — the beloved,
The free, the proud, the beautiful! whose eye
Grew fix'd before them, while a people's breath
Was hush'd, and its one soul bound in the thought of death!

XVIII.

It might be that, amidst the countless throng,
There swell'd some heart with pity's weight oppress'd:
For the wide stream of human love is strong;
And woman, on whose fond and faithful breast
Childhood is rear'd, and at whose knee the sigh
Of its first prayer is breathed — she, too, was nigh.
But life is dear, and the free footstep bless'd,
And home a sunny place, where each may fill
Some eye with glistening smiles,—and therefore all were still.

IX.

All still, — youth, courage, strength! — a winter laid,
A chain of palsy cast, on might and mind!
Still, as at noon a southern forest's shade,
They stood, those breathless masses of mankind,
Still, as a frozen torrent! But the wave
Soon leaps to foaming freedom; they, the brave,
Endured — they saw the martyr's place assign'd
In the red flames — whence is the withering spell
That numbs each human pulse? They saw, and thought it well.

X.

And I, too, thought it well! That very morn
From a far land I came, yet round me clung
The spirit of my own. No hand had torn
With a strong grasp away the veil which hung
Between mine eyes and truth. I gazed, I saw
Dimly, as through a glass. In silent awe
I watch'd the fearful rites; and if there sprung
One rebel feeling from its deep founts up,
Shuddering, I flung it back, as guilt's own poison-cup.

XI.

But I was waken'd as the dreamers waken,
Whom the shrill trumpet and the shriek of dread
Rouse up at midnight, when their walls are taken,
And they must battle till their blood is shed
On their own threshold floor. A path for light
Through my torn breast was shatter'd by the might
Of the swift thunder-stroke; and freedom's tread
Came in through ruins, late, yet not in vain,
Making the blighted place all green with life again.

XXII.

Still darkly, slowly, as a sullen mass
Of cloud o'ersweeping, without wind, the sky,
Dream-like I saw the sad procession pass,
And mark'd its victims with a tearless eye.
They moved before me but as pictures, wrought
Each to reveal some secret of man's thought,
On the sharp edge of sad mortality;
Till in his place came one — oh! could it be?
My friend, my heart's first friend! — and did I gaze on thee!

XXIII.

On thee! with whom in boyhood I had play'd,
At the grape-gatherings, by my native streams;
And to whose eye my youthful soul had laid
Bare, as to heaven's, its glowing world of dreams;
And by whose side midst warriors I had stood,
And in whose helm was brought — oh, earn'd with blood! —
The fresh wave to my lips, when tropic beams
Smote on my fever'd brow! Ay, years had pass'd,
Severing our paths, brave friend! — and *thus* we met at last!

XXIV.

I see it still — the lofty mien thou borest!
On thy pale forehead sat a sense of power —
The very look that once thou brightly worest,
Cheering me onward through a fearful hour,
When we were girt by Indian bow and spear,
Midst the white Andes — even as mountain deer,
Hemm'd in our camp; but through the javelin shower
We rent our way, a tempest of despair!
And thou — hadst thou but died with thy true brethren there!

XXV.

I call the fond wish back — for thou hast perish'd
More nobly far, my Alvar! — making known
The might of truth;* and be thy memory cherish'd
With theirs, the thousands that around her throne
Have pour'd their lives out smiling, in that doom
Finding a triumph, if denied a tomb!
Ay, with their ashes hath the wind been sown,
And with the wind their spirit shall be spread,
Filling man's heart and home with records of the dead.

XXVI.

Thou Searcher of the soul! in whose dread sight
Not the bold guilt alone that mocks the skies,
But the scarce-own'd unwhisper'd thought of night,
As a thing written with the sunbeam lies;
Thou know'st — whose eye through shade and depth can see,
That this man's crime was but to worship thee,
Like those that made their hearts thy sacrifice,
The call'd of yore — wont by the Saviour's side
On the dim Olive Mount to pray at eventide

XXVII.

For the strong spirit will at times awake,
Piercing the mists that wrap her clay abode;
And, born of thee, she may not always take
Earth's accents for the oracles of God;
And even for this — O dust, whose mask is power!

* For a most interesting account of the Spanish Protestants, and the heroic devotion with which they met the spirit of persecution in the sixteenth century, see the *Quarterly Review*, No. 57, Art. "Quin's Visit to Spain."

Reed, that wouldst be a scourge thy little hour!
Spark, whereon yet the mighty hath not trod,
And therefore thou destroyest! — where were flown
Our hopes, if man were left to man's decree alone!

XXVIII.

But this I felt not yet. I could but gaze
On him, my friend; while that swift moment threw
A sudden freshness back on vanish'd days,
Like water-drops on some dim picture's hue;
Calling the proud time up, when first I stood
Where banners floated, and my heart's quick blood
Sprang to a torrent as the clarion blew,
And he — his sword was like a brother's worn,
That watches through the field his mother's youngest born.

XXIX.

But a lance met me in that day's career —
Senseless I lay amidst the o'ersweeping fight;
Wakening at last, how full, how strangely clear,
That scene on memory flash'd! — the shivery light,
Moonlight, on broken shields — the plain of slaughter,
The fountain-side, the low sweet sound of water —
And Alvar bending o'er me — from the night
Covering me with his mantle. All the past
Flow'd back; my soul's far chords all answer'd to the blast.

XXX.

Till, in that rush of visions, I became
As one that, by the bands of slumber wound,
Lies with a powerless but all-thrilling frame,
Intense in consciousness of sight and sound,
Yet buried in a wildering dream which brings

Loved faces round him, girt with fearful things!
Troubled even thus I stood, but chain'd and bound
On that familiar form mine eye to keep:
Alas! I might not fall upon his neck and weep!

XXXI.

He pass'd me — and what next? I look'd on two,
Following his footsteps to the same dread place,
For the same guilt — his sisters!* Well I knew
The beauty on those brows, though each young face
Was changed — so deeply changed! — a dungeon's air
Is hard for loved and lovely things to bear.
And ye, O daughters of a lofty race,
Queen-like Theresa! radiant Inez! — flowers
So cherish'd! were ye then but rear'd for those dark hours?

XXXII.

A mournful home, young sisters, had ye left!
With your lutes hanging hush'd upon the wall,
And silence round the aged man, bereft

---

* "A priest named Gonsales had, among other proselytes, gained over two young females, his sisters, to the Protestant faith. All three were confined in the dungeons of the Inquisition. The torture, repeatedly applied, could not draw from them the least evidence against their religious associates. Every artifice was employed to obtain a recantation from the two sisters, since the constancy and learning of Gonsales precluded all hopes of a theological victory. Their answer, if not exactly logical, is wonderfully simple and affecting: — 'We will die in the faith of our brother; he is too wise to be wrong, and too good to deceive us.' The three stakes on which they died were near each other. The priest had been gagged till the moment of lighting up the wood. The few minutes that he was allowed to speak he employed in comforting his sisters, with whom he sung the 109th Psalm, till the flames smothered their voices." — *Quarterly Review*, No. 57, Art. "Quin's Visit to Spain."

Of each glad voice once answering to his call.
Alas, that lonely father! doom'd to pine
For sounds departed in his life's decline;
And, midst the shadowing banners of his hall,
With his white hair to sit, and deem the name
A hundred chiefs had borne, cast down by you to shame!*

XXXIII.

And woe for you, midst looks and words of love,
And gentle hearts and faces, nursed so long!
How had I seen you in your beauty move,
Wearing the wreath, and listening to the song! —
Yet sat, even then, what seem'd the crowd to shun,
Half-veil'd upon the pale clear brow of one,
And deeper thoughts than oft to youth belong —
Thoughts, such as wake to evening's whispery sway,
Within the drooping shade of her sweet eyelids lay.

XXXIV.

And if she mingled with the festive train,
It was but as some melancholy star
Beholds the dance of shepherds on the plain,
In its bright stillness present, though afar.
Yet would she smile — and that, too, hath its smile —
Circled with joy which reach'd her not the while,
And bearing a lone spirit, not at war
With earthly things, but o'er their form and hue
Shedding too clear a light, too sorrowfully true.

* The names, not only of the immediate victims of the Inquisition were devoted to infamy, but those of all their relations were branded with the same indelible stain, which was likewise to descend as an inheritance to their latest posterity.

XXXV.

But the dark hours wring forth the hidden might
Which hath lain bedded in the silent soul,
A treasure all undreamt of, — as the night
Calls out the harmonies of streams that roll
Unheard by day. It seem'd as if her breast
Had hoarded energies, till then suppress'd
Almost with pain, and bursting from control,
And finding first that hour their pathway free:
Could a rose brave the storm, such might her emblem be!

XXXVI.

For the soft gloom whose shadow still had hung
On her fair brow, beneath its garlands worn,
Was fled; and fire, like prophecy's, had sprung
Clear to her kindled eye. It might be scorn —
Pride — sense of wrong; ay, the frail heart is bound
By these at times, even as with adamant round,
Kept so from breaking! Yet not *thus* upborne
She moved, though some sustaining passion's wave
Lifted her fervent soul — a sister for the brave!

XXXVII.

And yet, alas! to see the strength which clings
Round woman in such hours! — a mournful sight,
Though lovely! — an o'erflowing of the springs,
The full springs of affection, deep as bright!
And she, because her life is ever twined
With other lives, and by no stormy wind
May thence be shaken, and because the light
Of tenderness is round her, and her eye
Doth weep such passionate tears — therefore she thus can die.

XXXVIII.

Therefore didst *thou*, through that heart-shaking scene,
As through a triumph move; and cast aside
Thine own sweet thoughtfulness for victory's mien,
O faithful sister! cheering thus the guide,
And friend, and brother of thy sainted youth,
Whose hand had led thee to the source of truth,
Where thy glad soul from earth was purified;
Nor wouldst thou, following him through all the past,
That he should see thy step grow tremulous at last.

XXXIX.

For thou hadst made no deeper love a guest,
Midst thy young spirit's dreams, than that which grows
Between the nurtured of the same fond breast,
The shelter'd of one roof; and thus it rose
Twined in with life. How is it that the hours
Of the same sport, the gathering early flowers
Round the same tree, the sharing one repose,
And mingling one first prayer in murmurs soft,
From the heart's memory fade in this world's breath so oft?

XL.

But thee that breath hath touch'd not; thee, nor him,
The true in all things found! — and thou wert blest
Even then, that no remember'd change could dim,
The perfect image of affection, press'd
Like armour to thy bosom! Thou hadst kept
Watch by thy brother's couch of pain, and wept,
Thy sweet face covering with thy robe, when rest
Fled from the sufferer; thou hadst bound his faith
Unto thy soul; one light, one hope ye chose — one death.

XLI.

So didst thou pass on brightly! — but for her,
Next in that path, how may *her* doom be spoken!
All Merciful! to think that such things were,
And *are*, and seen by men with hearts unbroken!
To think of that fair girl, whose path had been
So strew'd with rose-leaves, all one fairy scene!
And whose quick glance came ever as a token
Of hope to drooping thought, and her glad voice
As a free bird's in spring, that makes the woods rejoice!

XLII.

And she to die! — she loved the laughing earth
With such deep joy in its fresh leaves and flowers!
Was not her smile even as the sudden birth
Of a young rainbow, colouring vernal showers?
Yes! but to meet her fawn-like step, to hear
The gushes of wild song, so silvery clear,
Which oft, unconsciously, in happier hours
Flow'd from her lips, was to forget the sway
Of Time and Death below, blight, shadow, dull decay!

XLIII.

Could this change be? The hour, the scene, where last
I saw that form, came floating o'er my mind:
A golden vintage-eve; the heats were pass'd,
And, in the freshness of the fanning wind,
Her father sat where gleam'd the first faint star
Through the lime-boughs; and with her light guitar,
She, on the greensward at his feet reclined,
In his calm face laugh'd up; some shepherd lay
Singing, as childhood sings on the lone hills at play.

XLIV.

And now — oh, God! — the bitter fear of death,
The sore amaze, the faint o'ershadowing dread,
Had grasp'd her! — panting in her quick-drawn breath,
And in her white lips quivering. Onward led,
She look'd up with her dim bewilder'd eyes.
And there smiled out her own soft brilliant skies,
Far in their sultry southern azure spread,
Glowing with joy, but silent! — still they smiled,
Yet sent down no reprieve for earth's poor trembling child.

XLV.

Alas! that earth had all too strong a hold,
Too fast, sweet Inez! on thy heart, whose bloom
Was given to early love, nor knew how cold
The hours which follow. There was one, with whom,
Young as thou wert, and gentle, and untried,
Thou mightst, perchance, unshrinkingly have died:
But he was far away; and with thy doom
Thus gathering, life grew so intensely dear,
That all thy slight frame shook with its cold mortal fear!

XLVI.

No aid! — thou too didst pass! — and all had pass'd,
The fearful — and the desperate — and the strong!
Some like the bark that rushes with the blast,
Some like the leaf swept shiveringly along;
And some as men that have but one more field
To fight, and then may slumber on their shield, —
Therefore they arm in hope. But now the throng
Roll'd on, and bore me with their living tide,
Even as a bark wherein is left no power to guide.

Mrs. Hemans.

XLVII.

Wave swept on wave. We reach'd a stately square,
Deck'd for the rites. An altar stood on high,
And gorgeous, in the midst: a place for prayer,
And praise, and offering. Could the earth supply
No fruits, no flowers for sacrifice, of all
Which on her sunny lap unheeded fall?
No fair young firstling of the flock to die,
As when before their God the patriarchs stood? —
Look down! man brings thee, heaven! his brother's guiltless
  blood!

XLVIII.

Hear its voice, hear! — a cry goes up to thee,
From the stain'd sod; make thou thy judgment known
On him the shedder! — let his portion be
The fear that walks at midnight — give the moan
In the wind haunting him, a power to say,
"Where is thy brother?" — and the stars a ray
To search and shake his spirit, when alone
With the dread splendour of their burning eyes!
So shall earth own thy will — Mercy, not sacrifice!

XLIX.

Sounds of triumphant praise! the mass was sung —
Voices that die not might have pour'd such strains!
Through Salem's towers might that proud chant have rung
When the Most High, on Syria's palmy plains,
Had quell'd her foes! — so full it swept, a sea
Of loud waves jubilant, and rolling free!
  — Oft when the wind, as through resounding fanes,
Hath fill'd the choral forests with its power,
Some deep tone brings me back the music of that hour.

L.

It died away; — the incense-cloud was driven
Before the breeze — the words of doom were said;
And the sun faded mournfully from heaven:
He faded mournfully, and dimly red,
Parting in clouds from those that look'd their last,
And sigh'd — "Farewell, thou sun!" Eve glow'd and pass'd;
Night — midnight and the moon — came forth and shed
Sleep, even as dew, on glen, wood, peopled spot —
Save one — a place of death — and there men slumber'd not.

LI.

'Twas not within the city —* but in sight
Of the snow-crown'd sierras, freely sweeping,
With many an eagle's eyrie on the height,
And hunter's cabin, by the torrent peeping
Far off: and vales between, and vineyards lay,
With sound and gleam of waters on their way,
And chestnut woods, that girt the happy sleeping
In many a peasant home! — the midnight sky
Brought softly that rich world round those who came to die.

LII.

The darkly glorious midnight sky of Spain,
Burning with stars! What had the torches' glare
To do beneath that temple, and profane
Its holy radiance? By their wavering flare,
I saw beside the pyres — I see thee *now*,
O bright Theresa! with thy lifted brow,

---

* The piles erected for these executions were without the towns, and the final scene of an Auto da Fé was sometimes, from the length of the preceding ceremonies, delayed till midnight.

And thy clasp'd hands, and dark eyes fill'd with prayer!
And thee, sad Inez! bowing thy fair head,
And mantling up thy face, all colourless with dread!

LIII.

And Alvar, Alvar! — I beheld thee too,
Pale, steadfast, kingly: till thy clear glance fell
On that young sister; then perturb'd it grew,
And all thy labouring bosom seem'd to swell
With painful tenderness. Why came I there,
That troubled image of my friend to bear
Thence, for my after-years? — a thing to dwell
In my heart's core, and on the darkness rise,
Disquieting my dreams with its bright mournful eyes?

LIV.

Why came I? — oh! the heart's deep mystery! — Why
In man's last hour doth vain affection's gaze
Fix itself down on struggling agony,
To the dimm'd eyeballs freezing as they glaze?
It might be — yet the power to will seem'd o'er —
That my soul yearn'd to hear his voice once more!
But mine was fetter'd! — mute in strong amaze,
I watch'd his features as the night-wind blew,
And torch-light or the moon's pass'd o'er their marble hue.

LV.

The trampling of a steed! A tall white steed,
Rending his fiery way the crowds among —
A storm's way through a forest — came at speed,
And a wild voice cried "Inez!" Swift she flung
The mantle from her face, and gazed around,
With a faint shriek at that familiar sound;

And from his seat a breathless rider sprung,
And dash'd off fiercely those who came to part,
And rush'd to that pale girl, and clasp'd her to his heart.

LVI.

And for a moment all around gave way
To that full burst of passion! On his breast,
Like a bird panting yet from fear, she lay,
But blest — in misery's very lap — yet blest!
O love, love, strong as death! — from such an hour
Pressing out joy by thine immortal power;
Holy and fervent love! had earth but rest
For thee and thine, this world were all too fair!
How could we thence be wean'd to die without despair?

LVII.

But she — as falls a willow from the storm,
O'er its own river streaming — thus reclined
On the youth's bosom hung her fragile form,
And clasping arms, so passionately twined
Around his neck — with such a trusting fold,
A full deep sense of safety in their hold,
As if naught earthly might th' embrace unbind!
Alas! a child's fond faith, believing still
Its mother's breast beyond the lightning's reach to kill!

LVIII.

Brief rest! upon the turning billow's height
A strange sweet moment of some heavenly strain,
Floating between the savage gusts of night,
That sweep the seas to foam! Soon dark again
The hour — the scene; th' intensively present rush'd
Back on her spirit, and her large tears gush'd

Like blood-drops from a victim — with swift rain
Bathing the bosom where she lean'd that hour,
As if her life would melt into th' o'erswelling shower.

LIX.

But he whose arm sustain'd her! — oh, I knew
'Twas vain! — and yet he hoped — he fondly strove
Back from her faith her sinking soul to woo,
As life might yet be hers! A dream of love
Which could not look upon so fair a thing,
Remembering how like hope, like joy, like spring,
Her smile was wont to glance, her step to move,
And deem that men indeed, in very truth,
Could mean the sting of death for her soft flowering youth!

LX.

He woo'd her back to life. "Sweet Inez, live!
My blessed Inez! — visions have beguiled
Thy heart; abjure them! thou wert form'd to give
And to find joy; and hath not sunshine smiled
Around thee ever? Leave me not, mine own!
Or earth will grow too dark! — for thee alone,
Thee have I loved, thou gentlest! from a child,
And borne thine image with me o'er the sea,
Thy soft voice in my soul. Speak! Oh! yet live for me!"

LXI.

She look'd up wildly; there were anxious eyes
Waiting that look — sad eyes of troubled thought,
Alvar's — Theresa's! Did her childhood rise,
With all its pure and home-affections fraught,
In the brief glance? She clasp'd her hands — the strife
Of love, faith, fear, and that vain dream of life,

Within her woman's breast so deeply wrought,
It seem'd as if a reed so slight and weak
Must, in the rending storm not quiver only — break!

LXII.

And thus it was. The young cheek flush'd and faded,
As the swift blood in currents came and went,
And hues of death the marble brow o'ershaded,
And the sunk eye a watery lustre sent
Through its white fluttering lids. Then tremblings pass'd
O'er the frail form, that shook it as the blast
Shakes the sere leaf, until the spirit rent
Its way to peace — the fearful way unknown.
Pale in love's arms she lay — *she!* — what had loved was gone!

LXIII.

Joy for thee, trembler! — thou redeem'd one, joy!
Young dove set free! — earth, ashes, soulless clay,
Remain'd for baffled vengeance to destroy.
Thy chain was riven! Nor hadst thou cast away
Thy hope in thy last hour! — though love was there
Striving to wring thy troubled soul from prayer,
And life seem'd robed in beautiful array,
Too fair to leave! — but this might be forgiven,
Thou wert so richly crown'd with precious gifts of heaven!

LXIV.

But woe for him who felt the heart grow still,
Which, with its weight of agony, had lain
Breaking on his! Scarce could the mortal chill
Of the hush'd bosom, ne'er to heave again,
And all the silence curdling round the eye,
Bring home the stern belief that she could die —

That she indeed could die! — for, wild and vain
As hope might be, his soul *had* hoped: 'twas o'er —
Slowly his failing arms dropp'd from the form they bore.

LXV.

They forced him from that spot. It might be well,
That the fierce reckless words by anguish wrung
From his torn breast, all aimless as they fell,
Like spray-drops from the strife of torrents flung,
Were mark'd as guilt. There are who note these things
Against the smitten heart; its breaking strings
— On whose low thrills once gentle music hung —
With a rude hand of touch unholy trying,
And numbering then as crimes, the deep, strange tones replying.

LXVI.

But ye in solemn joy, O faithful pair!
Stood gazing on your parted sister's dust;
I saw your features by the torch's glare,
And they were brightening with a heavenward trust!
I saw the doubt, the anguish, the dismay,
Melt from my Alvar's glorious mien away;
And peace was there — the calmness of the just!
And, bending down the slumb'rer's brow to kiss,
"Thy rest is won," he said, "sweet sister! Praise for this!"

LXVII.

I started as from sleep; — yes! — he had spoken —
A breeze had troubled memory's hidden source!
At once the torpor of my soul was broken —
Thought, feeling, passion, woke in tenfold force.
There are soft breathings in the southern wind,
That so your ice-chains, O ye streams! unbind,

And free the foaming swiftness of your course!
I burst from those that held me back, and fell
Even on his neck, and cried — "Friend! brother! fare thee
    well!"

LXVIII.

Did *he* not say "Farewell?" Alas! no breath
Came to mine ear. Hoarse murmurs from the throng
Told that the mysteries in the face of death
Had from their eager sight been veil'd too long.
And we were parted as the surge might part
Those that would die together, true of heart.
His hour was come — but in mine anguish strong,
Like a fierce swimmer through the midnight sea,
Blindly I rush'd away from that which was to be.

LXIX.

Away — away I rush'd; but swift and high
The arrowy pillars of the firelight grew,
Till the transparent darkness of the sky
Flush'd to a blood-red mantle in their hue;
And, phantom-like, the kindling city seem'd
To spread, float, wave, as on the wind they stream'd,
With their wild splendour chasing me! I knew
The death-work was begun — I veil'd mine eyes,
Yet stopp'd in spell-bound fear to catch the victims' cries.

LXX.

What heard I then? — a ringing shriek of pain,
Such as for ever haunts the tortured ear?
I heard a sweet and solemn-breathing strain
Piercing the flame, untremulous and clear!
The rich, triumphal tones! — I knew them well,
As they came floating with a breezy swell!

Man's voice was there — a clarion-voice to cheer
In the mid-battle — ay, to turn the flying;
Woman's — that might have sung of heaven beside the dying!

LXI.

It was a fearful, yet a glorious thing
To hear that hymn of martyrdom, and know
That its glad stream of melody could spring
Up from th' unsounded gulfs of human woe!
Alvar! Theresa! — what is deep? what strong?
— God's breath within the soul! It fill'd that song
From your victorious voices! But the glow
On the hot air and lurid skies increased:
Faint grew the sounds — more faint: I listen'd — they had ceased!

LXII.

And thou indeed hadst perish'd, my soul's friend!
I might form other ties — but thou alone
Couldst with a glance the veil of dimness rend,
By other years o'er boyhood's memory thrown!
Others might aid me onward: thou and I
Had mingled the fresh thoughts that early die,
Once flowering — never more! And thou wert gone!
Who could give back my youth, my spirit free,
Or be in aught again what thou hadst been to me?

LXIII.

And yet I wept thee not, thou true and brave!
I could not weep — there gather'd round thy name
Too deep a passion, *Thou* denied a grave!
Thou, with the blight flung on thy soldier's fame!
Had I not known thy heart from childhood's time?
Thy heart of hearts? — and couldst thou die for crime?

No! had all earth decreed that death of shame,
I would have set, against all earth's decree,
Th' inalienable trust of my firm soul in thee!

LXXIV.

There are swift hours in life — strong, rushing hours,
That do the work of tempests in their might!
They shake down things that stood as rocks and towers
Unto th' undoubting mind; they pour in light
Where it but startles — like a burst of day
For which th' uprooting of an oak makes way;
They sweep the colouring mists from off our sight;
They touch with fire thought's graven page, the roll
Stamp'd with past years — and lo! it shrivels as a scroll!

LXXV.

And this was of such hours! The sudden flow
Of my soul's tide seem'd whelming me; the glare
Of the red flames, yet rocking to and fro,
Scorch'd up my heart with breathless thirst for air,
And solitude, and freedom. It had been
Well with me then, in some vast desert scene,
To pour my voice out, for the winds to bear
On with them, wildly questioning the sky,
Fiercely the untroubled stars, of man's dim destiny.

LXXVI.

I would have call'd, adjuring the dark cloud;
To the most ancient heavens I would have said —
"Speak to me! show me truth!"* — through night aloud

* For one of the most powerful and impressive pictures perhaps ever drawn, of a young mind struggling against habit and superstition in its

I would have cried to him, the newly dead,
"Come back! and show me truth!" My spirit seem'd
Gasping for some free burst, its darkness teem'd
With such pent storms of thought! Again I fled,
I fled, a refuge from man's face to gain,
Scarce conscious when I paused, entering a lonely fane.

LXXVII.

A mighty minster, dim, and proud, and vast!
Silence was round the sleepers whom its floor
Shut in the grave; a shadow of the past,
A memory of the sainted steps that wore
Erewhile its gorgeous pavement, seem'd to brood
Like mist upon the stately solitude;
A halo of sad fame to mantle o'er
Its white sepulchral forms of mail-clad men;
And all was hush'd as night in some deep Alpine glen.

LXXVIII.

More hush'd, far more! — for there the wind sweeps by,
Or the woods tremble to the streams' loud play;
Here a strange echo made my very sigh
Seem for the place too much a sound of day!
Too much my footsteps broke the moonlight, fading,
Yet arch through arch in one soft flow pervading.
And I stood still: prayer, chant had died away;
Yet past me floated a funereal breath
Of incense. I stood still — as before God and death.

first aspirations after truth, see the admirable *Letters from Spain by Don Leucadio Doblado.*

LXXIX.

For thick ye girt me round, ye long departed!*
Dust — imaged forms — with cross, and shield, and crest;
It seem'd as if your ashes would have started
Had a wild voice burst forth above your rest!
Yet ne'er, perchance, did worshipper of yore
Bear to your thrilling presence what *I* bore
Of wrath, doubt, anguish, battling in the breast!
I could have pour'd out words, on that pale air,
To make your proud tombs ring. No, no! I could not *there!*

LXXX.

Not midst those aisles, through which a thousand years,
Mutely as clouds, and reverently, had swept;
Not by those shrines, which yet the trace of tears
And kneeling votaries on their marble kept!
Ye were too mighty in your pomp of gloom
And trophied age, O temple, altar, tomb!
And you, ye dead! — for in that faith ye slept,
Whose weight had grown a mountain's on my heart,
Which could not *there* be loosed. I turn'd me to depart.

LXXXI.

I turn'd: what glimmer'd faintly on my sight —
Faintly, yet brightening as a wreath of snow

---

* "You walk from end to end over a floor of tombstones, inlaid in brass with the forms of the departed, mitres, and crosiers, and spears, and shields, and helmets, all mingled together — all worn into glass-like smoothness by the feet and the knees of long-departed worshippers. Around, on every side, each in their separate chapel, sleep undisturbed from age to age the venerable ashes of the holiest or the loftiest that of old came thither to worship — their images and their dying prayers sculptured among the resting-places of their remains." — From a beautiful description of ancient Spanish Cathedrals, in *Peter's Letters to his Kinsfolk.*

Seen through dissolving haze? The moon, the night,
Had waned, and dawn pour'd in — gray, shadowy, slow,
Yet dayspring still! A solemn hue it caught,
Piercing the storied windows, darkly fraught
With stoles and draperies of imperial glow;
And, soft and sad, that colouring gleam was thrown
Where, pale, a pictured form above the altar shone.

LXXXII.

Thy form, thou Son of God! — a wrathful deep,
With foam, and cloud, and tempest round Thee spread,
And such a weight of night! — a night, when sleep
From the fierce rocking of the billows fled.
A bark show'd dim beyond Thee, with its mast
Bow'd, and its rent sail shivering to the blast;
But, like a spirit in thy gliding tread,
Thou, as o'er glass, didst walk that stormy sea
Through rushing winds, which left a silent path for Thee.

LXXXIII.

So still thy white robes fell! — no breath of air
Within their long and slumb'rous folds had sway.
So still the waves of parted, shadowy hair
From thy clear brow flow'd droopingly away!
Dark were the heavens above thee, Saviour! — dark
The gulfs, Deliverer! round the straining bark!
But Thou! — o'er all thine aspect and array
Was pour'd one stream of pale, broad, silvery light:
Thou wert the single star of that all-shrouding night!

LXXXIV.

Aid for one sinking! Thy lone brightness gleam'd
On his wild face, just lifted o'er the wave,

With its worn, fearful, *human* look, that seem'd
To cry, through surge and blast — "I perish — save!"
Not to the winds — not vainly! Thou wert nigh,
Thy hand was stretch'd to fainting agony,
Even in the portals of th' unquiet grave!
O Thou that art the life! and yet didst bear
Too much of mortal woe to turn from mortal prayer!

LXXXV.

But was it not a thing to rise on death,
With its remember'd light, that face of thine,
Redeemer! dimm'd by this world's misty breath,
Yet mournfully, mysteriously divine?
Oh! that calm, sorrowful, prophetic eye,
With its dark depths of grief, love, majesty!
And the pale glory of the brow! — a shrine
Where power sat veil'd, yet shedding softly round
What told that *Thou* couldst be but for a time uncrown'd!

LXXXVI.

And, more than all, the heaven of that sad smile!
The lip of mercy, our immortal trust!
Did not that look, that very look, erewhile
Pour its o'ershadow'd beauty on the dust?
Wert thou not such when earth's dark cloud hung o'er
    Thee? —
Surely thou wert! My heart grew hush'd before Thee,
Sinking, with all its passions, as the gust
Sank at thy voice, along its billowy way:
What had I there to do but kneel, and weep, and pray?

LXXXVII.

Amidst the stillness rose my spirit's cry,
Amidst the dead — "By that full cup of woe,
Press'd from the fruitage of mortality,
Saviour! for Thee — give light! that I may know
If by *thy* will, in thine all-healing name,
Men cast down human hearts to blighting shame,
And early death; and say, if this be so,
  Where, then, is mercy? Whither shall we flee,
So unallied to hope, save by our hold on Thee?

LXXXVIII.

"But didst Thou not, the deep sea brightly treading,
Lift from despair that struggler with the wave?
And wert Thou not, sad tears, yet awful, shedding,
Beheld a weeper at a mortal's grave?
And is this weight of anguish, which they bind
On life — this searing to the quick of mind,
That but to God its own free path would crave —
  This crushing out of hope and love, and youth,
Thy will, indeed? Give light! that I may know the truth!

LXXXIX.

"For my sick soul is darken'd unto death,
With shadows from the suffering it hath seen;
The strong foundations of mine ancient faith
Sink from beneath me — whereon shall I lean?
Oh! if from thy pure lips was wrung the sigh
Of the dust's anguish! if like man to die —
And earth round *him* shuts heavily — hath been
  Even to *Thee* bitter, aid me! guide me! turn
My wild and wandering thoughts back from their starless
  bourne!"

XC.

And calm'd I rose: but how the while had risen
Morn's orient sun, dissolving mist and shade!
Could there indeed be wrong, or chain, or prison,
In the bright world such radiance might pervade?
It fill'd the fane, it mantled the pale form
Which rose before me through the pictured storm,
Even the gray tombs it kindled, and array'd
    With life! — How hard to see thy race begun,
And think man wakes to grief, wakening to *thee*, O Sun!

XCI.

I sought my home again; and thou, my child,
There at thy play beneath yon ancient pine,
With eyes, whose lightning laughter* hath beguiled
A thousand pangs, thence flashing joy to mine;
Thou in thy mother's arms, a babe, didst meet
My coming with young smiles, which yet, though sweet,
Seem'd on my soul all mournfully to shine,
    And ask a happier heritage for thee,
Than but in turn the blight of human hope to see.

XCII.

Now sport, for thou art free! the bright birds chasing,
Whose wings waft star-like gleams from tree to tree;
Or with the fawn, thy swift wood-playmate, racing,
Sport on, my joyous child! for thou art free!
Yes, on that day I took thee to my heart,
And inly vow'd, for thee a better part
To choose; that so thy sunny bursts of glee

---

* "El' *lampeggiar* de l'angelico riso." — PETRARCH.

Should wake no more dim thoughts of far-seen woe,
But, gladdening fearless eyes, flow on — as now they flow.

XCIII.

Thou hast a rich world round thee — mighty shades
Weaving their gorgeous tracery o'er thy head,
With the light melting through their high arcades,
As through a pillar'd cloister's;* but the dead
Sleep not beneath; nor doth the sunbeam pass
To marble shrines through rainbow-tinted glass;
Yet thou, by fount and forest-murmur led
To worship, thou art blest! to thee is shown
Earth in her holy pomp, deck'd for her God alone.

---

* "Sometimes their discourse was held in the deep shades of moss-grown forests, whose gloom and interlaced boughs first suggested that Gothic architecture beneath whose pointed arches, where they had studied and prayed, the parti-coloured windows shed a tinged light; scenes which the gleams of sunshine, penetrating the deep foliage, and flickering on the variegated turf below, might have recalled to their memory." — Webster's Oration on the Landing of the Pilgrim Fathers in New England. — See Hodgson's *Letters from North America*, vol. ii. p. 305.

PART II.

> Wie diese treue liebe Seele
> Von ihrem Glauben voll,
>   Der ganz allein
> Ihr selig machend ist, sich heilig quäle,
> Dass sie den liebsten Mann verloren halten soll. — FAUST.

> I never shall smile more — but all my days
> Walk with still footsteps and with humble eyes,
> An everlasting hymn within my soul. — WILSON.

I.

Bring me the sounding of the torrent-water,
With yet a nearer swell! Fresh breeze, awake!*
And river, darkening ne'er with hues of slaughter
Thy wave's pure silvery green, — and shining lake,
Spread far before my cabin, with thy zone
Of ancient woods, ye chainless things and lone!
Send voices through the forest aisles, and make
Glad music round me, that my soul may dare,
Cheer'd by such tones, to look back on a dungeon's air!

II.

O Indian hunter of the desert's race!
That with the spear at times, or bended bow,

---

* The varying sounds of waterfalls are thus alluded to in an interesting work of Mrs. Grant's. "On the opposite side the view was bounded by steep hills, covered with lofty pines, from which a waterfall descended, which not only gave animation to the sylvan scene, but was the best barometer imaginable; foretelling by its varied and intelligible sounds every approaching change, not only of the weather but of the wind." — *Memoirs of an American Lady*, vol. i. p. 143.

Dost cross my footsteps in thy fiery chase
Of the swift elk or blue hill's flying roe;
Thou that beside the red night-fire thou heapest,
Beneath the cedars and the star-light sleepest,
T'hou know'st not, wanderer — never may'st thou know! —
Of the dark holds wherewith man cumbers earth,
To shut from human eyes the dancing seasons' mirth.

III.

There, fetter'd down from day, to think the while
How bright in heaven the festal sun is glowing,
Making earth's loneliest places, with his smile,
Flush like the rose; and how the streams are flowing
With sudden sparkles through the shadowy grass,
And water-flowers, all trembling as they pass;
And how the rich, dark summer trees are bowing
With their full foliage: this to know, and pine
Bound unto midnight's heart, seems a stern lot — 'twas mine!

IV.

Wherefore was this? Because my soul had drawn
Light from the Book whose words are graved in light!
There, at its well-head, had I found the dawn,
And day, and noon of freedom: but too bright
It shines on that which man to man hath given,
And call'd the truth — the very truth, from heaven!
And therefore seeks he in his brother's sight
To cast the mote; and therefore strives to bind,
With his strong chains, to earth what is not earth's — the
 mind!

V.

It is a weary and a bitter task
Back from the lip the burning word to keep,

And to shut out heaven's air with falsehood's mask,
And in the dark urn of the soul to heap
Indignant feelings — making e'en of thought
A buried treasure, which may but be sought
When shadows are abroad — and night — and sleep.
I might not brook it long — and thus was thrown
Into that grave-like cell, to wither there alone.

VI.

And I, a child of danger, whose delights
Were on dark hills and many-sounding seas —
I, that amidst the Cordillera heights
Had given Castilian banners to the breeze,
And the full circle of the rainbow seen
There, on the snows;* and in my country been
A mountain wanderer, from the Pyrenees
To the Morena crags — how left I not
Life, or the soul's life, quench'd on that sepulchral spot?

VII.

Because *Thou* didst not leave me, O my God!
Thou wert with those that bore the truth of old
Into the deserts from th' oppressor's rod,
And made the caverns of the rock their fold;
And in the hidden chambers of the dead,
Our guiding lamp with fire immortal fed;
And met when stars met, by their beams to hold
The free heart's communing with Thee, — and Thou
Wert in the midst, felt, own'd — the Strengthener then as
   now!

---

* The circular rainbows, occasionally seen amongst the Andes, are described by Ulloa.

VIII.

Yet once I sank. Alas! man's wavering mind!
Wherefore and whence the gusts that o'er it blow?
How they bear with them, floating uncombined,
The shadows of the past, that come and go,
As o'er the deep the old long-buried things
Which a storm's working to the surface brings!
Is the reed shaken, — and must *we* be so,
 With every wind? So, Father! must we be,
Till we can fix undimm'd our steadfast eyes on Thee.

IX.

Once my soul died within me. What had thrown
That sickness o'er it? Even a passing thought
Of a clear spring, whose side, with flowers o'er-grown,
Fondly and oft my boyish steps had sought!
Perchance the damp roof's water-drops that fell
Just then, low tinkling through my vaulted cell,
Intensely heard amidst the stillness, caught
 Some tone from memory, of the music, welling
Ever with that fresh rill, from its deep rocky dwelling.

X.

But so my spirit's fever'd longings wrought,
Wakening, it might be, to the faint, sad sound,
That from the darkness of the walls they brought
A loved scene round me, visibly around.*

---

* Many striking instances of the vividness with which the mind, when strongly excited, has been known to renovate past impressions, and embody them into visible imagery, are noticed and accounted for in Dr. Hibbert's *Philosophy of Apparitions.* The following illustrative passage is quoted in the same work, from the writings of the late Dr. Ferriar: — "I remember that, about the age of fourteen, it was a source of great amuse-

Yes! kindling, spreading, brightening, hue by hue,
Like stars from midnight, through the gloom, it grew,
That haunt of youth, hope, manhood! — till the bound
Of my shut cavern seem'd dissolved, and I
Girt by the solemn hills and burning pomp of sky.

II.

I look'd — and lo! the clear, broad river flowing
Past the old Moorish ruin on the steep,
The lone tower dark against a heaven all glowing,
Like seas of glass and fire! — I saw the sweep
Of glorious woods far down the mountain side,
And their still shadows in the gleaming tide.
And the red evening on its waves asleep;
And midst the scene — oh! more than all — there smiled
My child's fair face, and hers, the mother of my child!

ment to myself, if I had been viewing any interesting object in the course of the day, such as a romantic ruin, a fine seat, or a review of a body of troops, as soon as evening came on, if I had occasion to go into a dark room, the whole scene was brought before my eyes with a brilliancy equal to what it had possessed in daylight, and remained visible for several minutes. I have no doubt that dismal and frightful images have been thus presented to young persons after scenes of domestic affliction or public horror."

The following passage from the *Alcazar of Seville*, a tale or historical sketch, by the Author of *Doblado's Letters*, affords a further illustration of this subject. "When, descending fast into the vale of years, I strongly fix my mind's eye on those narrow, shady, silent streets, where I breathed the scented air which came rustling through the surrounding groves; where the footsteps re-echoed from the clean watered porches of the houses, and where every object spoke of quiet and contentment; . . . . . . the objects around me begin to fade into a mere delusion, and not only the thoughts, but the external sensations, which I then experienced, revive with a reality that almost makes me shudder — it has so much the character of a trance or vision."

XII.

With their soft eyes of love and gladness raised
Up to the flushing sky, as when we stood
Last by that river, and in silence gazed
On the rich world of sunset. But a flood
Of sudden tenderness my soul oppress'd;
And I rush'd forward, with a yearning breast,
To clasp — alas! — a vision! Wave and wood,
And gentle faces, lifted in the light
Of day's last hectic blush, all melted from my sight.

XIII.

Then darkness! — oh! th' unutterable gloom
That seem'd as narrowing round me, making less
And less my dungeon, when, with all its bloom,
That bright dream vanish'd from my loneliness!
It floated off, the beautiful! yet left
Such deep thirst in my soul, that thus bereft,
I lay down, sick with passion's vain excess,
And pray'd to die. How oft would sorrow weep
Her weariness to death, if he might come like sleep!

XIV.

But I was roused — and how? It is no tale,
Even midst *thy* shades, thou wilderness! to tell.
I would not have my boy's young cheek made pale,
Nor haunt his sunny rest with what befell
In that drear prison-house. His eye must grow
More dark with thought, more earnest his fair brow,
More high his heart in youthful strength must swell;
So shall it fitly burn when all is told:
Let childhood's radiant mist the free child yet enfold.

XV.

It is enough that through such heavy hours
As wring us by our fellowship of clay,
I lived, and undegraded. We have powers
To snatch th' oppressor's bitter joy away!
Shall the wild Indian for his savage fame
Laugh and expire, and shall not Truth's high name
Bear up her martyrs with all-conquering sway?
It is enough that torture may be vain:
I had seen Alvar die — the strife was won from Pain.

XVI.

And faint not, heart of man! Though years wane slow,
There have been those that from the deepest caves,
And cells of night, and fastnesses below
The stormy dashing of the ocean waves,
Down, farther down than gold lies hid, have nursed
A quenchless hope, and watch'd their time, and burst
On the bright day, like wakeners from the graves!
I was of such at last! — unchain'd I trode
This green earth, taking back my freedom from my God!

XVII.

That was an hour to send its fadeless trace
Down life's far-sweeping tide! A dim, wild night,
Like sorrow, hung upon the soft moon's face,
Yet how my heart leap'd in her blessed light!
The shepherd's light — the sailor's on the sea —
The hunter's homeward from the mountains free,
Where its lone smile makes tremulously bright
The thousand streams! — I could but gaze through tears.
Oh! what a sight is heaven, thus first beheld for years!

XVIII.

The rolling clouds! — they have the whole blue space
Above to sail in — all the dome of sky!
My soul shot with them in their breezy race
O'er star and gloom; but I had yet to fly,
As flies the hunted wolf. A secret spot
And strange, I knew — the sunbeam knew it not, —
Wildest of all the savage glens that lie
In far sierras, hiding their deep springs,
And traversed but by storms, or sounding eagles' wings.

XIX.

Ay, and I met the storm there! I had gain'd
The covert's heart with swift and stealthy tread:
A moan went past me, and the dark trees rain'd
Their autumn foliage rustling on my head;
A moan — a hollow gust — and there I stood
Girt with majestic night, and ancient wood,
And foaming water. — Thither might have fled
The mountain Christian with his faith of yore,
When Afric's tambour shook the ringing western shore!

XX.

But through the black ravine the storm came swelling:
— Mighty thou art amidst the hills, thou blast!
In thy lone course the kingly cedars felling,
Like plumes upon the path of battle cast!
A rent oak thunder'd down beside my cave,
Booming it rush'd, as booms a deep sea wave;
A falcon soar'd; a startled wild-deer pass'd;
A far-off bell toll'd faintly through the roar.
How my glad spirit swept forth with the winds once more!

XXI.

And with the arrowy lightnings! — for they flash'd,
Smiting the branches in their fitful play,
And brightly shivering where the torrents dash'd
Up, even to crag and eagle's nest, their spray!
And there to stand amidst the pealing strife,
The strong pines groaning with tempestuous life,
And all the mountain-voices on their way, —
Was it not joy? 'Twas joy in rushing might,
After those years that wove but one long dead of night!

XXII.

There came a softer hour, a lovelier moon,
And lit me to my home of youth again,
Through the dim chestnut shade, where oft at noon,
By the fount's flashing burst, my head had lain
In gentle sleep. But now I pass'd as one
That may not pause where wood-streams whispering run,
Or light sprays tremble to a bird's wild strain;
Because th' avenger's voice is in the wind,
The foe's quick, rustling step close on the leaves behind.

XXIII.

My home of youth! Oh! if indeed to part
With the soul's loved ones be a mournful thing,
When we go forth in buoyancy of heart,
And bearing all the glories of our spring
For life to breathe on, — is it less to meet,
When these are faded? — who shall call it sweet?
Even though love's mingling tears may haply bring
Balm as they fall, too well their heavy showers
Teach us how much is lost of all that once was ours!

XXIV.

Not by the sunshine, with its golden glow,
Nor the green earth, nor yet the laughing sky,
Nor the fair flower-scents,* as they come and go
In the soft air, like music wandering by;
— Oh! not by these, th' unfailing, are we taught
How time and sorrow on our frames have wrought;
But by the sadden'd eye, the darken'd brow
Of kindred aspect, and the long dim gaze,
Which tells us *we* are changed — how changed from other days!

XXV.

Before my father, in my place of birth,
I stood an alien. On the very floor
Which oft had trembled to my boyish mirth,
The love that rear'd me knew my face no more!
There hung the antique armour, helm and crest,
Whose every stain woke childhood in my breast;
There droop'd the banner, with the marks it bore
Of Paynim spears; and I, the worn in frame
And heart, what there was I? — another and the same!

XXVI.

Then bounded in a boy, with clear, dark eye —
How should *he* know his father? When we parted,
From the soft cloud which mantles infancy,
His soul, just wakening into wonder, darted

---

* "For because the breath of flowers is farre sweeter in the aire (where it comes and goes like the warbling of musick) than in the hand, therefore nothing is more fit for that delight than to know what be the flowers and plants which doe best perfume the air." — LORD BACON's *Essay on Gardens.*

Its first looks round. Him follow'd one, the bride
Of my young days, the wife how loved and tried!
Her glance met mine — I could not speak — she started
With a bewilder'd gaze — until there came
Tears to my burning eyes, and from my lips her name.

XXVII.

She knew me then! I murmur'd "*Leonor!*"
And her heart answer'd! Oh! the voice is known
First from all else, and swiftest to restore
Love's buried images, with one low tone
That strikes like lightning, when the cheek is faded,
And the brow heavily with thought o'ershaded,
And all the brightness from the aspect gone!
— Upon my breast she sunk, when doubt was fled,
Weeping as those may weep, that meet in woe and dread.

XXVIII.

For there we might not rest. Alas! to leave
Those native towers, and know that they must fall
By slow decay, and none remain to grieve
When the weeds cluster'd on the lonely wall!
We were the last — my boy and I — the last
Of a long line which brightly thence had pass'd!
My father bless'd me as I left his hall —
With his deep tones and sweet, though full of years,
He bless'd me there, and bathed my child's young head with
    tears.

XXIX.

I had brought sorrow on his gray hairs down,
And cast the darkness of my branded name
(For so *he* deem'd it) on the clear renown,
My own ancestral heritage of fame.

And yet he bless'd me! Father! if the dust
Lie on those lips benign, my spirit's trust
Is to behold thee yet, where grief and shame
Dim the bright day no more; and thou wilt know
That not through guilt thy son thus bow'd thine age with woe!

XXX.

And thou, my Leonor! that unrepining,
If sad in soul, didst quit all else for me,
When stars, the stars that earliest rise, are shining,
How their soft glance unseals each thought of thee!
For on our flight they smiled; their dewy rays,
Through the last olives, lit thy tearful gaze
Back to the home we never more might see.
So pass'd we on, like earth's first exiles, turning
Fond looks where hung the sword above their Eden burning.

XXXI.

It was a woe to say, "Farewell, my Spain!
The sunny and the vintage land, farewell!"
— I could have died upon the battle-plain
For thee, my country! but I might not dwell
In thy sweet vales, at peace. The voice of song
Breathes, with the myrtle scent, thy hills along;
The citron's glow is caught from shade and dell:
But what are these? upon thy flowery sod
I might not kneel, and pour my free thoughts out to God!

XXXII.

O'er the blue deep I fled, the chainless deep!
Strange heart of man! that e'en midst woe swells high,
When through the foam he sees his proud bark sweep,
Flinging out joyous gleams to wave and sky!

Yes! it swells high, whate'er he leaves behind,
His spirit rises with the rising wind;
For, wedded to the far futurity,
On, on, it bears him ever, and the main
Seems rushing, like his hope, some happier shore to gain.

XXXIII.

Not thus is woman. Closely *her* still heart
Doth twine itself with e'en each lifeless thing
Which, long remember'd, seem'd to bear its part
In her calm joys. For ever would she cling,
A brooding dove, to that sole spot of earth
Where she hath loved, and given her children birth,
And heard their first sweet voices. There may spring
Array no path, renew no flower, no leaf,
But hath its breath of home, its claim to farewell grief.

XXXIV.

I look'd on Leonor, — and if there seem'd
A cloud of more than pensiveness to rise
In the faint smiles that o'er her features gleam'd,
And the soft darkness of her serious eyes,
Misty with tender gloom, I call'd it naught
But the fond exile's pang, a lingering thought
Of her own vale, with all its melodies
And living light of streams. Her soul would rest
Beneath your shades, I said, bowers of the gorgeous West!

XXXV.

Oh, could we live in visions! could we hold
Delusion faster, longer, to our breast,
When it shuts from us, with its mantle's fold,
That which we see not, and are therefore blest!

But they, our loved and loving — they to whom
We have spread out our souls in joy and gloom,
Their looks and accents, unto ours address'd,
Have been a language of familiar tone
Too long to breathe, at last, dark sayings and unknown.

XXXVI.

I told my heart, 'twas but the exile's woe
Which press'd on that sweet bosom; I deceived
My heart but half: a whisper, faint and low,
Haunting it ever, and at times believed,
Spoke of some deeper cause.   How oft we seem
Like those that dream, and *know* the while they dream —
Midst the soft falls of airy voices grieved
And troubled, while bright phantoms round them play,
By a dim sense that all will float and fade away!

XXXVII.

Yet, as if chasing joy, I woo'd the breeze
To speed me onward with the wings of morn.
Oh! far amidst the solitary seas,
Which were not made for man, what man hath borne,
Answering their moan with his! — what *thou* didst bear,
My lost and loveliest! while that secret care
Grew terror, and thy gentle spirit, worn
By its dull brooding weight, gave way at last,
Beholding me as one from hope for ever cast!

XXXVIII.

For unto thee, as through all change, reveal'd
Mine inward being lay.   In other eyes
I had to bow me yet, and make a shield,
To fence my burning bosom, of disguise;

By the still hope sustain'd, ere long to win
Some sanctuary, whose green retreats within
My thoughts unfetter'd to their source might rise,
Like songs and scents of morn. But thou didst look
Through all my soul, and thine e'en unto fainting shook.

XXXIX.

Fallen, fallen, I seem'd — yet, oh! not less beloved,
Though from thy love was pluck'd the early pride,
And harshly by a gloomy faith reproved,
And sear'd with shame! Though each young flower had died,
There was the root, — strong, living, not the less
That all it yielded now was bitterness;
Yet still such love as quits not misery's side,
Nor drops from guilt its ivy-like embrace,
Nor turns away from death's its pale heroic face.

XL.

Yes! thou hadst follow'd me through fear and flight!
Thou wouldst have follow'd had my pathway led
E'en to the scaffold; had the flashing light
Of the raised axe made strong men shrink with dread,
Thou, midst the hush of thousands, wouldst have been
With thy clasp'd hands beside me kneeling seen,
And meekly bowing to the shame thy head —
The shame! — oh! making beautiful to view
The might of human love — fair thing! so bravely true!

XLI.

There was thine agony — to love so well
Where fear made love life's chastener. Heretofore,
Whate'er of earth's disquiet round thee fell,
Thy soul, o'erpassing its dim bounds, could soar

Away to sunshine, and thy clear eye speak
Most of the skies when grief most touch'd thy cheek.
Now, that far brightness faded, never more
Could thou lift heavenwards for its hope thy heart,
Since at heaven's gate it seem'd that thou and I must part.

XLII.

Alas! and life hath moments when a glance —
(If thought to sudden watchfulness be stirr'd) —
A flush — a fading of the cheek, perchance —
A word — less, less — the *cadence* of a word,
Lets in our gaze the mind's dim veil beneath,
Thence to bring haply knowledge fraught with death!
Even thus, what never from thy lip was heard
Broke on my soul. I knew that in thy sight
I stood, however beloved, a recreant from the light.

XLIII.

Thy sad, sweet hymn, at eve, the seas along, —
Oh! the deep soul it breathed! — the love, the woe,
The fervour, pour'd in that full gush of song,
As it went floating through the fiery glow
Of the rich sunset! — bringing thoughts of Spain,
With all their vesper voices, o'er the main,
Which seem'd responsive in its murmuring flow.
"*Ave sanctissima!*" — how oft that lay
Hath melted from my heart the martyr strength away!

> Ave, sanctissima!
> 'Tis nightfall on the sea;
> Ora pro nobis!
> Our souls rise to thee!

Watch us, while shadows lie
  O'er the dim waters spread;
Hear the heart's lonely sigh —
  Thine too hath bled!

Thou that hast look'd on death,
  Aid us when death is near!
Whisper of heaven to faith;
  Sweet Mother, hear!

  Ora pro nobis!
The wave must rock our sleep,
  Ora, Mater, ora!
Thou star of the deep!

XLIV.

"*Ora pro nobis, Mater!*" — What a spell
Was in those notes, with day's last glory dying
On the flush'd waters — seem'd they not to swell
From the far dust wherein my sires were lying
With crucifix and sword? Oh! yet how clear
Comes their reproachful sweetness to mine ear!
"*Ora*" — with all the purple waves replying,
All my youth's visions rising in the strain —
And I had thought it much to bear the rack and chain!

XLV.

Torture! the sorrow of affection's eye,
Fixing its meekness on the spirit's core,
Deeper, and teaching more of agony,
May pierce than many swords! — and this I bore
With a mute pang. Since I had vainly striven
From its free springs to pour the truth of heaven
Into thy trembling soul, my Leonor!

Silence rose up where hearts no hope could share:
Alas! for those that love, and may not blend in prayer!

XLVI.

We could not pray together midst the deep,
Which, like a floor of sapphire, round us lay,
Through days of splendour, nights too bright for sleep,
Soft, solemn, holy! We were on our way
Unto the mighty Cordillera land,
With men whom tales of that world's golden strand
Had lured to leave their vines. Oh! who shall say
What thoughts rose in us, when the tropic sky
Touch'd all its molten seas with sunset's alchemy!

XLVII.

Thoughts no more mingled! Then came night — th' intense
Dark blue — the burning stars! I saw *thee* shine
Once more in thy serene magnificence,
O Southern Cross!* as when thy radiant sign

---

* "The pleasure we felt on discovering the Southern Cross was warmly shared by such of the crew as had lived in the colonies. In the solitude of the seas we hail a star as a friend from whom we have long been separated. Among the Portuguese and the Spaniards peculiar motives seem to increase this feeling; a religious sentiment attaches them to a constellation, the form of which recalls the sign of the faith planted by their ancestors in the deserts of the New World. . . . . . It has been observed at what hour of the night, in different seasons, the Cross of the South is erect or inclined. It is a time-piece that advances very regularly near four minutes a-day, and no other group of stars exhibits to the naked eye an observation of time so easily made. How often have we heard our guides exclaim, in the savannahs of Venezuela, or in the desert extending from Lima to Truxillo, 'Midnight is past — the Cross begins to bend!' How often these words reminded us of that affecting scene where Paul and Virginia, seated near the source of the river of La-

First drew my gaze of youth. No, not as then;
I had been stricken by the darts of men
Since those fresh days; and now thy light divine
Look'd on mine anguish, while within me strove
The still small voice against the might of suffering love.

XLVIII.

But thou, the clear, the glorious! thou wert pouring
Brilliance and joy upon the crystal wave,
While she that met thy ray with eyes adoring,
Stood in the lengthening shadow of the grave!
Alas! I watch'd her dark religious glance,
As it still sought thee through the heaven's expanse,
Bright Cross! and knew not that I watch'd what gave
But passing lustre — shrouded soon to be —
A soft light found no more — no more on earth or sea!

XLIX.

I knew not all — yet something of unrest
Sat on my heart. Wake, ocean-wind! I said;
Waft us to land, in leafy freshness drest,
Where, through rich clouds of foliage o'er her head,
Sweet day may steal, and rills unseen go by,
Like singing voices, and the green earth lie
Starry with flowers, beneath her graceful tread!
But the calm bound us midst the glassy main:
Ne'er was her step to bend earth's living flowers again.

taniers, conversed together for the last time; and where the old man, at the sight of the Southern Cross, warns them that it is time to separate." — Dr Humboldt's *Travels.*

L.

Yes! as if heaven upon the waves were sleeping,
Vexing my soul with quiet, there they lay,
All moveless, through their blue transparence keeping
The shadows of our sails, from day to day;
While she —— oh! strongest is the strong heart's woe —
And yet I live! I feel the sunshine's glow —
And I am he that look'd, and saw decay
Steal o'er the fair of earth, th' adored too much! —
It is a fearful thing to love what death may touch.

LI.

A fearful thing that love and death may dwell
In the same world! She faded on — and I,
Blind to the last, there needed death to tell
My trusting soul that she *could* fade to die!
Yet, ere she parted, I had mark'd a change;
But it breathed hope — 'twas beautiful, though strange:
Something of gladness in the melody
Of her low voice, and in her words a flight
Of airy thought — alas! too perilously bright!

LII.

And a clear sparkle in her glance, yet wild,
And quick, and eager, like the flashing gaze
Of some all-wondering and awakening child,
That first the glories of the earth surveys.
How could it thus deceive me? She had worn
Around her, like the dewy mists of morn,
A pensive tenderness through happiest days;
And a soft world of dreams had seem'd to lie
Still in her dark, and deep, and spiritual eye.

LIII.

And I could hope in that strange fire! — she died,
She died, with all its lustre on her mien!
The day was melting from the waters wide,
And through its long bright hours her thoughts had been,
It seem'd, with restless and unwonted yearning,
To Spain's blue skies and dark sierras turning;
For her fond words were all of vintage-scene,
And flowering myrtle, and sweet citron's breath:
Oh! with what vivid hues life comes back oft on death!

LIV.

And from her lips the mountain-songs of old,
In wild, faint snatches, fitfully had sprung;
Songs of the orange bower, the Moorish hold,
The "*Rio verde*,"* on her soul that hung,
And thence flow'd forth. But now the sun was low,
And watching by my side its last red glow,
That ever stills the heart, once more she sung
Her own soft "*Ora, Mater!*" and the sound
Was e'en like love's farewell — so mournfully profound.

LV.

The boy had dropp'd to slumber at our feet;
"And I have lull'd him to his smiling rest
Once more!" she said. I raised him — it was sweet,
Yet sad, to see the perfect calm, which bless'd

---

* "Rio verde! rio verde!" the popular Spanish romance, known to the English reader in Percy's translation: —

"Gentle river! gentle river!
Lo, thy streams are stain'd with gore;
Many a brave and noble captain
Floats along thy willow'd shore," etc.

His look that hour: for now her voice grew weak,
And on the flowery crimson of his cheek,
With her white lips, a long, long kiss she press'd,
Yet light, to wake him not. Then sank her head
Against my bursting heart. What did I clasp? — The dead!

LVI.

I call'd! To call what answers not our cries —
By what we loved to stand unseen, unheard —
With the loud passion of our tears and sighs,
To see but some cold glittering ringlet stirr'd;
And in the quench'd eye's fixedness to gaze,
All vainly searching for the parted rays —
This is what waits us! Dead! — with that chill word
To link our bosom-names! For this we pour
Our souls upon the dust — nor tremble to adore!

LVII.

But the true parting came! I look'd my last
On the sad beauty of that slumbering face:
How could I think the lovely spirit pass'd
Which there had left so tenderly its trace?
Yet a dim awfulness was on the brow —
No! not like sleep to look upon art thou,
Death, Death! She lay, a thing for earth's embrace,
To cover with spring-wreaths. For earth's? — the wave
That gives the bier no flowers, makes moan above her grave!

LVIII.

On the mid-seas a knell! — for man was there,
Anguish and love — the mourner with his dead!
A long, low-rolling knell — a voice of prayer —
Dark glassy waters, like a desert spread —

And the pale-shining Southern Cross on high,
Its faint stars fading from a solemn sky,
Where mighty clouds before the dawn grew red:
Were these things round me? Such o'er memory sweep
Wildly, when aught brings back that burial of the deep.

LIX.

Then the broad, lonely sunrise! — and the plash
Into the sounding waves!* Around her head
They parted, with a glancing moment's flash,
Then shut — and all was still. And now thy bed
Is of their secrets, gentlest Leonor!
Once fairest of young brides! — and never more,
Loved as thou wert, may human tear be shed
Above thy rest! No mark the proud seas keep,
To show where he that wept may pause again to weep!

LX.

So the depths took thee! Oh! the sullen sense
Of desolation in that hour compress'd!
Dust going down, a speck, amidst th' immense
And gloomy waters, leaving on their breast
The trace a weed might leave there! Dust! — the thing
Which to the heart was as a living spring
Of joy, with fearfulness of love possess'd,
Thus sinking! Love, joy, fear, all crush'd to this —
And the wide heaven so far — so fathomless th' abyss!

* De Humboldt, in describing the burial of a young Asturian at sea, mentions the entreaty of the officiating priest, that the body, which had been brought upon deck during the night, might not be committed to the waves until after sunrise, in order to pay it the last rites according to the usage of the Romish Church.

LXI.

Where the line sounds not, where the wrecks lie low,
What shall wake thence the dead? Blest, blest, are they
That earth to earth entrust, for they may know
And tend the dwelling whence the slumberer's clay
Shall rise at last; and bid the young flowers bloom
That waft a breath of hope around the tomb;
And kneel upon the dewy turf to pray!
But thou, what cave hath dimly chamber'd *thee?*
Vain dreams! — oh! art thou not where there is no more
    sea?*

LXII.

The wind rose free and singing: when for ever,
O'er that sole spot of all the watery plain,
I could have bent my sight with fond endeavour
Down, where its treasure was, its glance to strain;
Then rose the reckless wind! Before our prow
The white foam flash'd — ay, joyously, and thou
Wert left with all the solitary main
Around thee — and thy beauty in my heart,
And thy meek, sorrowing love — oh! where could *that* depart?

LXIII.

I will not speak of woe; I may not tell —
Friend tells not such to friends — the thoughts which rent
My fainting spirit, when its wild farewell
Across the billows to thy grave was sent,
Thou, there most lonely! He that sits above,
In his calm glory, will forgive the love
His creatures bear each other, even if blent

---

* "And there was no more sea." — *Revelation*, xxi. 1.

With a vain worship; for its close is dim
Ever with grief which leads the wrung soul back to Him!

LXIV.

And with a milder pang if now I bear
To think of thee in thy forsaken rest,
If from my heart be lifted the despair,
The sharp remorse with healing influence press'd,
If the soft eyes that visit me in sleep
Look not reproach, though still they seem to weep;
It is that He my sacrifice hath bless'd,
And fill'd my bosom, through its inmost cell,
With a deep chastening sense that all at last is well.

LXV.

Yes! thou art now — Oh! wherefore doth the thought
Of the wave dashing o'er thy long bright hair,
The sea-weed into its dark tresses wrought,
The sand thy pillow — thou that wert so fair!
Come o'er me still! Earth, earth! — it is the hold
Earth ever keeps on that of earthly mould!
But *thou* art breathing now in purer air,
I well believe, and freed from all of error,
Which blighted here the root of thy sweet life with terror.

LXVI.

And if the love, which here was passing light,
Went with what died not — oh! that *this* we knew,
But this! — that through the silence of the night,
Some voice, of all the lost ones and the true,
Would speak, and say, if in their far repose,
We are yet aught of what we were to those
We call the dead! Their passionate adieu,

Was it but breath, to perish? Holier trust
Be mine! — thy love *is* there, but purified from dust!

LXVII.

A thing all heavenly! — clear'd from that which hung
As a dim cloud between us, heart and mind!
Loosed from the fear, the grief, whose tendrils flung
A chain so darkly with its growth entwined.
This is my hope! — though when the sunset fades,
When forests rock the midnight on their shades,
When tones of wail are in the rising wind,
Across my spirit some faint doubt may sigh;
For the strong hours *will* sway this frail mortality!

LXVIII.

We have been wand'rers since those days of woe,
Thy boy and I! As wild birds tend their young,
So have I tended him — my bounding roe!
The high Peruvian solitudes among;
And o'er the Andes' torrents borne his form,
Where our frail bridge had quiver'd midst the storm.*
But there the war-notes of my country rung,

---

* The bridges over many deep chasms amongst the Andes are pendulous, and formed only of the fibres of equinoctial plants. Their tremulous motion is thus alluded to in one of the stanzas of *Gertrude of Wyoming:* —

> "Anon some wilder portraiture he draws,
> Of nature's savage glories he would speak;
> The loneliness of earth, that overawes,
> Where, resting by the tomb of old Cacique,
> The lama-driver on Peruvia's peak
> Nor voice nor living motion marks around,
> But storks that to the boundless forest shriek,
> Or wild-cane arch, high flung o'er gulf profound,
> That fluctuates when the storms of El Dorado sound."

And, smitten deep of heaven and man, I fled
To hide in shades unpierced a mark'd and weary head.

LXIX.

But he went on in gladness — that fair child!
Save when at times his bright eye seem'd to dream,
And his young lips, which then no longer smiled,
Ask'd of his mother! That was but a gleam
Of memory, fleeting fast; and then his play
Through the wide Llanos* cheer'd again our way,
And by the mighty Oronoco stream,**
On whose lone margin we have heard at morn,
From the mysterious rocks, the sunrise-music borne:

LXX.

So like a spirit's voice! a harping tone,
Lovely, yet ominous to mortal ear —
Such as might reach us from a world unknown,
Troubling man's heart with thrills of joy and fear!
'Twas sweet! — yet those deep southern shades oppress'd
My soul with stillness, like the calms that rest
On melancholy waves:*** I sigh'd to hear
Once more earth's breezy sounds, her foliage fann'd,
And turn'd to seek the wilds of the red hunter's land.

* Llanos, or savannahs, the great plains in South America.

** De Humboldt speaks of these rocks on the shores of the Oronoco. Travellers have heard from time to time subterraneous sounds proceed from them at sunrise, resembling those of an organ. He believes in the existence of this mysterious music, although not fortunate enough to have heard it himself; and thinks that it may be produced by currents of air issuing through the crevices.

*** The same distinguished traveller frequently alludes to the extreme stillness of the air in the equatorial regions of the New World, and particularly on the thickly wooded shores of the Oronoco. "In this neighbourhood," he says, "no breath of wind ever agitates the foliage."

LXXI.

And we have won a bower of refuge now,
In this fresh waste, the breath of whose repose
Hath cool'd, like dew, the fever of my brow,
And whose green oaks and cedars round me close
As temple walls and pillars, that exclude
Earth's haunted dreams from their free solitude;
All, save the image and the thought of those
Before us gone — our loved of early years,
Gone where affection's cup hath lost the taste of tears.

LXXII.

I see a star — eve's first-born! — in whose train
Past scenes, words, looks, come back. The arrowy spire
Of the lone cypress, as of wood-girt fane,
Rests dark and still amidst a heaven of fire;
The pine gives forth its odours, and the lake
Gleams like one ruby, and the soft winds wake,
Till every string of nature's solemn lyre
Is touch'd to answer; its most secret tone
Drawn from each tree, for each hath whispers all its own.

LXXIII.

And hark! another murmur on the air,
Not of the hidden rills or quivering shades! —
That is the cataract's, which the breezes bear,
Filling the leafy twilight of the glades
With hollow surge-like sounds, as from the bed
Of the blue, mournful seas, that keep the dead:
But *they* are far! The low sun here pervades
Dim forest arches, bathing with red gold
Their stems, till each is made a marvel to behold, —

LXIV.

Gorgeous, yet full of gloom! In such an hour,
The vesper-melody of dying bells
Wanders through Spain, from each gray convent's tower
O'er shining rivers pour'd and olive dells,
By every peasant heard, and muleteer,
And hamlet, round my home: and I am here,
Living again through all my life's farewells,
In these vast woods, where farewell ne'er was spoken
And sole I lift to heaven a sad heart — yet unbroken!

LXV.

In such an hour are told the hermit's beads;
With the white sail the seaman's hymn floats by:
Peace be with all! whate'er their varying creeds,
With all that send up holy thoughts on high!
Come to me, boy! By Guadalquiver's vines,
By every stream of Spain, as day declines,
Man's prayers are mingled in the rosy sky.
We, too, will pray; nor yet unheard, my child!
Of Him whose voice *we* hear at eve amidst the wild.

LXVI.

At eve? Oh, through all hours! From dark dreams oft
Awakening, I look forth, and learn the might
Of solitude, while thou art breathing soft,
And low, my loved one! on the breast of night.
I look forth on the stars — the shadowy sleep
Of forests — and the lake whose gloomy deep
Scuds up red sparkles to the fire-flies' light:
A lonely world! — even fearful to man's thought,
But for His presence felt, whom here my soul hath sought.

CRITICAL ANNOTATIONS ON "THE FOREST SANCTUARY."

[In the autumn of 1824 Mrs. Hemans began the poem which, in point of finish and consecutiveness, if not in popularity, may be considered her principal work, and which she herself inclined to look upon as her best. 'I am at present,' she wrote to one always interested in her literary occupations, 'engaged upon a poem of some length, the idea of which was suggested to me by some passages in your friend Mr. Blanco White's delightful writings.* It relates to the sufferings of a Spanish Protestant, in the time of Philip the Second, and is supposed to be narrated by the sufferer himself, who escapes to America. I am very much interested in my subject, and hope to complete the poem in the course of the winter.' The progress of this work was watched with great interest in her domestic circle, and its touching descriptions would often extract a tribute of tears from the fireside auditors. When completed, a family consultation was held as to its name. Various titles were proposed and rejected, till that of 'The Forest Sanctuary' was suggested by her brother, and finally decided upon. Though finished early in 1825, the poem was not published till the following year, when it was brought out in conjunction with the 'Lays of Many Lands,' and a collection of miscellaneous pieces." — *Memoir*, p. 81.

"Mrs. Hemans may be considered as the representative of a new school of poetry, or, to speak more precisely, her poetry discovers characteristics of the highest kind, which belong almost exclusively to that of latter times, and have been the result of the gradual advancement, and especially the moral progress of mankind. It is only when man, under the influence of true religion, feels himself connected with whatever is infinite, that his affections and powers are fully developed. The poetry of an immortal being must be of a different character from that of an earthly being. But, in recurring to the classic poets of antiquity, we find that in their conceptions the element of religious faith was wanting. Their mythology was to them no object of sober belief; and, had it been so, was adapted not to produce but to annihilate devotion. They had no thought of regarding the universe as created, animated, and ruled by God's all-powerful and omniscient goodness." — PROFESSOR NORTON in *Christian Examiner*.

"We will now say a few words of 'The Forest Sanctuary;' but it so abounds with beauty, is so highly finished, and animated by so generous a spirit of moral heroism, that we can do no justice to our views of it in the narrow space which our limits allow us. A Spanish Protestant flies from persecution at home to religious liberty in America. He has imbibed the spirit of our own fathers, and his mental struggles are described in verses, with which the descendants of the pilgrims must know how to sympathise. We dare not enter on an analysis. From one scene at sea, in the second part, we will make a few extracts. The exile is attended by his wife and child, but his wife remains true to the faith of her fathers.

* "Letters from Spain by Don Leucadio Doblado."

"'Ora pro nobis, Mater!' what a spell
    Was in those notes,'" etc.

"But we must cease making extracts, for we could not transfer all that is beautiful in the poem without transferring the whole." — *North American Review*, April 1827.

"Mrs. Hemans considered this poem as almost, if not altogether, the best of her works. She would sometimes say, that in proportion to the praise which had been bestowed upon other of her less carefully meditated and shorter compositions, she thought it had hardly met with its fair share of success; for it was the first continuous effort in which she dared to write from the fulness of her own heart — to listen to the promptings of her genius freely and fearlessly. The subject was suggested by a passage in one of the letters of Don Leucadio Doblado, and was wrought upon by her with that eagerness and fervour which almost command corresponding results. I have heard Mrs. Hemans say, that the greater part of this poem was written in no more picturesque a retreat than a laundry, to which, as being detached from the house, she resorted for undisturbed quiet and leisure. When she read it, while in progress, to her mother and sister, they were surprised to tears at the increased power displayed in it. She was not prone to speak with self-contentment of her own works, but, perhaps, *the one* favourite descriptive passage was that picture of a sea-burial in the second canto, —

'—— She lay a thing for earth's embrace,' etc.

"The whole poem, whether in its scenes of superstition — the Auto da Fé, the dungeon, the flight, or in its delineation of the mental conflicts of its hero — or in its forest pictures of the free West, which offer such a delicious repose to the mind, is full of happy thoughts and turns of expression. Four lines of peculiar delicacy and beauty recur to me as I write, too strongly to be passed by. They are from a character of one of the martyr sisters.

'And if she mingled with the festive train,
    It was but as some melancholy star
Beholds the dance of shepherds on the plain,
    In its bright stillness present, though afar'

"But the entire episode of 'Queen-like Teresa — radiant Inez,' is wrought up with a nerve and an impulse which men of renown have failed to reach. The death of the latter, if, perhaps, it be a little too romantic for the stern realities of the scene, is so beautifully told, that it cannot be read without strong feeling, nor carelessly remembered. And most beautiful, too, are the sudden outbursts of thankfulness — of the quick happy consciousness of liberty with which the narrator of this ghastly sacrifice interrupts the tale, to reassure himself, 'Sport on, my happy child! for thou art free.' The character of the convert's wife, Leonor, devotedly clinging to his fortunes, without a reproach or a murmur, while her heart trembles before him as though she were in the presence of a lost spirit, is one of those in which Mrs. Hemans' individual mode of thought and manner of expression are most happily impersonated. As a whole, she was hardly wrong in her own estimate of this poem; and, on recently turning to it, I have been surprised to find how well it bears the tests and trials with which it is only either fit or rational to examine works of the highest order of mind." — CHORLEY's *Memorials of Mrs. Hemans*, p. 196-7.

"If taste and elegance be titles to enduring fame, we might venture securely to promise that rich boon to the author before us, who adds to those great merits a tenderness and loftiness of feeling, and an ethereal purity of sentiment, which could only emanate from the soul of a woman. She must beware of becoming too voluminous, and must not venture again on any thing so long as 'The Forest Sanctuary.' But if the next generation inherits our taste for short poems, we are persuaded it will not readily allow her to be forgotten. For we do not hesitate to say that she is, beyond all comparison, the most touching and accomplished writer of occasional verses that our literature has yet to boast of." — LORD JEFFREY, in *Edinburgh Review*, October 1829.]

TALES AND HISTORIC SCENES.

THE LAST CONSTANTINE.

> . . . . "Thou strivest nobly,
> When hearts of sterner stuff perhaps had sunk;
> And o'er thy fall, if it be so decreed,
> Good men will mourn, and brave men will shed tears.
> . . . .
> . . . . Fame I look not for;
> But to sustain, in Heaven's all-seeing eye,
> Before my fellow man, in mine own sight,
> With graceful virtue and becoming pride,
> The dignity and honour of a man,
> Thus station'd as I am, I will do all
> That man may do."
> Miss Baillie's "Constantine Palæologus."

I.

The fires grew pale on Rome's deserted shrines,
In the dim grot the Pythia's voice had died;
— Shout for the City of the Constantines,
The rising city of the billow-side,
The City of the Cross! — great ocean's bride,
Crown'd with her birth she sprung! Long ages past,
And still she look'd in glory o'er the tide,
Which at her feet barbaric riches cast,
Pour'd by the burning East, all joyously and fast.

II.

Long ages past! — they left her porphyry halls
Still trod by kingly footsteps. Gems and gold
Broider'd her mantle, and her castled walls
Frown'd in their strength; yet there were signs which told
The days were full. The pure high faith of old
Was changed; and on her silken couch of sleep
She lay, and murmur'd if a rose-leaf's fold
Disturb'd her dreams; and call'd her slaves to keep
  Their watch, that no rude sound might reach her o'er the deep.

III.

But there are sounds that from the regal dwelling
Free hearts and fearless only may exclude;
'Tis not alone the wind at midnight swelling,
Breaks on the soft repose by luxury woo'd!
There are unbidden footsteps, which intrude
Where the lamps glitter and the wine-cup flows;
And darker hues have stain'd the marble, strew'd
With the fresh myrtle and the short-lived rose;
  And Parian walls have rung to the dread march of foes.

IV.

A voice of multitudes is on the breeze,
Remote, yet solemn as the night-storm's roar
Through Ida's giant-pines! Across the seas
A murmur comes, like that the deep winds bore
From Tempe's haunted river to the shore
Of the reed-crown'd Eurotas; when, of old,
Dark Asia sent her battle-myriads o'er
  Th' indignant wave, which would not be controll'd,
But past the Persian's chain in boundless freedom roll'd.

v.

And it is thus again! Swift oars are dashing
The parted waters, and a light is cast
On their white foam-wreaths, from the sudden flashing
Of Tartar spears, whose ranks are thickening fast.
There swells a savage trumpet on the blast,
A music of the deserts, wild and deep,
Wakening strange echoes, as the shores are pass'd
Where low midst Ilion's dust her conquerors sleep,
O'ershadowing with high names each rude sepulchral heap.

vi.

War from the West! — the snows on Thracian hills
Are loosed by Spring's warm breath; yet o'er the lands
Which Hæmus girds, the chainless mountain-rills
Pour down less swiftly than the Moslem bands.
War from the East! — midst Araby's lone sands,
More lonely now the few bright founts may be,
While Ismael's bow is bent in warrior-hands
Against the Golden City of the sea.*
— Oh! for a soul to fire thy dust, Thermopylæ!

vii.

Hear yet again, ye mighty! — Where are they
Who, with their green Olympic garlands crown'd,
Leap'd up in proudly beautiful array,
As to a banquet gathering, at the sound

---

* The army of Mohammed the Second, at the siege of Constantinople, was thronged with fanatics of all sects and nations, who were not enrolled amongst the regular troops. The Sultan himself marched upon the city from Adrianople; but his army must have been principally collected in the Asiatic provinces, which he had previously visited.

Of Persia's clarion? Far and joyous round,
From the pine forests, and the mountain snows,
And the low sylvan valleys, to the bound
Of the bright waves, at freedom's voice they rose!
— Hath it no thrilling tone to break the tomb's repose?

VIII.

They slumber with their swords! — the olive shades
In vain are whispering their immortal tale!
In vain the spirit of the past pervades
The soft winds, breathing through each Grecian vale.
Yet must *thou* wake, though all unarm'd and pale,
Devoted City! Lo! the Moslem's spear,
Red from its vintage, at thy gates; his sail
Upon thy waves, his trumpet in thine ear!
— Awake! and summon those, who yet perchance may hear!

IX.

Be hush'd, thou faint and feeble voice of weeping!
Lift ye the banner of the Cross on high,
And call on chiefs, whose noble sires are sleeping
In their proud graves of sainted chivalry,
Beneath the palms and cedars, where they sigh
To Syrian gales! The sons of each brave line
From their baronial halls shall hear your cry,
And seize the arms which flash'd round Salem's shrine,
And wield for you the swords once waved for Palestine!

X.

All still, all voiceless! — and the billow's roar
Alone replies! Alike *their* soul is gone
Who shared the funeral-feast on Œta's shore,
And *theirs* that o'er the field of Ascalon

Swell'd the crusaders' hymn! Then gird thou on
'Thine armour, Eastern Queen! and meet the hour
Which waits thee ere the day's fierce work is done
With a strong heart: so may thy helmet tower
Unshiver'd through the storm, for generous hope is power!

XI.

But linger not, — array thy men of might!
The shores, the seas, are peopled with thy foes.
Arms through thy cypress groves are gleaming bright.
And the dark huntsmen of the wild repose
Beneath the shadowy marble porticoes
Of thy proud villas. Nearer and more near,
Around thy walls the sons of battle close;
Each hour, each moment, hath its sound of fear,
Which the deep grave alone is charter'd not to hear!

XII.

Away! bring wine, bring odours, to the shade*
Where the tall pine and poplar blend on high!
Bring roses, exquisite, but soon to fade!
Snatch every brief delight, — since we must die! —
Yet is the hour, degenerate Greeks! gone by,
For feast in vine-wreath'd bower or pillar'd hall;
Dim gleams the torch beneath yon fiery sky,
And deep and hollow is the tambour's call,
And from the startled hand th' untasted cup will fall.

XIII.

The night — the glorious oriental night,
Hath lost the silence of her purple heaven,

* "Huc vina, et unguenta, et nimium breves
Flores amœnæ ferre jube rosæ." — HORACE.

With its clear stars! The red artillery's light,
Athwart her worlds of tranquil splendour driven,
To the still firmament's expanse hath given
Its own fierce glare, wherein each cliff and tower
Starts wildly forth; and now the air is riven
With thunder-bursts, and now dull smoke-clouds lower,
Veiling the gentle moon, in her most hallow'd hour.

XIV.

Sounds from the waters, sounds upon the earth,
Sounds in the air, of battle! Yet with these
A voice is mingling, whose deep tones give birth
To faith and courage! From luxurious ease
A gallant few have started! O'er the seas,
From the Seven Towers,* their banner waves its sign;
And Hope is whispering in the joyous breeze,
Which plays amidst its folds. That voice was *thine;*
Thy soul was on that band, devoted Constantine.

XV.

Was Rome thy parent? Didst thou catch from *her*
The fire that lives in thine undaunted eye?
— That city of the throne and sepulchre
Had given proud lessons how to reign and die!
Heir of the Cæsars! did that lineage high,
Which, as a triumph to the grave, hath pass'd
With its long march of spectred imagery,**

---

* The castle of the Seven Towers is mentioned in the Byzantine history, as early as the sixth century of the Christian era, as an edifice which contributed materially to the defence of Constantinople; and it was the principal bulwark of the town on the coast of the Propontis, in the later periods of the empire. For a description of this building, see Pouqueville's *Travels.*

** An allusion to the Roman custom of carrying in procession, at the funerals of their great men, the images of their ancestors.

Th' heroic mantle o'er thy spirit cast?
Thou! of an eagle-race the noblest and the last!

XVI.

Vain dreams! Upon that spirit hath descended
Light from the living Fountain, whence each thought
Springs pure and holy! In that eye is blended
A spark, with earth's triumphal memories fraught,
And, far within, a deeper meaning, caught
From worlds unseen. A hope, a lofty trust,
Whose resting-place on buoyant wing is sought
('Though through its veil seen darkly from the dust)
In realms where Time no more hath power upon the just.

XVII.

Those were proud days, when on the battle-plain,
And in the sun's bright face, and midst th' array
Of awe-struck hosts, and circled by the slain,
The Roman cast his glittering mail away,*

* The following was the ceremony of consecration with which Decius devoted himself in battle: — He was ordered by Valerius, the Pontifex Maximus, to quit his military habit, and put on the robe he wore in the senate. Valerius then covered his head with a veil, commanded him to put forth his hand under his robe to his chin, and, standing with both feet upon a javelin, to repeat these words: — "O Janus, Jupiter, Mars, Romulus, Bellona! and ye, Lares and Novensiles! All you heroes who dwell in heaven! and all ye gods who rule over us and our enemies — especially ye gods of hell! — I honour you, invoke you, and humbly entreat you to prosper the arms of the Romans, and to transfer all fear and terror from them to their enemies; and I do, for the safety of the Roman people, and their legions, devote myself, and with myself the army and auxiliaries of the enemy, to the infernal gods, and the goddess of the earth." Decius then, girding his robe around them, mounted his horse, and rode full speed into the thickest of the enemy's battalions. The Latins were, for a while, thunderstruck at this spectacle; but at length recovering themselves, they discharged a shower of darts, under which the Consul fell.

And while a silence, as of midnight, lay
O'er breathless thousands at his voice who started,
Call'd on the unseen terrific powers that sway
　The heights, the depths, the shades; then, fearless-hearted,
Girt on his robe of death, and for the grave departed!

XVIII.

But then, around him as the javelins rush'd,
From earth to heaven swell'd up the loud acclaim;
And, ere his heart's last free libation gush'd,
With a bright smile, the warrior caught his name
Far-floating on the winds! And Victory came,
And made the hour of that immortal deed
A life, in fiery feeling! Valour's aim
Had sought no loftier guerdon. Thus to bleed
Was to be Rome's high star!— He died — and had his meed.

XIX.

But praise — and dearer, holier praise be theirs,
Who, in the stillness and the solitude
Of hearts press'd earthwards by a weight of cares,
Uncheer'd by Fame's proud hope, th' ethereal food
Of restless energies, and only view'd
By Him whose eye, from his eternal throne,
Is on the soul's dark places; have subdued
And vow'd themselves with strength till then unknown,
To some high martyr-task, in secret and alone.

XX.

Theirs be the bright and sacred names, enshrined
Far in the bosom! for their deeds belong,
Not to the gorgeous faith which charm'd mankind
With its rich pomp of festival and song,

Garland, and shrine, and incense-bearing throng;
But to that Spirit, hallowing, as it tries
Man's hidden soul in whispers, yet more strong
Than storm or earthquake's voice; for *thence* arise
All that mysterious world's unseen sublimities.

XXI.

Well might *thy* name, brave Constantine! awake
Such thought, such feeling! — But the scene again
Bursts on my vision, as the day-beams break
Through the red sulphurous mists: the camp, the plain,
The terraced palaces, the dome-capt fane,
With its bright cross fix'd high in crowning grace;
Spears on the ramparts, galleys on the main,
And, circling all with arms, that turban'd race —
The sun, the desert, stamp'd in each dark haughty face.

XXII.

Shout, ye seven hills! Lo! Christian pennons streaming
Red o'er the waters!* Hail, deliverers, hail!
Along your billowy wake the radiance gleaming,
Is Hope's own smile! They crowd the swelling sail,
On, with the foam, the sunbeam and the gale,
Borne, as a victor's car! The batteries pour
Their clouds and thunders; but the rolling veil
Of smoke floats up the exulting winds before!
— And oh! the glorious burst of that bright sea and shore!

* See Gibbon's animated description of the arrival of five Christian ships, with men and provisions, for the succour of the besieged, not many days before the fall of Constantinople. — *Decline and Fall of the Roman Empire*, vol. xii. p. 215.

XXIII.

The rocks, waves, ramparts, Europe's, Asia's coast,
All throng'd! one theatre for kingly war!
A monarch, girt with his barbaric host,
Points o'er the beach his flashing scimitar!
Dark tribes are tossing javelins from afar,
Hands waving banners o'er each battlement,
Decks, with their serried guns, array'd to bar
The promised aid: but hark! a shout is sent
Up from the noble barks! — the Moslem line is rent!

XXIV.

On, on through rushing flame and arrowy shower,
The welcome prows have cleft their rapid way;
And, with the shadows of the vesper hour,
Furl'd their white sails, and anchor'd in the bay.
Then were the streets with song and torch-fire gay,
Then the Greek wines flow'd mantling in the light
Of festal halls; and there was joy! — the ray
Of dying eyes, a moment wildly bright —
The sunset of the soul, ere lost to mortal sight.

XXV.

For vain that feeble succour! Day by day
Th' imperial towers are crumbling, and the sweep
Of the vast engines, in their ceaseless play,
Comes powerful, as when heaven unbinds the deep!
— Man's heart is mightier than the castled steep,
Yet will it sink when earthly hope is fled;
Man's thoughts work darkly in such hours, and sleep
Flies far; and in *their* mien, the walls who tread,
Things by the brave untold may fearfully be read!

XXVI.

It was a sad and solemn task, to hold
Their midnight-watch on that beleaguer'd wall!
As the sea-wave beneath the bastions roll'd,
A sound of fate was in its rise and fall;
The heavy clouds were as an empire's pall,
The giant shadows of each tower and fane
Lay like the grave's; a low mysterious call
Breathed in the wind, and, from the tented plain,
A voice of omens rose with each wild martial strain,

XXVII.

For they might catch the Arab chargers neighing,
The Thracian drum, the Tartar's drowsy song;
Might almost hear the soldan's banner swaying,
The watchword mutter'd in some eastern tongue.
Then flash'd the gun's terrific light along
The marble streets, all stillness — not repose;
And boding thoughts came o'er them, dark and strong;
For heaven, earth, air, speak auguries to those
Who see their number'd hours fast pressing to the close.

XXVIII.

But strength is from the Mightiest! There is one
Still in the breach and on the rampart seen,
Whose cheek shows paler with each morning sun,
And tells in silence how the night hath been
In kingly halls a vigil: yet serene
The ray set deep within his thoughtful eye;
And there is that in his collected mien,
To which the hearts of noble men reply
With fires, partaking not this frame's mortality!

XXIX.

Yes! call it not of lofty minds the fate
To pass o'er earth in brightness but alone;
High power was made their birthright, to create
A thousand thoughts responsive to their own!
A thousand echoes of their spirit's tone
Start into life, where'er their path may be,
Still following fast; as when the wind hath blown
O'er Indian groves,* a wanderer wild and free,
Kindling and bearing flames afar from tree to tree!

XXX.

And it is thus with thee! thy lot is cast
On evil days, thou Cæsar! — yet the few,
That set their generous bosom to the blast
Which rocks thy throne — the fearless and the true,
Bear hearts wherein thy glance can still renew
The free devotion of the years gone by,
When from bright dreams th' ascendant Roman drew
Enduring strength! States vanish — ages fly —
But leave one task unchanged — to suffer and to die!

XXXI.

These are our nature's heritage. But thou,
The crown'd with empire! thou wert call'd to share

---

* "The summits of the lofty rocks in the Carnatic, particularly about the Ghauts, are sometimes covered with the bamboo tree, which grows in thick clumps, and is of such uncommon aridity that, in the sultry season of the year, the friction occasioned by a strong dry wind will literally produce sparks of fire, which, frequently setting the woods in a blaze, exhibit to the spectator stationed in a valley surrounded by rocks, a magnificent though imperfect circle of fire." — *Notes to* KINDERSLEY's *Specimens of Hindoo Literature.*

A cup more bitter. On thy fever'd brow
The semblance of that buoyant hope to wear,
Which long had pass'd away; alone to bear
The rush and pressure of dark thoughts, that came
As a strong billow in their weight of care,
And with all this to smile! For earth-born frame
These are stern conflicts, yet they pass, unknown to fame!

XXXII.

Her glance is on the triumph, on the field,
On the red scaffold; and where'er, in sight
Of human eyes, the human soul is steel'd
To deeds that seem as of immortal might,
Yet are proud Nature's! But her meteor-light
Can pierce no depths, no clouds; it falls not where
In silence, and in secret, and in night,
The noble heart doth wrestle with despair,
And rise more strong than death from its unwitness'd prayer.

XXXIII.

Men have been firm in battle; they have stood
With a prevailing hope on ravaged plains,
And won the birthright of their hearths with blood,
And died rejoicing, midst their ancient fanes,¹
That so their children, undefiled with chains,
Might worship there in peace. But they that stand
When not a beacon o'er the wave remains,
Link'd but to perish with a ruin'd land,
Where Freedom dies with them — call *these* a martyr-band!

XXXIV.

But the world heeds them not. Or if, perchance,
Upon their strife it bend a careless eye,

It is but as the Roman's stoic glance
Fell on that stage, where man's last agony
Was made *his* sport, who, knowing *one* must die,
Reck'd not *which* champion; but prepared the strain,
And bound the bloody wreath of victory,
To greet the conqueror; while, with calm disdain,
The vanquish'd proudly met the doom he met in vain.

XXXV.

The hour of Fate comes on! and it is fraught
With *this* of Liberty, that now the need
Is past to veil the brow of anxious thought,
And clothe the heart, which still beneath must bleed,
With Hope's fair-seeming drapery. We are freed
From tasks like these by misery: one alone
Is left the brave, and rest shall be thy meed,
Prince, watcher, wearied one! when thou hast shown
How brief the cloudy space which parts the grave and throne.

XXXVI.

The signs are full. They are not in the sky,
Nor in the many voices of the air,
Nor the swift clouds. No fiery hosts on high
Toss their wild spears: no meteor banners glare,
No comet fiercely shakes its blazing hair;
And yet the signs are full: too truly seen
In the thinn'd ramparts, in the pale despair
Which lends one language to a people's mien,
And in the ruin'd heaps where wall and towers have been!

XXXVII.

It is a night of beauty: such a night
As, from the sparry grot or laurel-shade,

Or wave in marbled cavern rippling bright,
Might woo the nymphs of Grecian fount and glade
To sport beneath its moonbeams, which pervade
Their forest haunts; a night to rove alone
Where the young leaves by vernal winds are sway'd,
And the reeds whisper with a dreamy tone
Of melody that seems to breathe from worlds unknown;

XXXVIII.

A night to call from green Elysium's bowers
The shades of elder bards; a night to hold
Unseen communion with th' inspiring powers
That made deep groves their dwelling-place of old;
A night for mourners, o'er the hallow'd mould,
To strew sweet flowers — for revellers to fill
And wreathe the cup — for sorrows to be told
Which love hath cherish'd long. Vain thoughts! be still!
It is a night of fate, stamp'd with Almighty Will!

XXXIX.

It *should* come sweeping in the storm, and rending
The ancient summits in its dread career!
And with vast billows wrathfully contending,
And with dark clouds o'ershadowing every sphere!
But He, whose footstep shakes the earth with fear,
Passing to lay the sovereign cities low,
Alike in His omnipotence is near,
When the soft winds o'er spring's green pathway blow,
And when His thunders cleave the monarch mountain's brow.

XL.

The heavens in still magnificence look down
On the hush'd Bosphorus, whose ocean stream

Sleeps with its paler stars: the snowy crown
Of far Olympus,* in the moonlight gleam,
Towers radiantly, as when the Pagan's dream
Throng'd it with gods, and bent th' adoring knee;
— But that is past — and now the One Supreme
Fills not alone *those* haunts, but earth, air, sea,
And Time, which presses on to finish his decree.

XLI.

Olympus, Ida, Delphi! ye, the thrones
And temples of a visionary might,
Brooding in clouds above your forest zones,
And mantling thence the realms beneath with night:
Ye have look'd down on battles — Fear and Flight,
And arm'd Revenge, all hurrying past below! —
But there is yet a more appalling sight
For earth prepared than e'er, with tranquil brow,
Ye gazed on from your world of solitude and snow!

XLII.

Last night a sound was in the Moslem camp,
And Asia's hills re-echo'd to a cry
Of savage mirth! Wild horn and war-steeds' tramp
Blent with the shout of barbarous revelry,
The clash of desert-spears! Last night the sky
A hue of menace and of wrath put on,
Caught from red watch-fires, blazing far and high,
And countless as the flames in ages gone,
Streaming to heaven's bright queen from shadowy Lebanon!

* Those who steer their westward course through the middle of the Propontis may at once descry the high lands of Thrace and Bithynia, and never lose sight of the lofty summit of Mount Olympus, covered with eternal snows. — *Decline and Fall*, &c. vol. III. p. 8.

XLIII.

But all is stillness now. May this be sleep
Which wraps those Eastern thousands? Yes! perchance
Along yon moonlit shore and dark-blue deep,
Bright are their visions with the Houri's glance,
And they behold the sparkling fountains dance
Beneath the bowers of paradise that shed
Rich odours o'er the faithful; but the lance,
The bow, the spear, now round the slumberers spread,
Ere Fate fulfil such dreams, must rest beside the dead.

XLIV.

May this be sleep, this hush? — A sleepless eye
Doth hold its vigil midst that dusky race!
One that would scan th' abyss of destiny
E'en now is gazing on the skies to trace,
In those bright worlds, the burning isles of space,
Fate's mystic pathway: they the while, serene,
Walk in their beauty; but Mohammed's face
Kindles beneath their aspect,* and his mien,
All fired with stormy joy, by that soft light is seen.

XLV.

Oh! wild presumption of a conqueror's dream,
To gaze on those pure altar-fires, enshrined
In depths of blue infinitude, and deem
They shine to guide the spoiler of mankind
O'er fields of blood! But with the restless mind
It hath been ever thus! and they that weep
For worlds to conquer, o'er the bounds assign'd

---

* Mohammed II. was greatly addicted to the study of astrology. His calculations in this science led him to fix upon the morning of the 29th of May, as the fortunate hour for a general attack upon the city.

To human search, in daring pride would sweep,
As o'er the trampled dust wherein they soon must sleep.

XLVI.

But ye! that beam'd on Fate's tremendous night,
When the storm burst o'er golden Babylon;
And ye, that sparkled with your wonted light
O'er burning Salem, by the Roman won;
And ye, that calmly view'd the slaughter done
In Rome's own streets, when Alaric's trumpet-blast
Rang through the Capitol: bright spheres! roll on!
Still bright, though empires fall; and bid man cast
His humbled eyes to earth, and commune with the past.

XLVII.

For it hath mighty lessons! from the tomb,
And from the ruins of the tomb, and where,
Midst the wreck'd cities in the desert's gloom,
All tameless creatures make their savage lair,
Thence comes its voice, that shakes the midnight air,
And calls up clouds to dim the laughing day,
And thrills the soul; — yet bids us not despair,
But make one Rock our shelter and our stay,
Beneath whose shade all else is passing to decay!

XLVIII.

The hours move on. I see a wavering gleam
O'er the hush'd waters tremulously fall,
Pour'd from the Cæsars' palace; now the beam
Of many lamps is brightening in the hall,
And from its long arcades and pillars tall
Soft graceful shadows undulating lie
On the wave's heaving bosom, and recall

A thought of Venice, with her moonlight sky,
And festal seas and domes, and fairy pageautry.

XLIX.

But from that dwelling floats no mirthful sound!
The swell of flute and Grecian lyre no more,
Wafting an atmosphere of music round,
Tells the hush'd seaman, gliding past the shore,
How monarchs revel there! Its feasts are o'er —
Why gleam the lights along its colonnade?
— I see a train of guests in silence pour
Through its long avenues of terraced shade,
Whose stately founts and bowers for joy alone were made!

L.

In silence, and in arms! With helm — with sword —
These are no marriage garments! Yet e'en now
Thy nuptial feast should grace the regal board,
Thy Georgian bride should wreathe her lovely brow
With an imperial diadem!* — but thou,
O fated prince! art call'd, and these with thee,
To darker scenes; and thou hast learn'd to bow
Thine Eastern sceptre to the dread decree,
And count it joy enough to perish — being free!

LI.

On through long vestibules, with solemn tread,
As men, that in some time of fear and woe,
Bear darkly to their rest the noble dead,
O'er whom by day their sorrows may not flow,

---

* Constantine Palæologus was betrothed to a Georgian princess, and the very spring which witnessed the fall of Constantinople had been fixed upon as the time for conveying the imperial bride to that city.

The warriors pass: their measured steps are slow,
And hollow echoes fill the marble halls,
Whose long-drawn vistas open as they go
In desolate pomp; and from the pictured walls,
Sad seems the light itself which on their armour falls!

LII.

And they have reach'd a gorgeous chamber, bright
With all we dream of splendour; yet a gloom
Seems gather'd o'er it to the boding sight,
A shadow that anticipates the tomb!
Still from its fretted roof the lamps illume
A purple canopy, a golden throne;
But it is empty! — hath the stroke of doom
Fallen there already? Where is He, the One,
Born that high seat to fill, supremely and alone?

LIII.

Oh! there are times whose pleasure doth efface
Earth's vain distinctions! When the storm beats loud,
When the strong towers are tottering to their base,
And the streets rock, — who mingle in the crowd?
— Peasant and chief, the lowly and the proud,
Are in that throng! Yes, life hath many an hour
Which makes us kindred, by one chast'ning bow'd,
And feeling but, as from the storm we cower,
What shrinking weakness feels before unbounded power!

LIV.

Yet then that Power, whose dwelling is on high,
Its loftiest marvels doth reveal, and speak,
In the deep human heart more gloriously,
Than in the bursting thunder! Thence the weak,

They that seem'd form'd, as flower-stems, but to break
With the first wind, have risen to deeds whose name
Still calls up thoughts that mantle to the cheek,
And thrill the pulse! — Ay, strength no pangs could tame
Hath look'd from woman's eye upon the sword and flame!

LV.

And this is of such hours! — That throne is void,
And its lord comes uncrown'd. Behold him stand,
With a calm brow, where woes have not destroy'd
The Greek's heroic beauty, midst his band,
The gather'd virtue of a sinking land —
Alas! how scanty! Now is cast aside
All form of princely state; each noble hand
Is press'd by turns in his: for earthly pride
There is no room in hearts where earthly hope hath died!

LVI.

A moment's hush — and then he speaks — he speaks!
But not of hope! *that* dream hath long gone by:
His words are full of memory — as he seeks,
By the strong names of Rome and Liberty,
Which yet are living powers that fire the eye,
And rouse the heart of manhood; and by all
The sad yet grand remembrances, that lie
Deep with earth's buried heroes; to recall
The soul of other years, if but to grace their fall!

LVII.

His words are full of faith! — and thoughts, more high
Than Rome e'er knew, now fill his glance with light;
Thoughts which give nobler lessons how to die,
Than e'er were drawn from Nature's haughty might!

And to that eye, with all the spirit bright
Have theirs replied in tears, which may not shame
The bravest in such moments! 'Tis a sight
To make all earthly splendours cold and tame,
— That generous burst of soul, with its electric flame!

LVIII.

They weep — those champions of the Cross — they weep,
Yet vow themselves to death! Ay, midst that train,
Are martyrs, privileged in tears to steep
Their lofty sacrifice! The pang is vain,
And yet its gush of sorrow shall not stain
A warrior's sword. Those men are strangers here:*
The homes they never may behold again,
Lie far away, with all things blest and dear,
On laughing shores, to which their barks no more shall steer!

LIX.

Know'st thou the land where bloom the orange bowers?**
Where, through dark foliage, gleam the citron's dyes?
— It is their own. They see their fathers' towers
Midst its Hesperian groves in sunlight rise:
They meet, in soul, the bright Italian eyes
Which long and vainly shall explore the main
For their white sails' return: the melodies

---

* Many of the adherents of Constantine, in his last noble stand for the liberties, or rather the honour, of a falling empire, were foreigners, and chiefly Italians.

** This and the next line are an almost literal translation from a beautiful song of Goethe's: —

"Kennst du das Land, wo die Citronen blühn,
Im dunkeln Laub die Goldorangen glühn?" etc.

THE LAST CONSTANTINE.

Of that sweet land are floating o'er their brain —
Oh! what a crowded world one moment may contain!

LX.

Such moments come to thousands! — few may die
Amidst their native shades. The young, the brave,
The beautiful, whose gladdening voice and eye
Made summer in a parent's heart, and gave
Light to their peopled homes; o'er land and wave
Are scatter'd fast and far, as rose-leaves fall
From the deserted stem. They find a grave
Far from the shadow of th' ancestral hall,
A lonely bed is theirs, whose smiles were hope to all!

LXI.

But life flows on, and bears us with its tide,
Nor may we, lingering, by the slumberers dwell,
Though they were those once blooming at our side
In youth's gay home! Away! what sound's deep swell
Comes on the wind? — It is an empire's knell,
Slow, sad, majestic, pealing through the night!
For the last time speaks forth the solemn bell
Which calls the Christians to their holiest rite,
With a funereal voice of solitary might.

LXII.

Again, and yet again! A startling power
In sounds like these lives ever; for they bear,
Full on remembrance, each eventful hour
Checkering life's crowded path. They fill the air
When conquerors pass, and fearful cities wear
A mien like joy's; and when your brides are led
From their paternal homes; and when the glare

Of burning streets on midnight's cloud waves red,
And when the silent house receives its guest — the dead.*

LXIII.

But to those tones what thrilling soul was given
On that last night of empire! As a spell
Whereby the life-blood to its source is driven,
On the chill'd heart of multitudes they fell.
Each cadence seem'd a prophecy, to tell
Of sceptres passing from their line away,
An angel-watcher's long and sad farewell,
The requiem of a faith's departing sway,
A throne's, a nation's dirge, a wail for earth's decay.

LXIV.

Again, and yet again! — from yon high dome,
Still the slow peal comes awfully; and they
Who never move, to rest in mortal home,
Shall throw the breastplate off at fall of day,
Th' imperial band, in close and arm'd array,
As men that from the sword must part no more,
Take through the midnight streets their silent way,
Within their ancient temple to adore,
Ere yet its thousand years of Christian pomp are o'er.

LXV.

It is the hour of sleep: yet few the eyes
O'er which forgetfulness her balm hath shed
In the beleaguer'd city. Stillness lies,
With moonlight, o'er the hills and waters spread,

---

* The idea expressed in this stanza is beautifully amplified in Schiller's poem, "Das Lied von der Glocke."

But not the less, with signs and sounds of dread,
The time speeds on. No voice is raised to greet
The last brave Constantine; and yet the tread
Of many steps is in the echoing street,
And pressure of pale crowds, scarce conscious why they meet.

LXVI.

Their homes are luxury's yet; why pour they thence
With a dim terror in each restless eye?
Hath the dread car which bears the pestilence,
In darkness, with its heavy wheels roll'd by,
And rock'd their palaces, as if on high
The whirlwind pass'd? From couch and joyous board
Hath the fierce phantom beckon'd them to die!*
— No! — what are these? — for them a cup is pour'd
More dark with wrath, — *man* comes — the spoiler and the
    sword.

LXVII.

Still, as the monarch and his chieftains pass
Through those pale throngs, the streaming torchlight
    throws.
On some wild form, amidst the living mass,
Hues, deeply red like lava's, which disclose
What countless shapes are worn by mortal woes!
Lips bloodless, quivering limbs, hands clasp'd in prayer,
Starts, tremblings, hurryings, tears; all outward shows
Betokening inward agonies, were there:
Greeks! Romans! all but such as image brave despair!

---

* It is said to be a Greek superstition that the plague is announced by the heavy rolling of an invisible chariot, heard in the streets at midnight; and also by the appearance of a gigantic spectre, who summons the devoted person by name.

LXVIII.

But high above that scene, in bright repose,
And beauty borrowing from the torches' gleams
A mien of life, yet where no life-blood flows,
But all instinct with loftier being seems,
Pale, grand, colossal: lo! th' embodied dreams
Of yore! — Gods, heroes, bards, in marble wrought,
Look down, as powers, upon the wild extremes
Of mortal passion! Yet 'twas man that caught,
And in each glorious form enshrined immortal thought!

LXIX.

Stood ye not thus amidst the streets of Rome?
That Rome which witness'd, in her sceptred days,
So much of noble death? When shrine and dome,
Midst clouds of incense, rang with choral lays,
As the long triumph pass'd, with all its blaze
Of regal spoil, were ye not proudly borne,
O sovereign forms! concentring all the rays
Of the soul's lightnings? — did ye not adorn
The pomp which earth stood still to gaze on, and to mourn?

LXX.

Hath it been thus? — Or did ye grace the halls,
Once peopled by the mighty? Haply there,
In your still grandeur, from the pillar'd walls
Serene ye smiled on banquets of despair,*
Where hopeless courage wrought itself to dare
The stroke of its deliverance, midst the glow
Of living wreaths, the sighs of perfumed air,

---

* Many instances of such banquets, given and shared by persons resolved upon death, might be adduced from ancient history. That of Vibius Virius, at Capua, is amongst the most memorable.

The sound of lyres, the flower-crown'd goblet's flow.
— Behold again! — high hearts make nobler offerings now!

LXXI.

The stately fane is reach'd — and at its gate
The warriors pause. On life's tumultuous tide
A stillness falls, while he whom regal state
Hath mark'd from all, to be more sternly tried
By suffering, speaks: each ruder voice hath died,
While his implores forgiveness! — "If there be
One midst your throngs, my people! whom, in pride
Or passion, I have wrong'd; such pardon free
As mortals hope from heaven, accord that man to me!"

LXXII.

But all is silence; and a gush of tears
Alone replies! He hath not been of those
Who, fear'd by many, pine in secret fears
Of all; th' environ'd but by slaves and foes,
To whom day brings not safety, night repose,
For they have *heard the voice cry*, "*Sleep no more!*"
Of them he hath not been, nor such as close
Their hearts to misery, till the time is o'er,
When it speaks low and kneels th' oppressor's throne before!

LXXIII.

He hath been loved. But who may trust to love
Of a degenerate race? — in other mould
Are cast the free and lofty hearts that prove
Their faith through fiery trials. Yet behold,
And call him not forsaken! — thoughts untold
Have lent his aspect calmness, and his tread
Moves firmly to the shrine. What pomps unfold

Within its precincts! Isles and seas have shed
Their gorgeous treasures there, around th' imperial dead.

LXXIV.

'Tis a proud vision — that most regal pile
Of ancient days! The lamps are streaming bright
From its rich altar, down each pillar'd aisle,
Whose vista fades in dimness; but the sight
Is lost in splendours, as the wavering light
Develops on those walls the thousand dyes
Of the vein'd marbles, which array their height,
And from yon dome, the lode-star of all eyes,*
Pour such an iris-glow as emulates the skies.

LXXV.

But gaze thou not on these; though heaven's own hues
In their soft clouds and radiant tracery vie —
Though tints, of sun-born glory, may suffuse
Arch, column, rich mosaic — pass thou by
The stately tombs, where Eastern Cæsars lie,
Beneath their trophies: pause not here; for know,
A deeper source of all sublimity
Lives in man's bosom, than the world can show
In nature or in art — above, around, below.

LXXVI.

Turn thou to mark (though tears may dim thy gaze)
The steel-clad group before yon altar-stone:
Heed not though gems and gold around it blaze;
Those heads unhelm'd, those kneeling forms alone,

* For a minute description of the marbles, jaspers, and porphyries, employed in the construction of St. Sophia, see *The Decline and Fall*, &c., vol. vii. p. 120.

Thus bow'd, look glorious here. The light is thrown
Full from the shrine on one, a nation's lord,
A sufferer! but his task shall soon be done —
E'en now, as Faith's mysterious cup is pour'd,
See to that noble brow, peace, not of earth, restored!

LXXVII.

The rite is o'er. The band of brethren part,
Once — and *but* once — to meet on earth again!
Each, in the strength of a collected heart,
To dare what man may dare — and know 'tis vain!
The rite is o'er: and thou, majestic fane!
The glory is departed from thy brow! —
Be clothed with dust! — the Christian's farewell strain
Hath died within these walls; thy Cross must bow,
Thy kingly tombs be spoil'd, the golden shrines laid low!

LXXVIII.

The streets grow still and lonely — and the star,
The last bright lingerer in the path of morn,
Gleams faint; and in the very lap of war,
As if young Hope with twilight's ray were born,
Awhile the city sleeps: her throngs, o'erworn
With fears and watchings, to their homes retire.
Nor is the balmy air of dayspring torn
With battle-sounds;* the winds in sighs expire,
And quiet broods in mists that veil the sunbeam's fire.

---

* The assault of the city took place at daybreak, and the Turks were strictly enjoined to advance in silence, which had also been commanded, on pain of death, during the preceding night. This circumstance is finely alluded to by Miss Baillie, in her tragedy of *Constantine Palæologus:* —

"Silent shall be the march; nor drum, nor trump,
Nor clash of arms, shall to the watchful foe

LXXIX.

The city sleeps! Ay! on the combat's eve,
And by the scaffold's brink, and midst the swell
Of angry seas, hath Nature won reprieve
Thus from her cares. The brave have slumber'd well,
And e'en the fearful, in their dungeon cell,
Chain'd between life and death. Such rest be thine,
For conflicts wait thee still! — yet who can tell,
In that brief hour, how much of heaven may shine
Full on thy spirit's dream! — Sleep, weary Constantine!

LXXX.

Doth the blast rise? — the clouded east is red,
As if a storm were gathering; and I hear.
What seems like heavy rain-drops, or the tread,
The soft and smother'd step of those that fear
Surprise from ambush'd foes. Hark! yet more near
It comes, a many-toned and mingled sound;
A rustling, as of winds, where boughs are sere —
A rolling, as of wheels that shake the ground
From far; a heavy rush, like seas that burst their bound!

LXXXI.

Wake! wake! They come from sea and shore ascending
In hosts your ramparts! Arm ye for the day!
Who now may sleep amidst the thunders rending,
Through tower and wall, a path for their array?

> Our near approach betray: silent and soft
> As the pard's velvet foot on Libya's sands,
> Slow stealing with crouch'd shoulders on her prey."
> CONSTANTINE PALÆOLOGUS, act. iv.

"The march and labour of thousands," must, however, as Gibbon observes, "have inevitably produced a strange confusion of discordant clamours, which reached the ears of the watchmen on the towers."

Hark! how the trumpet cheers them to the prey,
With its wild voice, to which the seas reply;
And the earth rocks beneath their engines' sway,
And the far hills repeat their battle-cry,
Till that fierce tumult seems to shake the vaulted sky!

LXXXII.

They fail not now, the generous band, that long
Have ranged their swords around a falling throne;
Still in those fearless men the walls are strong,
Hearts such as rescue empires, are their own!
— Shall those high energies be vainly shown?
No! from their towers th' invading tide is driven
Back, like the Red Sea waves, when God had blown
With his strong winds! The dark-brow'd ranks are riven:*
Shout, warriors of the Cross! — for victory is of Heaven!

LXXXIII.

Stand firm! Again the Crescent host is rushing,
And the waves foam, as on the galleys sweep,
With all their fires and darts, though blood is gushing
Fast o'er their sides, as rivers to the deep.
Stand firm! — there yet is hope; th' ascent is steep,
And from on high no shaft descends in vain.
— But those that fall swell up the mangled heap,
In the red moat, the dying and the slain,
And o'er that fearful bridge the assailants mount again!

---

* "After a conflict of two hours, the Greeks still maintained and preserved their advantage," says Gibbon. The strenuous exertions of the janisaries first turned the fortune of the day.

LXXXIV.

Oh! the dread mingling, in that awful hour,
Of all terrific sounds! — the savage tone
Of the wild horn, the cannon's peal, the shower
Of hissing darts, the crash of walls o'erthrown,
The deep dull tambour's beat — man's voice alone
Is there unheard! Ye may not catch the cry
Of trampled thousands — prayer, and shriek, and moan,
All drown'd, as that fierce hurricane sweeps by,
But swell the unheeded sum earth pays for victory!

LXXXV.

War-clouds have wrapt the city! — through their dun
O'erloaded canopy, at times a blaze
As of an angry storm-presaging sun,
From the Greek fire shoots up!* and lightning rays
Flash, from the shock of sabres, through the haze,
And glancing arrows cleave the dusky air!
— Ah! *this* is in the compass of our gaze,
But fearful things unknown, untold, are there —
Workings of wrath and death, and anguish, and despair!

LXXXVI.

Woe, shame and woe! — A chief, a warrior flies,
A red-cross champion, bleeding, wild, and pale!
— Oh God! that Nature's passing agonies
Thus, o'er the spark which dies not, should prevail!

---

* "A circumstance that distinguishes the siege of Constantinople is the union of the ancient and modern artillery. The bullet and the battering-ram were directed against the same wall; nor had the discovery of gunpowder superseded the use of the liquid and inextinguishable fire." — *Decline and Fall*, &c., vol. xii. p. 215.

Yes! rend the arrow from thy shatter'd mail,
And stanch the blood-drops, Genoa's fallen son!*
Fly swifter yet! the javelins pour as hail!
— But there are tortures which thou canst not shun:
The spirit is *their* prey — thy pangs are but begun!

LXXXVII.

Oh, happy in their homes, the noble dead!
The seal is set on their majestic fame;
Earth has drunk deep the generous blood they shed,
Fate has no power to dim their stainless name!
They may not, in one bitter moment, shame
Long glorious years. From many a lofty stem
Fall graceful flowers, and eagle hearts grow tame,
And stars drop, fading from the diadem;
But the bright *past* is theirs — there is no change for *them!*

LXXXVIII.

Where art thou, Constantine? — where death is reaping
His sevenfold harvest! — where the stormy light,
Fast as th' artillery's thunderbolts are sweeping,
Throws meteor-bursts o'er battle's noonday-night!
Where the towers rock and crumble from their height,
As to the earthquake, and the engines ply
Like red Vesuvio; and where human might
Confronts all this, and still brave hearts beat high,
While scimitars ring loud on shivering panoply.

---

* "The immediate loss of Constantinople may be ascribed to the bullet, or arrow, which pierced the gauntlet of John Justiniani, (a Genoese chief). The sight of his blood and exquisite pain appalled the courage of the chief, whose arms and counsels were the firmest rampart of the city." *Decline and Fall*, &c., vol. xii. p. 229.

LXXXIX.

Where art thou, Constantine? — where Christian blood
Hath bathed the walls in torrents, and in vain!
Where faith and valour perish in the flood,
Whose billows, rising o'er their bosoms, gain
Dark strength each moment; where the gallant slain
Around the banner of the Cross lie strew'd
Thick as the vine-leaves on th' autumnal plain;
Where all, save one high spirit, is subdued,
And through the breach press on th' o'erwhelming multitude.

XC.

Now is he battling midst a host alone,
As the last cedar stems awhile the sway
Of mountain storms, whose fury hath o'erthrown
Its forest-brethren in their green array!
And he hath cast his purple robe away,
With its imperial bearings, that his sword
An iron ransom from the chain may pay,
And win, what haply fate may yet accord,
A soldier's death — the all now left an empire's lord!

XCI.

Search for him now where bloodiest lie the files
Which once were men, the faithful and the brave!
Search for him now where loftiest rise the piles
Of shatter'd helms and shields which could not save,
And crests and banners never more to wave
In the free winds of heaven! He is of those
O'er whom the host may rush, the tempest rave,
And the steeds trample, and the spearmen close,
Yet wake them not! — so deep their long and last repose!

XCII.

Woe to the vanquish'd! — thus it hath been still
Since Time's first march! Hark, hark, a people's cry!
Ay, now the conquerors in the streets fulfil
Their task of wrath! In vain the victims fly;
Hark! now each piercing tone of agony
Blends in the city's shriek! The lot is cast.
Slaves! 'twas your *choice* thus, rather thus, to die,
Than where the warrior's blood flows warm and fast,
And roused and mighty hearts beat proudly to the last!

XCIII.

Oh! well doth freedom battle! Men have made,
E'en midst their blazing roofs, a noble stand,
And on the floors, where once their children play'd,
And by the hearths, round which their household band
At evening met; ay, struggling hand to hand,
Within the very chambers of their sleep,
There have they taught the spoilers of the land
In chainless hearts what fiery strength lies deep,
To guard free homes! But ye! — kneel, tremblers! kneel, and weep!

XCIV.

'Tis eve — the storm hath died, the valiant rest
Low on their shields; the day's fierce work is done,
And blood-stain'd seas and burning towers attest
Its fearful deeds. An empire's race is run!
Sad, midst his glory, looks the parting sun
Upon the captive city. Hark! a swell
(Meet to proclaim barbaric war-fields won)
Of fierce triumphal sounds, that wildly tell
The Soldan comes within the Cæsars' halls to dwell!

XCV.

Yes! with the peal of cymbal and of gong,
He comes: the Moslem treads those ancient halls!
But all is stillness there, as death had long
Been lord alone within those gorgeous walls.
And half that silence of the grave appals
The conqueror's heart. Ay! thus, with triumph's hour,
Still comes the boding whisper, which recalls
A thought of those impervious clouds that lower
O'er grandeur's path, a sense of some far mightier Power!

XCVI.

"The owl upon Afrasiab's towers hath sung
Her watch-song,* and around th' imperial throne
The spider weaves his web!" — Still darkly hung
That verse of omen, as a prophet's tone,
O'er his flush'd spirit. Years on years have flown
To prove its truth: kings pile their domes in air,
That the coil'd snake may bask on sculptured stone,
And nations clear the forest, to prepare
For the wild fox and wolf more stately dwellings there!

XCVII.

But thou! that on thy ramparts proudly dying,
As a crown'd leader in such hours should die,

---

* Mohammed II., on entering, after his victory, the palace of the Byzantine emperors, was strongly impressed with the silence and desolation which reigned within its precincts. "A melancholy reflection on the vicissitudes of human greatness forced itself on his mind, and he repeated an elegant distich of Persian poetry: 'The spider has wove his web in the imperial palace, and the owl hath sung her watch-song on the towers of Afrasiab.'" — *Decline and Fall*, &c., vol. XII. p. 240.

Upon thy pyre of shiver'd spears art lying,
With the heavens o'er thee for a canopy,
And banners for thy shroud! No tear, no sigh,
Shall mingle with thy dirge; for thou art now
Beyond vicissitude! Lo! rear'd on high,
The Crescent blazes, while the Cross must bow —
But where no change can reach, there, Constantine, art thou!

XCVIII.

"After life's fitful fever thou sleep'st well!"
We may not mourn thee! Sceptred chiefs, from whom
The earth received her destiny, and fell
Before them trembling — to a sterner doom
Have oft been call'd. For them the dungeon's gloom,
With its cold starless midnight, hath been made
More fearful darkness, where, as in a tomb,
Without a tomb's repose, the chain hath weigh'd
Their very soul to dust, with each high power decay'd.

XCIX.

Or in the eye of thousands they have stood,
To meet the stroke of death; but not like thee!
From bonds and scaffolds hath appeal'd *their* blood,
But thou didst fall unfetter'd, arm'd, and free,
And kingly to the last! And if it be,
That from the viewless world, whose marvels none
Return to tell, a spirit's eye can see
The things of earth: still may'st thou hail the sun,
Which o'er thy land shall dawn, when freedom's fight is won!

C.

And the hour comes, in storm! A light is glancing
Far through the forest gods's Arcadian shades!

— "Tis not the moonbeam, tremulously dancing,
Where lone Alpheus bathes his haunted glades.
A murmur, gathering power, the air pervades,
Round dark Cithæron and by Delphi's steep;
— 'Tis not the song and lyre of Grecian maids,
Nor pastoral reed that lulls the vales to sleep,
Nor yet the rustling pines, nor yet the sounding deep!

CI.

Arms glitter on the mountains, which of old
Awoke to freedom's first heroic strain,
And by the streams, once crimson, as they roll'd
The Persian helm and standard to the main;
And the blue waves of Salamis again
Thrill to the trumpet; and the tombs reply,
With their ten thousand echoes, from each plain,
Far as Platæa's, where the mighty lie,
Who crown'd so proudly there the bowl of liberty!*

CII.

Bright land, with glory mantled o'er by song!
Land of the vision-peopled hills, and streams,
And fountains, whose deserted banks along
Still the soft air with inspiration teems;
Land of the graves, whose dwellers shall be themes
To verse for ever; and of ruin'd shrines,
That scarce look desolate beneath such beams,
As bathe in gold thine ancient rocks and pines?
— When shall thy sons repose in peace beneath their vines?

* One of the ceremonies by which the battle of Platæa was annually commemorated was, to crown with wine a cup called the *Bowl of Liberty*, which was afterwards poured forth in libation.

CIII.

Thou wert not made for bonds, nor shame, nor fear!
— Do the hoar oaks and dark-green laurels wave
O'er Mantinea's earth? — doth Pindus rear
His snows, the sunbeam and the storm to brave?
And is there yet on Marathon a grave?
And doth Eurotas lead his silvery line
By Sparta's ruins? And shall man, a slave,
Bow'd to the dust, amid such scenes repine?
— If e'er a soil was mark'd for freedom's step, 'tis thine!

CIV.

Wash from that soil the stains with battle-showers.
— Beneath Sophia's dome the Moslem prays,
The Crescent gleams amidst the olive-bowers,
In the Comneni's halls the Tartar sways:*
But not for long! — the spirit of those days,
When the three hundred made their funeral pile
Of Asia's dead, is kindling, like the rays
Of thy rejoicing sun, when first his smile
Warms the Parnassian rock, and gilds the Delian isle.

CV.

If then 'tis given thee to arise in might,
Trampling the scourge, and dashing down the chain,
Pure be thy triumphs, as thy name is bright!
The cross of victory should not know a stain!
So may that faith once more supremely reign,

* The Comneni were amongst the most distinguished of the families who filled the Byzantine throne in the declining years of the Eastern Empire.

Through which we lift our spirits from the dust!
And deem not, e'en when virtue dies in vain,
She dies forsaken; but repose our trust
On Him whose ways are dark, unsearchable — but just.

ANNOTATION ON "THE LAST CONSTANTINE."

["The present publication appears to us, (Dr. Morehead in *Constable's Magazine*, Sept. 1823,) in every respect superior to any thing Mrs. Hemans has yet written; more powerful in particular passages — more interesting in the narrative part — as pathetic and delicate in the reflective — as elaborately faultless in its versification — as copious in imagery. Of the longer poems, 'The Last Constantine' is our favourite. . . . . . The leading features of Constantine's character seem to be taken from the unequal, but, on the whole, admirable play of *Constantine Palæologus* by the gifted rival of our authoress, Joanna Baillie; and the picture of that enduring and Christian courage which, in the midst of a ruined city and a fallen state, sustained the last of the Cæsars, when all earthly hope and help had failed him, is eminently touching and poetical. The following stanzas appear to us particularly beautiful:

'Sounds from the waters, sounds upon the earth,
Sounds in the air, of battle,' etc.

The following stanzas, too, in which the leading idea of Constantine's character is still more fully brought out, are likewise excellent: —

'It was a sad and solemn task to hold
Their midnight watch on that beleaguer'd wall,' etc.

These are splendid passages, justly conceived, admirably expressed, full of eloquence and melody; and the poem contains many others equally beautiful. As we have already hinted, the story might have been better told — or rather, there is scarcely any story at all; but the reader is borne down the stream of pensive reflection so gently, and so easily, that he scarcely perceives the want of it."]

THE WIDOW OF CRESCENTIUS.

["In the reign of Otho III. Emperor of Germany, the Romans, excited by their Consul, Crescentius, who ardently desired to restore the ancient glory of the Republic, made a bold attempt to shake off the Saxon yoke, and the authority of the popes, whose vices rendered them objects of universal contempt. The Consul was besieged by Otho in the Mole of Hadrian, which long afterwards continued to be called the Tower of Crescentius. Otho, after many unavailing attacks upon this fortress, at last entered into negotiations; and, pledging his imperial word to respect the life of Crescentius, and the rights of the Roman citizens, the unfortunate leader was betrayed into his power, and immediately beheaded, with many of his partisans. Stephania, his widow, concealing her affliction and her resentment for the insults to which she had been exposed, secretly resolved to revenge her husband and herself. On the return of Otho from a pilgrimage to Mount Gargano, which perhaps a feeling of remorse had induced him to undertake, she found means to be introduced to him, and to gain his confidence; and a poison administered by her was soon afterwards the cause of his painful death." — SISMONDI, *History of the Italian Republics*, vol. i.]

"L'orage peut briser en un moment les fleurs qui tiennent encore la tête lovée." — MAD. DE STAEL.

MIDST Tivoli's luxuriant glades,
Bright-foaming falls, and olive shades,
Where dwelt, in days departed long,
The sons of battle and of song,
No tree, no shrub its foliage rears
But o'er the wrecks of other years,
Temples and domes, which long have been
The soil of that enchanted scene.

There the wild fig-tree and the vine
O'er Hadrian's mouldering villa twine;*

* "J'étais allé passer quelque jours seuls à Tivoli. Je parcourus les environs, et surtout celles de la Villa Adriana. Surpris par la pluie au

The cypress, in funereal grace,
Usurps the vanish'd column's place;
O'er fallen shrine and ruin'd frieze
The wall-flower rustles in the breeze;
Acanthus-leaves the marble hide
They once adorn'd in sculptured pride;
And nature hath resumed her throne
O'er the vast works of ages flown.

Was it for this that many a pile,
Pride of Ilissus and of Nile,
To Anio's banks the image lent
Of each imperial monument?*
Now Athens weeps her shatter'd fanes,
Thy temples, Egypt, strew thy plains;
And the proud fabrics Hadrian rear'd
From Tibur's vale have disappear'd.

milieu de ma course, je me réfugiai dans les Salles des *Thermes* voisins du *Pécile*, (monumens de la villa,) sous un figuier qui avait renversé le pan d'un mur en s'élevant. Dans un petit salon octogone, ouvert devant moi, une vigne vierge avait percé la voûte de l'édifice, et son gros cep lisse, rouge, et tortueux, montait le long du mur comme un serpent. Autour de moi, à travers les arcades des ruines, s'ouvraient des points de vue sur la Campagne Romaine. Des buissons de sureau remplissaient les salles désertes où venaient se réfugier quelques merles solitaires. Les fragmens de maçonnerie étaient tapissées de feuilles de scolopendre, dont la verdure satinée se dessinait comme un travail en mosaïque sur la blancheur des marbres; çà et là de hauts cyprès remplaçaient les colonnes tombées dans ces palais de la Mort; l'acanthe sauvage rampait à leurs pieds, sur des débris, comme si la nature s'était plu à reproduire sur ces chefs-d'œuvre mutilés d'architecture, l'ornement de leur beauté passée." CHATEAUBRIAND's *Souvenirs d'Italie*.

* The gardens and buildings of Hadrian's villa were copies of the most celebrated scenes and edifices in his dominions — the Lyceum, the Academia, the Prytaneum of Athens, the Temple of Serapis at Alexandria, the Vale of Tempe, &c.

We need no prescient sibyl there
The doom of grandeur to declare;
Each stone, where weeds and ivy climb,
Reveals some oracle of Time;
Each relic utters Fate's decree —
The future as the past shall be.

Halls of the dead! in Tibur's vale,
Who now shall tell your lofty tale?
Who trace the high patrician's dome,
The bard's retreat, the hero's home?
When moss-clad wrecks alone record
There dwelt the world's departed lord,
In scenes where verdure's rich array
Still sheds young beauty o'er decay,
And sunshine on each glowing hill
Midst ruins finds a dwelling still.

Sunk is thy palace — but thy tomb,
Hadrian! hath shared a prouder doom.*
Though vanish'd with the days of old
Its pillars of Corinthian mould;

---

* The mausoleum of Hadrian, now the castle of St. Angelo, was first converted into a citadel by Belisarius, in his successful defence of Rome against the Goths. "The lover of the arts," says Gibbon, "must read with a sigh that the works of Praxiteles and Lysippus were torn from their lofty pedestals, and hurled into the ditch on the heads of the besiegers." He adds, in a note, that the celebrated Sleeping Faun of the Barberini palace was found, in a mutilated state, when the ditch of St. Angelo was cleansed under Urban VIII. In the middle ages, the Moles Hadriani was made a permanent fortress by the Roman government, and bastions, outworks, &c. were added to the original edifice, which had been stripped of its marble covering, its Corinthian pillars, and the brazen cone which crowned its summit.

Though the fair forms by sculpture wrought,
Each bodying some immortal thought,
Which o'er that temple of the dead
Serene but solemn beauty shed,
Have found, like glory's self, a grave
In time's abyss or Tiber's wave;*
Yet dreams more lofty and more fair
Than art's bold hand hath imaged o'er,
High thoughts of many a mighty mind
Expanding when all else declined,
In twilight years, when only they
Recall'd the radiance pass'd away,
Have made that ancient pile their home,
Fortress of freedom and of Rome.

There he, who strove in evil days
Again to kindle glory's rays,
Whose spirit sought a path of light
For those dim ages far too bright —
Crescentius — long maintain'd the strife
Which closed but with its martyr's life,
And left th' imperial tomb a name,
A heritage of holier fame.
There closed De Brescia's mission high,
From thence the patriot came to die;**

---

* "Les plus beaux monumens des arts, les plus admirables statues, ont été jetées dans le Tibre, et sont cachées sous ses flots. Qui sait si, pour les chercher, on ne le détournera pas un jour de son lit? Mais quand on songe que les chefs-d'œuvres du génie humain sont peut-être là devant nous, et qu'un œil plus perçant les verrait à travers les ondes, l'on éprouve je ne sais quelle émotion, qui renaît à Rome sans cesse sous diverses formes, et fait trouver une société pour la pensée dans les objets physiques, muets partout ailleurs." — Mad. de Stael.

** Arnold de Brescia, the undaunted and eloquent champion of Roman

And thou, whose Roman soul the last
Spoke with the voice of ages past,*
Whose thoughts so long from earth had fled
To mingle with the glorious dead,
That midst the world's degenerate race
They vainly sought a dwelling-place,
Within that house of death didst brood
O'er visions to thy ruin woo'd.
Yet, worthy of a brighter lot,
Rienzi, be thy faults forgot!
For thou, when all around thee lay
Chain'd in the slumbers of decay —
So sunk each heart, that mortal eye
Had scarce a *tear* for liberty —
Alone, amidst the darkness there,
Couldst gaze on Rome — yet not despair!**

liberty, after unremitting efforts to restore the ancient constitution of the republic, was put to death in the year 1155 by Adrian IV. This event is thus described by Sismondi, *Histoire des Republiques Italiennes*, vol. ii. pages 68 and 69. "Le préfet demeura dans le château Saint Ange avec son prisonnier: il lo fit transporter un matin sur la place destinée aux exécutions, devant la porte du peuple. Arnaud de Brescia, élevé sur un bûcher, fut attaché à un poteau, en face du Corso. Il pouvoit mesurer des yeux les trois longues rues qui aboutissoient devant son échafaud; elles font presqu' une moitié de Rome. C'est là qu'habitoient les hommes qu'il avoit si souvent appelés à la liberté. Ils reposoient encore en paix, ignorant le danger de leur législateur. Le tumulte de l'exécution et la flamme du bûcher réveillèrent les Romains; ils s'armèrent, ils accoururent, mais trop tard; et les cohortes du pape repoussèrent, avec leurs lances, ceux qui, n'ayant pu sauver Arnaud, vouloient du moins recueillir ses cendres comme de précieuses reliques."

* "Posterity will compare the virtues and failings of this extraordinary man; but in a long period of anarchy and servitude, the name of Rienzi has often been celebrated as the deliverer of his country, and the last of the Roman patriots." — Gibbon's *Decline and Fall*, &c. vol. xii. p. 369.

** "Le consul Terentius Varron avoit foi honteusement jusqu'à Venouse.

'Tis morn — and nature's richest dyes
Are floating o'er Italian skies;
Tints of transparent lustre shine
Along the snow-clad Apennine;
The clouds have left Soracte's height,
And yellow Tiber winds in light,
Where tombs and fallen fanes have strew'd
The wide Campagna's solitude.
'Tis sad amidst that scene to trace
Those relics of a vanish'd race;
Yet, o'er the ravaged path of time —
Such glory sheds that brilliant clime,
Where nature still, though empires fall,
Holds her triumphant festival —
E'en desolation wears a smile,
Where skies and sunbeams laugh the while;
And heaven's own light, earth's richest bloom,
Array the ruin and the tomb.

But she, who from yon convent tower
Breathes the pure freshness of the hour;
She, whose rich flow of raven hair
Streams wildly on the morning air,
Heeds not how fair the scene below,
Robed in Italia's brightest glow.
Though throned midst Latium's classic plains
Th' Eternal City's towers and fanes,

Cet homme, de la plus basse naissance, n'avoit été élevé au consulat que pour mortifier la noblesse; mais le sénat ne voulut pas jouir de ce malheureux triomphe; il vit combien il étoit nécessaire qu'il s'attirât dans cette occasion la confiance du peuple — il alla au-devant de Varron, et le remercia de ce qu'il n'avoit pas *désespéré de la république.*" — Montesquieu's *Grandeur et Décadence des Romains.*

THE WIDOW OF CRESCENTIUS.

And they, the Pleiades of earth,
The seven proud hills of Empire's birth,
Lie spread beneath; not now her glance
Roves o'er that vast sublime expanse;
Inspired, and bright with hope, 'tis thrown
On Adrian's massy tomb alone;
There, from the storm, when Freedom fled,
His faithful few Crescentius led;
While she, his anxious bride, who now
Bends o'er the scene her youthful brow,
Sought refuge in the hallow'd fane,
Which then could shelter, not in vain.

But now the lofty strife is o'er,
And Liberty shall weep no more.
At length imperial Otho's voice
Bids her devoted sons rejoice;
And he, who battled to restore
The glories and the rights of yore,
Whose accents, like the clarion's sound,
Could burst the dead repose around,
Again his native Rome shall see
The sceptred city of the free!
And young Stephania waits the hour
When leaves her lord his fortress-tower —
Her ardent heart with joy elate,
That seems beyond the reach of fate;
Her mien, like creature from above,
All vivified with hope and love.

Fair is her form, and in her eye
Lives all the soul of Italy;

A meaning lofty and inspired,
As by her native day-star fired;
Such wild and high expression, fraught
With glances of impassion'd thought,
As fancy sheds, in visions bright,
O'er priestess of the God of Light;
And the dark locks that lend her face
A youthful and luxuriant grace,
Wave o'er her cheek, whose kindling dyes
Seem from the fire within to rise,
But deepen'd by the burning heaven
To her own land of sunbeams given.
Italian art that fervid glow
Would o'er ideal beauty throw,
And with such ardent life express
Her high-wrought dreams of loveliness, —
Dreams which, surviving Empire's fall,
The shade of glory still recall.

But see! — the banner of the brave
O'er Adrian's tomb hath ceased to wave.
'Tis lower'd — and now Stephania's eye
Can well the martial train descry,
Who, issuing from that ancient dome,
Pour through the crowded streets of Rome.
Now from her watch-tower on the height,
With step as fabled wood-nymph's light,
She flies — and swift her way pursues
Through the lone convent's avenues.
Dark cypress groves, and fields o'erspread
With records of the conquering dead,
And paths which track a glowing waste,
She traverses in breathless haste;

And by the tombs where dust is shrined
Once tenanted by loftiest mind,
Still passing on, hath reach'd the gate
Of Rome, the proud, the desolate!
Throng'd are the streets, and, still renew'd,
Rush on the gathering multitude.
— Is it their high-soul'd chief to greet
That thus the Roman thousands meet?
With names that bid their thoughts ascend,
Crescentius! thine in song to blend;
And of triumphal day gone by
Recall th' inspiring pageantry?
— There is an air of breathless dread,
An eager glance, a hurrying tread;
And now a fearful silence round,
And now a fitful murmuring sound,
Midst the pale crowds, that almost seem
Phantoms of some tumultuous dream.
Quick is each step and wild each mien,
Portentous of some awful scene.
Bride of Crescentius! as the throng
Bore thee with whelming force along,
How did thine anxious heart beat high,
Till rose suspense to agony! —
Too brief suspense, that soon shall close,
And leave thy heart to deeper woes.

Who midst yon guarded precinct stands,
With fearless mien but fetter'd hands?
The ministers of death are nigh,
Yet a calm grandeur lights his eye;
And in his glance there lives a mind
Which was not form'd for chains to bind,

But cast in such heroic mould
As theirs, th' ascendant ones of old.
Crescentius! freedom's daring son,
Is this the guerdon thou hast won?
Oh, worthy to have lived and died
In the bright days of Latium's pride!
Thus must the beam of glory close
O'er the seven hills again that rose,
When at thy voice, to burst the yoke,
The soul of Rome indignant woke?
Vain dream! the sacred shields are gone,*
Sunk is the crowning city's throne:**
Th' illusions, that around her cast
Their guardian spells, have long been past.***

---

* Of the sacred bucklers, or *ancilia* of Rome, which were kept in the temple of Mars, Plutarch gives the following account: — "In the eighth year of Numa's reign, a pestilence prevailed in Italy; Rome also felt its ravages. While the people were greatly dejected, we are told that a brazen buckler fell from heaven into the hands of Numa. Of this he gave a very wonderful account, received from Egeria and the Muses; that the buckler was sent down for the preservation of the city, and should be kept with great care; that eleven others should be made as like it as possible in size and fashion, in order that, if any person were disposed to steal it, he might not be able to distinguish that which fell from heaven from the rest. He further declared, that the place, and the meadows about it, where he frequently conversed with the Muses, should be consecrated to those divinities; and that the spring which watered the ground should be sacred to the use of the Vestal Virgins, daily to sprinkle and purify their temple. The immediate cessation of the pestilence is said to have confirmed the truth of this account." — *Life of Numa.*

** "Who hath taken this counsel against Tyre, the *crowning city*, whose merchants are princes, whose traffickers are the honourable of the earth?" — *Isaiah*, chap. 23.

*** "Un mélange bizarre de grandeur d'âme et de foiblesse entroit dès cette époque (l'onzième siècle) dans le caractère des Romains. Un mouvement généreux vers les grandes choses faisoit place tout-à-coup à l'abatte-

Thy life hath been a shot-star's ray,
Shed o'er her midnight of decay;
Thy death at freedom's ruin'd shrine
Must rivet every chain — but thine.

Calm is his aspect, and his eye
Now fix'd upon the deep blue sky,
Now on those wrecks of ages fled
Around in desolation spread —
Arch, temple, column, worn and gray,
Recording triumphs pass'd away;
Works of the mighty and the free,
Whose steps on earth no more shall be,
Though their bright course hath left a trace
Nor years nor sorrows can efface.
Why changes now the patriot's mien,
Erewhile so loftily serene?
Thus can approaching death control
The might of that commanding soul?
No! — Heard ye not that thrilling cry
Which told of bitterest agony?
He heard it, and at once, subdued,
Hath sunk the hero's fortitude.

---

ment; ils passoient de la liberté la plus orageuse, à la servitude la plus avilissante. On auroit dit que les ruines et les portiques déserts de la capitale du monde, entretenoient ses habitans dans le sentiment de leur impuissance; au milieu de ces monumens de leur domination passée, les citoyens éprouvoient d'une manière trop décourageante leur propre nullité. Le nom des Romains qu'ils portoient ranimoit fréquemment leur enthousiasme, comme il le ranime encore aujourd'hui; mas bientôt la vue de Rome, du forum désert, des sept collines de nouveau rendues au pâturage des troupeaux, des temples désolés, des monumens tombant en ruine, les ramenoit à sentir qu'ils n'étoient plus les Romains d'autrefois."—SISMONDI, *Histoire des Républiques Italiennes*, vol. I. p. 172.

He heard it, and his heart too well
Whence rose that voice of woe can tell;
And midst the gazing throngs around
One well-known form his glance hath found —
One fondly loving and beloved,
In grief, in peril, faithful proved.
Yes! in the wildness of despair,
She, his devoted bride, is there.
Pale, breathless, through the crowd she flies,
The light of frenzy in her eyes:
But ere her arms can clasp the form
Which life ere long must cease to warm —
Ere on his agonising breast
Her heart can heave, her head can rest —
Check'd in her course by ruthless hands,
Mute, motionless, at once she stands;
With bloodless cheek and vacant glance,
Frozen and fix'd in horror's trance;
Spell-bound, as every sense were fled,
And thought o'erwhelm'd, and feeling dead;
And the light waving of her hair,
And veil, far floating on the air,
Alone, in that dread moment, show
She is no sculptured form of woe.

The scene of grief and death is o'er,
The patriot's heart shall throb no more;
But *hers* — so vainly form'd to prove
The pure devotedness of love,
And draw from fond affection's eye
All thought sublime, all feeling high —
When consciousness again shall wake,
Hath now no refuge but to break.

The spirit long inured to pain
May smile at fate in calm disdain,
Survive its darkest hour, and rise
In more majestic energies.
But in the glow of vernal pride,
If each warm hope *at once* hath died,
Then sinks the mind, a blighted flower,
Dead to the sunbeam and the shower;
A broken gem, whose inborn light
Is scatter'd — ne'er to re-unite.

PART II.

Hast thou a scene that is not spread
With records of thy glory fled?
A monument that doth not tell
The tale of liberty's farewell?
Italia! thou art but a grave
Where flowers luxuriate o'er the brave,
And nature gives her creatures birth
O'er all that hath been great on earth.
Yet smile thy heavens as once they smiled
When thou wert freedom's favour'd child:
Though fane and tomb alike are low,
Time hath not dimm'd thy sunbeam's glow;
And, robed in that exulting ray,
Thou seem'st to triumph o'er decay —
Oh, yet, though by thy sorrows bent,
In nature's pomp magnificent!
What marvel if, when all was lost
Still on thy bright enchanted coast,

Though many an omen warn'd him thence,
Linger'd the lord of eloquence.*
Still gazing on the lovely sky,
Whose radiance woo'd him — but to die?
Like him, *who* would not linger there,
Where heaven, earth, ocean, all are fair?
Who midst thy glowing scenes could dwell,
Nor bid awhile his griefs farewell?

---

* As for Cicero, he was carried to Astyra, where, finding a vessel, he immediately went on board, and coasted along to Circæum with a favourable wind. The pilots were preparing immediately to sail from thence, but whether it was that he feared the sea, or had not yet given up all his hopes in Cæsar, he disembarked, and travelled a hundred furlongs on foot, as if Rome had been the place of his destination. Repenting, however, afterwards, he left that road, and made again for the sea. He passed the night in the most perplexing and horrid thoughts; insomuch, that he was sometimes inclined to go privately into Cæsar's house, and stab himself upon the altar of his domestic gods, to bring the divine vengeance upon his betrayer. But he was deterred from this by the fear of torture. Other alternatives, equally distressful, presented themselves. At last he put himself in the hands of his servants, and ordered them to carry him by sea to Cajeta, where he had a delightful retreat in the summer, when the Etesian winds set in. There was a temple of Apollo on that coast, from which a flight of crows came with great noise towards Cicero's vessel as it was making land. They perched on both sides the sail-yard, where some sat croaking, and others pecking the ends of the ropes. All looked upon this as an ill omen; yet Cicero went on shore, and, entering his house, lay down to repose himself. In the meantime a number of the crows settled in the chamber-window, and croaked in the most doleful manner. One of them even entered it, and, alighting on the bed, attempted with its beak to draw off the clothes with which he had covered his face. On sight of this, the servants began to reproach themselves. 'Shall we,' said they, 'remain to be spectators of our master's murder? Shall we not protect him, so innocent and so great a sufferer as he is, when the brute creatures give him marks of their care and attention?' Then, partly by entreaty, partly by force, they got him into his litter, and carried him towards the sea." — PLUTARCH, *Life of Cicero.*

Hath not thy pure and genial air
Balm for all sadness but despair?*
No! there are pangs whose deep-worn trace
Not all thy magic can efface!
Hearts by unkindness wrung may learn
The world and all its gifts to spurn;
Time may steal on with silent tread,
And dry the tear that mourns the dead,
May change fond love, subdue regret,
And teach e'en vengeance to forget:
But thou, Remorse! there is no charm
Thy sting, avenger, to disarm!
Vain are bright suns and laughing skies
To soothe thy victim's agonies:
The heart once made thy burning throne,
Still, while it beats, is thine alone.

In vain for Otho's joyless eye
Smile the fair scenes of Italy,
As through her landscapes' rich array
Th' imperial pilgrim bends his way.
Thy form, Crescentius! on his sight
Rises when nature laughs in light,
Glides round him at the midnight hour,
Is present in his festal bower,
With awful voice and frowning mien,
By all but him unheard, unseen.
Oh! thus to shadows of the grave
Be every tyrant still a slave!

* "Now purer air
Meets his approach, and to the heart inspires
Vernal delight and joy, able to drive
All sadness but despair." — MILTON.

Where, through Gargano's woody dells,
O'er bending oaks the north wind swells,*

A sainted hermit's lowly tomb
Is bosom'd in umbrageous gloom,
In shades that saw him live and die
Beneath their waving canopy.
'Twas his, as legends tell, to share
The converse of immortals there;
Around that dweller of the wild
There " bright appearances" have smiled,**
And angel-wings at eve have been
Gleaming the shadowy boughs between.
And oft from that secluded bower
Hath breathed, at midnight's calmer hour,
A swell of viewless harps, a sound
Of warbled anthems pealing round.
Oh, none but voices of the sky
Might wake that thrilling harmony,

---

* Mount Gargano. "This ridge of mountains forms a very large promontory advancing into the Adriatic, and separated from the Apennines on the west by the plains of Lucera and San Severo. We took a ride into the heart of the mountains through shady dells and noble woods, which brought to our minds the venerable groves that in ancient times bent with the loud winds sweeping along the rugged sides of Garganus:
'Aquilonibus
Querceta Gargani laborant,
Et foliis viduantur orni.' — HORACE.
"There is still a respectable forest of evergreen and common oak, pine, hornbeam, chestnut, and manna-ash. The sheltered valleys are industriously cultivated, and seem to be blest with luxuriant vegetation." — SWINBURNE's *Travels*.

** "In yonder nether world where shall I seek
His bright appearances, or footstep trace?" — MILTON.

Whose tones, whose very echoes made
An Eden of the lonely shade!
Years have gone by; the hermit sleeps
Amidst Gargano's woods and steeps;
Ivy and flowers have half o'ergrown
And veil'd his low sepulchral stone:
Yet still the spot is holy, still
Celestial footsteps haunt the hill;
And oft the awe-struck mountaineer
Aërial vesper-hymns may hear
Around those forest-precincts float,
Soft, solemn, clear, but still remote.
Oft will Affliction breathe her plaint
To that rude shrine's departed saint,
And deem that spirits of the blest
There shed sweet influence o'er her breast.

   And thither Otho now repairs,
To soothe his soul with vows and prayers;
And if for him, on holy ground,
The lost one, Peace, may yet be found,
Midst rocks and forests, by the bed
Where calmly sleep the sainted dead,
She dwells, remote from heedless eye,
With nature's lonely majesty.

   Vain, vain the search! — his troubled breast
Nor vow nor penance lulls to rest:
The weary pilgrimage is o'er,
The hopes that cheer'd it are no more.
Then sinks his soul, and day by day
Youth's buoyant energies decay

The light of health his eye hath flown,
The glow that tinged his cheek is gone.
Joyless as one on whom is laid
Some baleful spell that bids him fade,
Extending its mysterious power
O'er every scene, o'er every hour:
E'en thus *he* withers; and to him
Italia's brilliant skies are dim.
He withers — in that glorious clime
Where Nature laughs in scorn of Time;
And suns, that shed on all below
Their full and vivifying glow,
From him alone their power withhold,
And leave his heart in darkness cold.
Earth blooms around him, heaven is fair —
He only seems to perish there.

Yet sometimes will a transient smile
Play o'er his faded cheek awhile,
When breathes his minstrel boy a strain
Of power to lull all earthly pain —
So wildly sweet, its notes might seem
Th' ethereal music of a dream,
A spirit's voice from worlds unknown,
Deep thrilling power in every tone!
Sweet is that lay! and yet its flow
Hath language only given to woe;
And if at times its wakening swell
Some tale of glory seems to tell,
Soon the proud notes of triumph die,
Lost in a dirge's harmony.
Oh! many a pang the heart hath proved,
Hath deeply suffer'd, fondly loved,

Ere the sad strain could catch from thence
Such deep impassion'd eloquence!
Yes! gaze on him, that minstrel boy —
He is no child of hope and joy!
Though few his years, yet have they been
Such as leave traces on the mien,
And o'er the roses of our prime
Breathe other blights than those of time.

Yet seems his spirit wild and proud,
By grief unsoften'd and unbow'd.
Oh! there are sorrows which impart
A sternness foreign to the heart,
And, rushing with an earthquake's power,
That makes a desert in an hour,
Rouse the dread passions in their course,
As tempests wake the billows' force! —
'Tis sad, on youthful Guido's face,
The stamp of woes like these to trace.
Oh! where can ruins awe mankind
Dark as the ruins of the mind?

His mien is lofty, but his gaze
Too well a wandering soul betrays:
His full dark eye at times is bright
With strange and momentary light,
Whose quick uncertain flashes throw
O'er his pale cheek a hectic glow:
And oft his features and his air
A shade of troubled mystery wear,
A glance of hurried wildness, fraught
With some unfathomable thought.

Whate'er that thought, still unexpress'd
Dwells the sad secret in his breast;
The pride his haughty brow reveals
All other passion well conceals —
He breathes each wounded feeling's tone
In music's eloquence alone;
His soul's deep voice is only pour'd
Through his full song and swelling chord.

 He seeks no friend, but shuns the train
Of courtiers with a proud disdain;
And, save when Otho bids his lay
Its half unearthly power essay
In hall or bower the heart to thrill,
His haunts are wild and lonely still.
Far distant from the heedless throng,
He roves old Tiber's banks along,
Where Empire's desolate remains
Lie scatter'd o'er the silent plains;
Or, lingering midst each ruin'd shrine
That strews the desert Palatine,
With mournful yet commanding mien,
Like the sad genius of the scene,
Entranced in awful thought appears
To commune with departed years.
Or at the dead of night, when Rome
Seems of heroic shades the home;
When Tiber's murmuring voice recalls
The mighty to their ancient halls;
When hush'd is every meaner sound,
And the deep moonlight-calm around
Leaves to the solemn scene alone
The majesty of ages flown —

A pilgrim to each hero's tomb,
He wanders through the sacred gloom;
And midst those dwellings of decay
At times will breathe so sad a lay,
So wild a grandeur in each tone,
'Tis like a dirge for empires gone!

   Awake thy pealing harp again,
But breathe a more exulting strain,
Young Guido! for awhile forgot
Be the dark secrets of thy lot,
And rouse th' inspiring soul of song
To speed the banquet's hour along! —
The feast is spread, and music's call
Is echoing through the royal hall,
And banners wave and trophies shine
O'er stately guests in glittering line;
And Otho seeks awhile to chase
The thoughts he never can erase,
And bid the voice, whose murmurs deep
Rise like a spirit on his sleep —
The still small voice of conscience — die,
Lost in the din of revelry.
On his pale brow dejection lowers,
But that shall yield to festal hours;
A gloom is in his faded eye,
But that from music's power shall fly;
His wasted cheek is wan with care,
But mirth shall spread fresh crimson there.
Wake, Guido! wake thy numbers high,
Strike the bold chord exultingly!
And pour upon the enraptured ear
Such strains as warriors love to hear!

Let the rich mantling goblet flow,
And banish aught resembling woe;
And if a thought intrude, of power
To mar the bright convivial hour,
Still must its influence lurk unseen,
And cloud the heart — but not the mien!

  Away, vain dream! — on Otho's brow,
Still darker lower the shadows now;
Changed are his features, now o'erspread
With the cold paleness of the dead;
Now crimson'd with a hectic dye,
The burning flush of agony!
His lip is quivering, and his breast
Heaves with convulsive pangs oppress'd;
Now his dim eye seems fix'd and glazed,
And now to heaven in anguish raised;
And as, with unavailing aid,
Around him throng his guests dismay'd,
He sinks — while scarce his struggling breath
Hath power to falter — "This is death!"

  Then rush'd that haughty child of song,
Dark Guido, through the awe-struck throng.
Fill'd with a strange delirious light,
His kindling eye shone wildly bright;
And on the sufferer's mien awhile
Gazing with stern vindictive smile,
A feverish glow of triumph dyed
His burning cheek, while thus he cried: —
"Yes! these are death-pangs — on thy brow
Is set the seal of vengeance now!

THE WIDOW OF CRESCENTIUS.

Oh! well was mix'd the deadly draught,
And long and deeply hast thou quaff'd;
And bitter as thy pangs may be,
They are but guerdons meet from me!
Yet these are but a moment's throes —
Howe'er intense, they soon shall close.
Soon shalt thou yield thy fleeting breath —
My life hath been a lingering death,
Since one dark hour of woe and crime,
A blood-spot on the page of time!

"Deem'st thou my mind of reason void?
It is not frenzied — but destroy'd!
Ay! view the wreck with shuddering thought —
That work of ruin thou hast wrought!
The secret of thy doom to tell,
My name alone suffices well!
Stephania! — once a hero's bride!
Otho! thou know'st the rest — *he died.*
Yes! trusting to a monarch's word,
The Roman fell, untried, unheard!
And thou, whose every pledge was vain,
How couldst *thou* trust in aught again?

"He died, and I was changed — my soul,
A lonely wanderer, spurn'd control.
From peace, and light, and glory hurl'd,
The outcast of a purer world,
I saw each brighter hope o'erthrown,
And lived for one dread task alone.
The task is closed, fulfill'd the vow —
The hand of death is on thee now.

Betrayer! in thy turn betray'd,
The debt of blood shall soon be paid!
Thine hour is come — the time hath been
My heart had shrunk from such a scene;
That feeling long is past — my fate
Hath made me stern as desolate.

"Ye that around me shuddering stand,
Ye chiefs and princes of the land!
Mourn ye a guilty monarch's doom?
Ye wept not o'er the patriot's tomb!
He sleeps unhonour'd — yet be mine
To share his low, neglected shrine.
His soul with freedom finds a home,
His grave is that of glory — Rome!
Are not the great of old with her,
That city of the sepulchre?
Lead me to death! and let me share,
The slumbers of the mighty there!"

The day departs — that fearful day
Fades in calm loveliness away:
From purple heavens its lingering beam
Seems melting into Tiber's stream,
And softly tints each Roman hill
With glowing light, as clear and still
As if, unstain'd by crime or woe,
Its hours had pass'd in silent flow.
The day sets calmly — it hath been
Mark'd with a strange and awful scene:
One guilty bosom throbs no more,
And Otho's pangs and life are o'er.

And thou, ere yet another sun
His burning race hath brightly run,
Released from anguish by thy foes,
Daughter of Rome! shalt find repose.
Yes! on thy country's lovely sky
Fix yet once more thy parting eye!
A few short hours — and all shall be
The silent and the past for thee.
Oh! thus with tempests of a day
We struggle, and we pass away,
Like the wild billows as they sweep,
Leaving no vestige on the deep!
And o'er thy dark and lowly bed
 The sons of future days shall tread,
The pangs, the conflicts, of thy lot,
By them unknown, by thee forgot.

ALARIC IN ITALY.

[After describing the conquest of Greece and Italy by the German and Scythian hordes united under the command of Alaric, the historian of *The Decline and Fall of the Roman Empire* thus proceeds: — "Whether fame, or conquest, or riches, were the object of Alaric, he pursued that object with an indefatigable ardour, which could neither be quelled by adversity nor satiated by success. No sooner had he reached the extreme land of Italy, than he was attracted by the neighbouring prospect of a fair and peaceful island. Yet even the possession of Sicily he considered only as an intermediate step to the important expedition which he already meditated against the continent of Africa. The straits of Rhegium and Messina are twelve miles in length, and, in the narrowest passage, about one mile and a half broad; and the fabulous monsters of the deep — the rocks of Scylla and the whirlpool of Charybdis — could terrify none but the most timid and unskilful mariners: yet, as soon as the first division of the Goths had embarked, a sudden tempest arose, which sunk or scattered many of the transports. Their courage was daunted by the terrors of a new element; and the whole design was defeated by the premature death of Alaric, which fixed, after a short illness, the fatal term of his conquests. The ferocious character of the barbarians was displayed in the funeral of a hero, whose valour and fortune they celebrated with mournful applause. By the labour of a captive multitude, they forcibly diverted the course of the Busentinus, a small river that washes the walls of Consentia. The royal sepulchre, adorned with the splendid spoils and trophies of Rome, was constructed in the vacant bed; the waters were then restored to their natural channel, and the secret spot where the remains of Alaric had been deposited was for ever concealed by the inhuman massacre of the prisoners who had been employed to execute the work." — *Decline and Fall of the Roman Empire*, vol. v. p. 329.]

  Heard ye the Gothic trumpet's blast?
  The march of hosts as Alaric pass'd?
  His steps have track'd that glorious clime,
  The birth-place of heroic time;
  But he, in northern deserts bred,
  Spared not the living for the dead, *
  Nor heard the voice whose pleading cries
  From temple and from tomb arise.
  He pass'd — the light of burning fanes
  Hath been his torch o'er Grecian plains;
  And woke they not — the brave, the free,
  To guard their own Thermopylæ?
  And left they not their silent dwelling,
  When Scythia's note of war was swelling?

 * After the taking of Athens by Sylla, "though such numbers were put to the sword, there were as many who laid violent hands upon themselves in grief for their sinking country. What reduced the best men among them to this despair of finding any mercy or moderate terms for Athens, was the well-known cruelty of Sylla: yet, partly by the intercession of Midias and Calliphon, and the exiles who threw themselves at his feet — partly by the entreaties of the senators who attended him in that expedition, and being himself satiated with blood besides, he was at last prevailed upon to stop his hand; and in compliment to the ancient Athenians, he said, 'he forgave the many for the sake of the few, the *living for the dead.*'" — Plutarch.

No! where the bold Three Hundred slept,
Sad freedom battled not — but wept!
For nerveless then the Spartan's hand,
And Thebes could rouse no Sacred Band;
Nor one high soul from slumber broke
When Athens own'd the northern yoke.

But was there none for *thee* to dare
The conflict, scorning to despair?
O City of the seven proud hills!
Whose name e'en yet the spirit thrills,
As doth a clarion's battle-call —
Didst thou, too, ancient empress, fall?
Did no Camillus from the chain
Ransom thy Capitol again?
Oh, who shall tell the days to be
No patriot rose to bleed for thee!

Heard ye the Gothic trumpet's blast?
The march of hosts as Alaric pass'd?
That fearful sound, at midnight deep,[*]
Burst on the Eternal City's sleep: —
How woke the mighty? She whose will
So long had bid the world be still,
Her sword a sceptre, and her eye
Th' ascendant star of destiny!

---

[*] "At the hour of midnight the Salarian gate was silently opened, and the inhabitants were awakened by the tremendous sound of the Gothic trumpet. Eleven hundred and sixty-three years after the foundation of Rome, the imperial city, which had subdued and civilised so considerable a portion of mankind, was delivered to the licentious fury of the tribes of Germany and Scythia." — *Decline and Fall of the Roman Empire*, vol. v. p. 311.

She woke — to view the dread army
Of Scythians rushing to their prey,
To hear her streets resound the cries
Pour'd from a thousand agonies!
While the strange light of flames, that gave
A ruddy glow to Tiber's wave,
Bursting in that terrific hour
From fane and palace, dome and tower,
Reveal'd the throngs, for aid divine,
Clinging to many a worshipp'd shrine:
Fierce fitful radiance wildly shed
O'er spear and sword, with carnage red,
Shone o'er the suppliant and the flying,
And kindled pyres for Romans dying.

Weep, Italy! alas, that e'er
Should tears alone thy wrongs declare!
The time hath been when *thy* distress
Had roused up empires for redress!
Now, her long race of glory run,
Without a combat Rome is won,
And from her plunder'd temples forth
Rush the fierce children of the North,
To share beneath more genial skies
Each joy their own rude clime denies.

Ye who on bright Campania's shore
Bade your fair villas rise of yore,
With all their graceful colonnades,
And crystal baths, and myrtle shades,
Along the blue Hesperian deep,
Whose glassy waves in sunshine sleep —

Beneath your olive and your vine
Far other inmates now recline;
And the tall plane, whose roots ye fed
With rich libations duly shed, *
O'er guests, unlike your vanish'd friends,
Its bowery canopy extends.
For them the southern heaven is glowing,
The bright Falernian nectar flowing;
For them the marble halls unfold,
Where nobler beings dwelt of old,
Whose children for barbarian lords
Touch the sweet lyre's resounding chords,
Or wreaths of Pæstan roses twine
To crown the sons of Elbe and Rhine.
Yet, though luxurious they repose
Beneath Corinthian porticoes —
While round them into being start
The marvels of triumphant art —
Oh! not for them hath Genius given
To Parian stone the fire of heaven,
Enshrining in the forms he wrought
A bright eternity of thought.
In vain the natives of the skies
In breathing marble round them rise,
And sculptured nymphs of fount or glade
People the dark-green laurel shade.
Cold are the conqueror's heart and eye
To visions of divinity;

* The plane-tree was much cultivated among the Romans, on account of its extraordinary shade; and they used to nourish it with wine instead of water, believing (as Sir W. Temple observes) that "this tree loved that liquor as well as those who used to drink it under its shade." — See the notes to Melmoth's *Pliny*.

And rude his hand which dares deface
The models of immortal grace.

   Arouse ye from your soft delights!
Chieftains! the war-note's call invites;
And other lands must yet be won,
And other deeds of havoc done.
Warriors! your flowery bondage break;
Sons of the stormy North, awake!
The barks are launching from the steep —
Soon shall the Isle of Ceres weep,*
And Afric's burning winds afar
Waft the shrill sounds of Alaric's war.
Where shall his race of victory close?
When shall the ravaged earth repose?
But hark! what wildly mingling cries
From Scythia's camp tumultuous rise?
Why swells dread Alaric's name on air?
A sterner conqueror hath been there!
A conqueror — yet his paths are peace,
He comes to bring the world's release;
He of the sword that knows no sheath,
The avenger, the deliverer — Death!

   Is then that daring spirit fled?
Doth Alaric slumber with the dead?
Tamed are the warrior's pride and strength,
And he and earth are calm at length.
The land where heaven unclouded shines,
Where sleep the sunbeams on the vines;

---

* Sicily was anciently considered as the favoured and peculiar dominion of Ceres.

The land by conquest made his own,
Can yield him now — a grave alone.
But his — her lord from Alp to sea —
No common sepulchre shall be!
Oh, make his tomb where mortal eye
Its buried wealth may ne'er descry!
Where mortal foot may never tread
Above a victor-monarch's bed.
Let not his royal dust be hid
'Neath star-aspiring pyramid;
Nor bid the gather'd mound arise,
To bear his memory to the skies.
Years roll away — oblivion claims
Her triumph o'er heroic names;
And hands profane disturb the clay
That once was fired with glory's ray;
And Avarice, from their secret gloom,
Drags e'en the treasures of the tomb.
But thou, O leader of the free!
That general doom awaits not thee:
Thou, where no step may e'er intrude,
Shalt rest in regal solitude,
Till, bursting on thy sleep profound,
The Awakener's final trumpet sound.
Turn ye the waters from their course,
Bid Nature yield to human force,
And hollow in the torrent's bed
A chamber for the mighty dead.
The work is done — the captive's hand
Hath well obey'd his lord's command.
Within that royal tomb are cast
The richest trophies of the past,

The wealth of many a stately dome,
The gold and gems of plunder'd Rome;
And when the midnight stars are beaming,
And ocean waves in stillness gleaming,
Stern in their grief, his warriors bear
The Chastener of the Nations there;
To rest at length from victory's toil,
Alone, with all an empire's spoil!

Then the freed current's rushing wave
Rolls o'er the secret of the grave;
Then streams the martyr'd captives' blood
To crimson that sepulchral flood,
Whose conscious tide alone shall keep
The mystery in its bosom deep.
Time hath past on since then — and swept
From earth the urns where heroes slept;
Temples of gods and domes of kings
Are mouldering with forgotten things;
Yet not shall ages e'er molest
The viewless home of Alaric's rest:
Still rolls, like them, the unfailing river,
The guardian of his dust for ever.

THE LAST BANQUET OF ANTONY AND CLEOPATRA.

["Antony, concluding that he could not die more honourably than in battle, determined to attack Cæsar at the same time both by sea and land. The night preceding the execution of this design, he ordered his servants at supper to render him their best services that evening, and fill the wine round pentifully, for the day following they might belong to another master, whilst he lay extended on the ground, no longer of consequence either to them or to himself. His friends were affected, and wept to hear him talk thus; which when he perceived, he encouraged them by assurances that his expectations of a glorious victory were at least equal to those of an honourable death. At the dead of night, when universal silence reigned through the city — a silence that was deepened by the awful thought of the ensuing day — on a sudden was heard the sound of musical instruments, and a noise which resembled the exclamations of Bacchanals. This tumultuous procession seemed to pass through the whole city, and to go out at the gate which led to the enemy's camp. Those who reflected on this prodigy concluded that Bacchus, the god whom Antony affected to imitate, had then forsaken him." — LANGHORNE'S *Plutarch*.]

Thy foes had girt thee with their dread array,
   O stately Alexandria! — yet the sound
Of mirth and music, at the close of day,
   Swell'd from thy splendid fabrics far around
O'er camp and wave. Within the royal hall,
   In gay magnificence the feast was spread;
And, brightly streaming from the pictured wall,
   A thousand lamps their trembling lustre shed
O'er many a column, rich with precious dyes,
'That tinge the marble's vein, 'neath Afric's burning skies.

And soft and clear that wavering radiance play'd
   O'er sculptured forms, that round the pillar'd scene
Calm and majestic rose, by art array'd
   In godlike beauty, awfully serene.

Oh! how unlike the troubled guests, reclined
    Round that luxurious board! — in every face
Some shadow from the tempest of the mind,
    Rising by fits, the searching eye might trace,
Though vainly mask'd in smiles which are not mirth,
But the proud spirit's veil thrown o'er the woes of earth.

Their brows are bound with wreaths, whose transient bloom
    May still survive the wearers — and the rose
Perchance may scarce be wither'd, when the tomb
    Receives the mighty to its dark repose!
The day must dawn on battle, and may set
    In death — but fill the mantling wine-cup high!
Despair is fearless, and the Fates e'en yet
    Lend her one hour for parting revelry.
They who the empire of the world possess'd
Would taste its joys again, ere all exchanged for rest.

Its joys! oh, mark yon proud Triumvir's mien,
    And read their annals on that brow of care!
Midst pleasure's lotus-bowers his steps have been:
    Earth's brightest pathway led him to despair.
Trust not the glance that fain would yet inspire
    The buoyant energies of days gone by;
There is delusion in its meteor fire,
    And all within is shame, is agony!
Away! the tear in bitterness may flow,
But there are smiles which bear a stamp of deeper woe.

Thy cheek is sunk, and faded as thy fame,
    O lost, devoted Roman! yet thy brow,
To that ascendant and undying name,
    Pleads with stern loftiness thy right e'en now.

Thy glory is departed, but hath left
  A lingering light around thee: in decay
Not less than kingly — though of all bereft,
  Thou seem'st as empire had not pass'd away.
Supreme in ruin! teaching hearts elate
A deep prophetic dread of still mysterious fate!

But thou, enchantress queen! whose love hath made
  His desolation — thou art by his side,
In all thy sovereignty of charms array'd,
  To meet the storm with still unconquer'd pride.
Imperial being! e'en though many a stain
  Of error be upon thee, there is power
In thy commanding nature, which shall reign
  O'er the stern genius of misfortune's hour;
And the dark beauty of thy troubled eye
E'en now is all illumed with wild sublimity.

Thine aspect, all impassion'd, wears a light
  Inspiring and inspired — thy cheek a dye,
Which rises not from joy, but yet is bright
  With the deep glow of feverish energy.
Proud siren of the Nile! thy glance is fraught
  With an immortal fire — in every beam
It darts, there kindles some heroic thought,
  But wild and awful as a sibyl's dream;
For thou with death hast communed to attain
Dread knowledge of the pangs that ransom from the chain.*

---

* Cleopatra made a collection of poisonous drugs, and being desirous to know which was least painful in the operation, she tried them on the capital convicts. Such poisons as were quick in their operation, she found to be attended with violent pain and convulsions; such as were milder were slow in their effect: she therefore applied herself to the exam-

And the stern courage by such musings lent,
　　Daughter of Afric! o'er thy beauty throws
The grandeur of a regal spirit, blent
　　With all the majesty of mighty woes:
While he, so fondly, fatally adored,
　　Thy fallen Roman, gazes on thee yet,
Till scarce the soul that once exulting soar'd
　　Can deem the day-star of its glory set;
Scarce his charm'd heart believes that power can be
In sovereign fate, o'er him thus fondly loved by thee.

But there is sadness in the eyes around,
　　Which mark that ruin'd leader, and survey
His changeful mien, whence oft the gloom profound
　　Strange triumph chases haughtily away.
"Fill the bright goblet, warrior guests!" he cries;
　　"Quaff, ere we part, the generous nectar deep!
Ere sunset gild once more the western skies
　　Your chief in cold forgetfulness may sleep;
While sounds of revel float o'er shore and sea,
And the red bowl again is crown'd — but not for me.

"Yet weep not thus. The struggle is not o'er,
　　O victors of Philippi! many a field
Hath yielded palms to us: one effort more!
　　By one stern conflict must our doom be seal'd.
Forget not, Romans! o'er a subject world
　　How royally your eagle's wing hath spread,
Though, from his eyrie of dominion hurl'd,
　　Now bursts the tempest on his crested head!

ination of venomous creatures; and at length she found that the bite of the asp was the most eligible kind of death, for it brought on a gradual kind of lethargy. — See PLUTARCH.

Yet sovereign still, if banish'd from the sky,
The sun's indignant bird, he must not drop — but die."

The feast is o'er. 'Tis night, the dead of night —
    Unbroken stillness broods o'er earth and deep;
From Egypt's heaven of soft and starry light
    The moon looks cloudless o'er a world of sleep.
For those who wait the morn's awakening beams,
    The battle-signal to decide their doom,
Have sunk to feverish rest and troubled dreams; —
    Rest that shall soon be calmer in the tomb;
Dreams dark and ominous, but *there* to cease,
When sleep the lords of war in solitude and peace.

Wake, slumberers! wake! Hark! heard ye not a sound
    Of gathering tumult? — Near and nearer still
Its murmur swells. Above, below, around,
    Bursts a strange chorus forth, confused and shrill.
Wake, Alexandria! through thy streets the tread
    Of steps unseen is hurrying, and the note
Of pipe, and lyre, and trumpet, wild and dread,
    Is heard upon the midnight air to float;
And voices, clamorous as in frenzied mirth,
Mingle their thousand tones, which are not of the earth.

These are no mortal sounds — their thrilling strain
    Hath more mysterious power, and birth more high;
And the deep horror chilling every vein
    Owns them of stern terrific augury.
Beings of worlds unknown! ye pass away,
    O ye invisible and awful throng!
Your echoing footsteps and resounding lay
    To Cæsar's camp exulting move along.

Thy gods forsake thee, Antony! the sky
By that dread sign reveals thy doom — "Despair and die!"*

HELIODORUS IN THE TEMPLE.

[From *Maccabees*, book II. chapter 3, verse 21. "Then it would have pitied a man to see the falling down of the multitude of all sorts, and the fear of the high priest, being in such an agony. — 22. They then called upon the Almighty Lord to keep the things committed of trust safe and sure, for those that had committed them. — 23. Nevertheless Heliodorus executed that which was decreed. — 24. Now as he was there present himself, with his guard about the treasury, the Lord of Spirits, and the Prince of all Power, caused a great apparition, so that all that presumed to come in with him were astonished at the power of God, and fainted, and were sore afraid. — 25. For there appeared unto them a horse with a terrible rider upon him, and adorned with a very fair covering; and he ran fiercely, and smote at Heliodorus with his fore-feet, and it seemed that he that sat upon the horse had complete harness of gold. — 26. Moreover, two other young men appeared before him, notable in strength, excellent in beauty, and comely in apparel, who stood by him on either side, and scourged him continually, and gave him many sore stripes. — 27. And Heliodorus fell suddenly to the ground, and was compassed with great darkness; but they that were with him took him up, and put him into a litter. — 28. Thus him that lately came with great train, and with all his guard into the said treasury, they carried out, being unable to help himself with his weapons, and manifestly they acknowledged the power of God. — 29. For he by the hand of God was cast down, and lay speechless without all hope of life."]

A SOUND of woe in Salem! mournful cries
  Rose from her dwellings — youthful cheeks were pale,
Tears flowing fast from dim and aged eyes,
  And voices mingling in tumultuous wail;
Hands raised to heaven in agony of prayer,
And powerless wrath, and terror, and despair.

* "To-morrow in the battle think on me,
  And fall thy edgeless sword; despair and die!"
                              Richard III.

HELIODORUS IN THE TEMPLE.

Thy daughters, Judah! weeping, laid aside
  The regal splendour of their fair array,
With the rude sackcloth girt their beauty's pride,
  And throng'd the streets in hurrying, wild dismay;
While knelt thy priest before His awful shrine
Who made of old renown and empire thine.

But on the spoiler moves! The temple's gate,
  The bright, the beautiful, his guards unfold;
And all the scene reveals its solemn state,
  Its courts and pillars, rich with sculptured gold;
And man with eye unhallow'd views th' abode,
The sever'd spot, the dwelling-place of God.

Where art thou, Mighty Presence! that of yore
  Wert wont between the cherubim to rest,
Veil'd in a cloud of glory, shadowing o'er
  Thy sanctuary the chosen and the blest?
Thou! that didst make fair Sion's ark thy throne,
And call the oracle's recess thine own!

Angel of God! that through the Assyrian host,
  Clothed with the darkness of the midnight hour,
To tame the proud, to hush the invader's boast,
  Didst pass triumphant in avenging power,
Till burst the day-spring on the silent scene,
And death alone reveal'd where thou hadst been.

Wilt thou not wake, O Chastener! in thy might,
  To guard thine ancient and majestic hill,
Where oft from heaven the full Shechinah's light
  Hath stream'd the house of holiness to fill?

Oh! yet once more defend thy loved domain,
Eternal One! Deliverer! rise again!

Fearless of thee, the plunderer undismay'd
  Hastes on, the sacred chambers to explore
Where the bright treasures of the fane are laid,
  The orphan's portion and the widow's store:
What recks *his* heart though age unsuccour'd die,
And want consume the cheek of infancy?

Away, intruders! — hark! a mighty sound!
  Behold, a burst of light! — away, away!
A fearful glory fills the temple round,
  A vision bright in terrible array!
And lo! a steed of no terrestrial frame,
His path a whirlwind and his breath a flame!

His neck is clothed with thunder,* and his mane
  Seems waving fire — the kindling of his eye
Is as a meteor — ardent with disdain
  His glance, his gesture, fierce in majesty!
Instinct with light he seems, and form'd to bear
Some dread archangel through the fields of air.

But who is he, in panoply of gold,
  Throned on that burning charger? Bright his form,
Yet in its brightness awful to behold,
  And girt with all the terrors of the storm!
Lightning is on his helmet's crest — and fear
Shrinks from the splendour of his brow severe.

---

* "Hast thou given the horse strength? Hast thou clothed his neck with thunder?" — *Job*, chap. xxxix. v. 19.

And by his side two radiant warriors stand,
   All arm'd, and kingly in commanding grace —
Oh! more than kingly — godlike! — sternly grand,
   Their port indignant, and each dazzling face
Beams with the beauty to immortals given,
Magnificent in all the wrath of heaven.

Then sinks each gazer's heart — each knee is bow'd
   In trembling awe; but, as to fields of fight,
Th' unearthly war-steed, rushing through the crowd,
   Bursts on their leader in terrific might;
And the stern angels of that dread abode
Pursue its plunderer with the scourge of God.

Darkness — thick darkness! — low on earth he lies,
   Rash Heliodorus — motionless and pale —
Bloodless his cheek, and o'er his shrouded eyes
   Mists, as of death, suspend their shadowy veil;
And thus th' oppressor, by his fear-struck train,
Is borne from that inviolable fane.

The light returns — the warriors of the sky
   Have pass'd, with all their dreadful pomp, away;
Then wakes the timbrel, swells the song on high
   Triumphant as in Judah's elder day;
Rejoice, O city of the sacred hill!
Salem, exult! thy God is with thee still.

THE MAREMMA.

[" NELLO DELLA PIETRA had espoused a lady of noble family at Sienna, named Madonna Pia. Her beauty was the admiration of Tuscany, and excited in the heart of her husband a jealousy, which, exasperated by false reports and groundless suspicions, at length drove him to the desperate resolution of Othello. It is difficult to decide whether the lady was quite innocent, but so Dante represents her. Her husband brought her into the Maremma, which, then as now, was a district destructive of health. He never told his unfortunate wife the reason of her banishment to so dangerous a country. He did not deign to utter complaint or accusation. He lived with her alone, in cold silence, without answering her questions, or listening to her remonstrances. He patiently waited till the pestilential air should destroy the health of this young lady. In a few months she died. Some chronicles, indeed, tell us that Nello used the dagger to hasten her death. It is certain that he survived her, plunged in sadness and perpetual silence. Dante had, in this incident, all the materials of an ample and very poetical narrative. But he bestows on it only four verses. He meets in Purgatory three spirits. One was a captain who fell fighting on the same side with him in the battle of Campaldino; the second, a gentleman assassinated by the treachery of the House of Este; the third was a woman unknown to the poet, and who, after the others had spoken, turned towards him with these words:—

'Recorditi di me; che son la Pia,
Siena mi fe, disfecemi Maremma;
Salsi colui che inanellata pria
Disposando m' avea con la sua gemma.'"

PURGATORIO, cant. v.

— *Edinburgh Review*, No. LVII.]

THERE are bright scenes beneath Italian skies,
Where glowing suns there purest light diffuse,
Uncultured flowers in wild profusion rise,
And nature lavishes her warmest hues;
But trust thou not her smile, her balmy breath —
Away! her charms are but the pomp of Death!

He in the vine-clad bowers, unseen, is dwelling,
Where the cool shade its freshness round thee throws;

THE MAREMMA.

His voice, in every perfumed zephyr swelling,
With gentlest whisper lures thee to repose;
And the soft sounds that through the foliage sigh
But woo thee still to slumber and to die.

Mysterious danger lurks, a syren there,
Not robed in terrors, or announced in gloom,
But stealing o'er thee in the scented air,
And veil'd in flowers, that smile to deck thy tomb;
How may we deem, amidst their deep array,
That heaven and earth but flatter to betray?

Sunshine, and bloom, and verdure! Can it be
That these but charm us with destructive wiles?
Where shall we turn, O Nature, if in *thee*
Danger is mask'd in beauty — death in smiles?
Oh! still the Circe of that fatal shore,
Where she, the Sun's bright daughter, dwelt of yore!

There, year by year, that secret peril spreads,
Disguised in loveliness, its baleful reign,
And viewless blights o'er many a landscape sheds,
Gay with the riches of the south, in vain;
O'er fairy bowers and palaces of state
Passing unseen, to leave them desolate.

And pillar'd halls, whose airy colonnades
Were form'd to echo music's choral tone,
Are silent now, amidst deserted shades,
Peopled by sculpture's graceful forms alone;
And fountains dash unheard, by lone alcoves,
Neglected temples, and forsaken groves.

And there, where marble nymphs, in beauty gleaming,
Midst the deep shades of plane and cypress rise.

By wave or grot might Fancy linger, dreaming
Of old Arcadia's woodland deities.
Wild visions! — there no sylvan powers convene:
Death reigns the genius of th' Elysian scene.

Ye, too, illustrious hills of Rome! that bear
Traces of mightier beings on your brow,
O'er you that subtle spirit of the air
Extends the desert of his empire now;
Broods o'er the wrecks of altar, fane, and dome,
And makes the Cæsars' ruin'd halls his home.

Youth, valour, beauty, oft have felt his power.
His crown'd and chosen victims: o'er their lot
Hath fond affection wept — each blighted flower
In turn was loved and mourn'd, and is forgot.
But one who perish'd, left a tale of woe,
Meet for as deep a sigh as pity can bestow.

A voice of music, from Sienna's walls,
Is floating joyous on the summer air;
And there art banquets in her stately halls,
And graceful revels of the gay and fair,
And brilliant wreaths the altar have array'd,
Where meet her noblest youth and loveliest maid.

To that young bride each grace hath Nature given
Which glows on Art's divinest dream: her eye
Hath a pure sunbeam of her native heaven —
Her cheek a tinge of morning's richest dye;
Fair as that daughter of the south, whose form
Still breathes and charms, in Vinci's colours warm.*

* An allusion to Leonardo da Vinci's picture of his wife Mona Lisa, supposed to be the most perfect imitation of nature ever exhibited in painting.

But is she blest? — for sometimes o'er her smile
A soft sweet shade of pensiveness is cast;
And in her liquid glance there seems awhile
To dwell some thought whose soul is with the past
Yet soon it flies — a cloud that leaves no trace,
On the sky's azure, of its dwelling-place.

Perchance, at times, within her heart may rise
Remembrance of some early love or woe,
Faded, yet scarce forgotten — in her eyes
Wakening the half-formed tear that may not flow,
Yet radiant seems her lot as aught on earth,
Where still some pining thought comes darkly o'er our mirth.

The world before her smiles — its changeful gaze
She hath not proved as yet; her path seems gay
With flowers and sunshine, and the voice of praise
Is still the joyous herald of her way;
And beauty's light around her dwells, to throw
O'er every scene its own resplendent glow.

Such is the young Bianca — graced with all
That nature, fortune, youth, at once can give;
Pure in their loveliness, her looks recall
Such dreams as ne'er life's early bloom survive;
And when she speaks, each thrilling tone is fraught
With sweetness, born of high and heavenly thought.

And he to whom are breathed her vows of faith
Is brave and noble — child of high descent,
He hath stood fearless in the ranks of death,
Mid slaughter'd heaps, the warrior's monument;
And proudly marshall'd his carroccio's* way
Amidst the wildest wreck of war's array.

* A sort of consecrated war-chariot.

And his the chivalrous commanding mien,
Where high-born grandeur blends with courtly grace;
Yet may a lightning glance at times be seen,
Of fiery passions, darting o'er his face,
And fierce the spirit kindling in his eye —
But e'en while yet we gaze, its quick wild flashes die.

And calmly can Pietra smile, concealing,
As if forgotten, vengeance, hate, remorse;
And veil the workings of each darker feeling,
Deep in his soul concentrating its force;
But yet he loves — Oh! who hath loved, nor known
Affection's power exalt the bosom all its own?

The days roll on — and still Bianca's lot
Seems as a path of Eden. Thou mightst deem
That grief, the mighty chastener, had forgot
To wake her soul from life's enchanted dream;
And, if her brow a moment's sadness wear,
It sheds but grace more intellectual there.

A few short years, and all is changed; her fate
Seems with some deep mysterious cloud o'ercast.
Have jealous doubts transform'd to wrath and hate,
The love whose glow expression's power surpass'd?
Lo! on Pietra's brow a sullen gloom
Is gathering day by day, prophetic of her doom.

Oh! can he meet that eye, of light serene,
Whence the pure spirit looks in radiance forth,
And view that bright intelligence of mien
Form'd to express but thoughts of loftiest worth,
Yet deem that vice within that heart can reign?
— How shall he e'er confide in aught on earth again?

In silence oft, with strange vindictive gaze,
Transient, yet fill'd with meaning, stern and wild,
Her features, calm in beauty, he surveys,
Then turns away, and fixes on her child
So dark a glance as thrills a mother's mind
With some vague fear scarce own'd, and undefined.

There stands a lonely dwelling, by the wave
Of the blue deep which bathes Italia's shore,
Far from all sounds, but rippling seas that lave
Gray rocks with foliage richly shadow'd o'er,
And sighing winds, that murmur through the wood,
Fringing the beach of that Hesperian flood.

Fair is that house of solitude — and fair
The green Maremma, far around it spread,
A sun-bright waste of beauty; yet an air
Of brooding sadness o'er the scene is shed,
No human footstep tracks the lone domain,
The desert of luxuriance glows in vain.

And silent are the marble halls that rise
'Mid founts, and cypress walks and olive groves:
All sleep in sunshine, 'neath cerulean skies,
And still around the sea-breeze lightly roves;
Yet every trace of man reveals alone,
That there life once hath flourish'd — and is gone.

There, till around them slowly, slowly stealing,
The summer air, deceit in every sigh,
Came fraught with death, its power no sign revealing,
Thy sires, Pietra, dwelt in days gone by;
And strains of mirth and melody have flow'd
Where stands, all voiceless now, the still abode.

And thither doth her Lord remorseless bear
Bianca with her child. His alter'd eye
And brow a stern and fearful calmness wear,
While his dark spirit seals their doom — to die;
And the deep bodings of his victim's heart
Tell her from fruitless hope at once to part.

It is the summer's glorious prime — and blending
Its blue transparence with the skies, the deep,
Each tint of heaven upon its breast descending,
Scarce murmurs as it heaves in glassy sleep,
And on its wave reflects, more softly bright,
That lovely shore of solitude and light.

Fragrance in each warm southern gale is breathing,
Deck'd with young flowers the rich Maremma glows,
Neglected vines the trees are wildly wreathing,
And the fresh myrtle in exuberance blows,
And, far around, a deep and sunny bloom
Mantles the scene, as garlands robe the tomb.

Yes! 'tis *thy* tomb, Bianca! fairest flower!
The voice that calls thee speaks in every gale,
Which, o'er thee breathing with insidious power,
Bids the young roses of thy cheek turn pale;
And fatal in its softness, day by day,
Steals from that eye some trembling spark away.

But sink not yet; for there are darker woes,
Daughter of Beauty! in thy spring-morn fading —
Sufferings more keen for thee reserved, than those
Of lingering death, which thus thine eye are shading!
Nerve then thy heart to meet that bitter lot:
'Tis agony — but soon to be forgot!

What deeper pangs maternal hearts can wring,
Than hourly to behold the spoiler's breath
Shedding, as mildews on the bloom of spring,
O'er Infancy's fair cheek the blight of death?
To gaze and shrink, as gathering shades o'ercast
The pale smooth brow, yet watch it to the last!

Such pangs were thine, young mother! Thou didst bend
O'er thy fair boy, and raise his drooping head;
And faint and hopeless, far from every friend,
Keep thy sad midnight vigils near his bed,
And watch his patient, supplicating eye
Fix'd upon thee — on thee! — who couldst no aid supply!

There was no voice to cheer thy lonely woe
Through those dark hours: to thee the wind's low sigh,
And the faint murmur of the ocean's flow,
Came like some spirit whispering — "He must die!"
And thou didst vainly clasp him to the breast,
His young and sunny smile so oft with hope had blest.

'Tis past — that fearful trial! — he is gone!
But thou, sad mourner! hast not long to weep;
The hour of nature's charter'd peace comes on,
And thou shalt share thine infant's holy sleep.
A few short sufferings yet — and death shall be
As a bright messenger from heaven to thee.

But ask not — hope not — one relenting thought
From him who doom'd thee thus to waste away,
Whose heart, with sullen, speechless vengeance fraught,
Broods in dark triumph o'er thy slow decay;
And coldly, sternly, silently can trace
The gradual withering of each youthful grace.

And yet the day of vain remorse shall come,
When thou, bright victim! on his dreams shalt rise
As an accusing angel — and thy tomb,
A martyr's shrine, be hallow'd in his eyes!
Then shall thine innocence his bosom wring,
More than thy fancied guilt with jealous pangs could sting.

Lift thy meek eyes to heaven — for all on earth,
Young sufferer! fades before thee. Thou art lone:
Hope, Fortune, Love, smiled brightly on thy birth,
Thine hour of death is all Affliction's own!
It is our task to suffer — and our fate
To learn that mighty lesson, soon or late.

The season's glory fades — the vintage lay
Through joyous Italy resounds no more;
But mortal loveliness hath pass'd away,
Fairer than aught in summer's glowing store.
Beauty and youth are gone — behold them such
As death hath made them with his blighting touch!

The summer's breath came o'er them — and they died!
Softly it came to give luxuriance birth,
Call'd forth young nature in her festal pride,
But bore to them their summons from the earth!
Again shall blow that mild, delicious breeze,
And wake to life and light all flowers — but these.

No sculptured urn, nor verse thy virtues telling,
O lost and loveliest one! adorns thy grave;
But o'er that humble cypress-shaded dwelling
The dew-drops glisten and the wild-flowers wave —
Emblems more meet, in transient light and bloom,
For thee, who thus didst pass in brightness to the tomb!

RECORDS OF WOMAN.

ARABELLA STUART

["THE LADY ARABELLA," as she has been frequently entitled, was descended from Margaret, eldest daughter of Henry VII., and consequently allied by birth to Elizabeth as well as James I. This affinity to the throne proved the misfortune of her life, as the jealousies which it constantly excited in her royal relatives, who were anxious to prevent her marrying, shut her out from the enjoyment of that domestic happiness which her heart appears to have so fervently desired. By a secret but early discovered union with William Seymour, son of Lord Beauchamp, she alarmed the cabinet of James, and the wedded lovers were immediately placed in separate confinement. From this they found means to concert a romantic plan of escape; and having won over a female attendant, by whose assistance she was disguised in male attire, Arabella, though faint from recent sickness and suffering, stole out in the night, and at last reached an appointed spot, where a boat and servants were in waiting. She embarked; and at break of day a French vessel engaged to receive her was discovered and gained. As Seymour, however, had not yet arrived, she was desirous that the vessel should lie at anchor for him; but this wish was overruled by her companions, who, contrary to her entreaties, hoisted sail, "which," says D'Israeli, "occasioned so fatal a termination to this romantic adventure. Seymour, indeed, had escaped from the Tower; he reached the wharf, and found his confidential man waiting with a boat, and arrived at Lee. The time passed; the waves were rising; Arabella was not there; but in the distance he descried a vessel. Hiring a fisherman to take him on board, he discovered, to his grief, on hailing it, that it was not the French ship charged with his Arabella; in despair and confusion he found another ship from Newcastle, which for a large sum altered its course, and landed him in Flanders." Arabella, meantime, whilst imploring her attendants to linger, and earnestly looking out for the expected boat of her husband, was overtaken in Calais Roads by a vessel in the king's service, and brought back to a captivity, under the suffering of which her mind and constitution gradually sank. "What passed in that dreadful imprisonment cannot perhaps be recovered for authentic history, but enough is known — that her mind grew impaired, that she finally lost her reason, and, if the duration of her imprisonment was short, that it was only terminated by her death. Some effusions, often begun and never ended, written and erased, incoherent and rational, yet remain among her papers." — D'Israeli's *Curiosities of Literature*.

The following poem, meant as some record of her fate, and the imagined fluctuations of her thoughts and feelings, is supposed to commence during the time of her first imprisonment, whilst her mind was yet buoyed up by the consciousness of Seymour's affection, and the cherished hope of eventual deliverance.]

"And is not love in vain
Torture enough without a living tomb?" BYRON.

"Fermossi al fin il cor che balzo tanto." PINDEMONTE.

I.

'Twas but a dream! I saw the stag leap free,
  Under the boughs where early birds were singing;
I stood o'ershadow'd by the greenwood tree,
  And heard, it seem'd, a sudden bugle ringing
Far through a royal forest. Then the fawn
Shot, like a gleam of light, from grassy lawn
To secret covert; and the smooth turf shook,
And lilies quiver'd by the glade's lone brook,
And young leaves trembled, as, in fleet career,
A princely band, with horn, and hound, and spear,
Like a rich masque swept forth. I saw the dance
Of their white plumes, that bore a silvery glance
Into the deep wood's heart; and all pass'd by
Save one — I met the smile of *one* clear eye,
Flashing out joy to mine. Yes, *thou* wert there,
Seymour! A soft wind blew the clustering hair
Back from thy gallant brow, as thou didst rein
Thy courser, turning from that gorgeous train,
And fling, methought, thy hunting spear away,
And, lightly graceful in thy green array,
Bound to my side. And we, that met and parted
  Ever in dread of some dark watchful power,

Won back to childhood's trust, and fearless-hearted,
  Blent the glad fulness of our thoughts that hour
Even like the mingling of sweet streams, beneath
Dim woven leaves, and midst the floating breath
Of hidden forest-flowers.

II.

'Tis past! I wake,
  A captive, and alone, and far from thee,
My love and friend! Yet fostering, for thy sake,
  A quenchless hope of happiness to be;
And feeling still my woman-spirit strong,
In the deep faith which lifts from earthly wrong
A heavenward glance. I know, I know our love
Shall yet call gentle angels from above,
By its undying fervour, and prevail —
Sending a breath, as of the spring's first gale,
Through hearts now cold; and, raising its bright face,
With a free gush of sunny tears, erase
The characters of anguish. In this trust,
I bear, I strive, I bow not to the dust,
That I may bring thee back no faded form,
No bosom chill'd and blighted by the storm,
But all my youth's first treasures, when we meet,
Making past sorrow, by communion, sweet.

III.

And thou too art in bonds! Yet droop thou not,
O my beloved! there is *one* hopeless lot,
But one, and that not ours. Beside the dead
There sits the grief that mantles up its head,
Loathing the laughter and proud pomp of light,
When darkness, from the vainly doting sight

Covers its beautiful!* If thou wert gone
  To the grave's bosom, with thy radiant brow —
If thy deep-thrilling voice, with that low tone
  Of earnest tenderness, which now, even now
Seems floating through my soul, were music taken
For ever from this world — oh! thus forsaken
Could I bear on? Thou livest, thou livest, thou'rt mine!
With this glad thought I make my heart a shrine,
And by the lamp which quenchless there shall burn,
Sit a lone watcher for the day's return.

IV.

And lo! the joy that cometh with the morning,
  Brightly victorious o'er the hours of care!
I have not watch'd in vain, serenely scorning
  The wild and busy whispers of despair!
Thou hast sent tidings, as of heaven — I wait
  The hour, the sign, for blessed flight to thee.
Oh! for the skylark's wing that seeks its mate
  As a star shoots! — but on the breezy sea
We shall meet soon. To think of such an hour!
  Will not my heart, o'erburden'd by its bliss,
Faint and give way within me, as a flower
  Borne down and perishing by noontide's kiss?
Yet shall I *fear* that lot — the perfect rest,
The full deep joy of dying on thy breast,
After long suffering won? So rich a close
Too seldom crowns with peace affection's woes.

---

* "Whoresoever you are, or in what state soever you be, it sufficeth me you are mine. Rachel wept and would not be comforted, *because her children were no more*. And that indeed, is the remediless sorrow, and none else!" — From a letter of Arabella Stuart's to her husband. -- See *Curiosities of Literature*.

ARABELLA STUART.

V.

Sunset! I tell each moment. From the skies
  The last red splendour floats along my wall
Like a king's banner! Now it melts, it dies!
  I see one star — I hear — 'twas not the call,
Th' expected voice; my quick heart throbb'd too soon.
I must keep vigil till yon rising moon
Shower down less golden light. Beneath her beam
Through my lone lattice pour'd, I sit and dream
Of summer lands afar, where holy love,
Under the vine or in the citron grove,
May breathe from terror.
                         Now the night grows deep,
And silent as its clouds, and full of sleep.
I hear my veins beat. Hark! a bell's slow chime!
My heart strikes with it. Yet again — 'tis time!
A step! — a voice! — or but a rising breeze?
Hark! — haste! — I come to meet thee on the seas!

. . . .

VI.

Now never more, oh; never, in the worth
Of its pure cause, let sorrowing love on earth
Trust fondly — never more! The hope is crush'd
That lit my life, the voice within me hush'd
That spoke sweet oracles; and I return
To lay my youth, as in a burial urn,
Where sunshine may not find it. All is lost!
No tempest met our barks — no billow toss'd;
Yet were they sever'd, even as we must be,
That so have loved, so striven our hearts to free
From their close-coiling fate! In vain — in vain!
The dark links meet, and clasp themselves again,

And press out life. Upon the deck I stood,
And a white sail came gliding o'er the flood,
Like some proud bird of ocean; then mine eye
Strain'd out, one moment earlier to descry
The form it ached for, and the bark's career
Seem'd slow to that fond yearning: it drew near,
Fraught with our foes! What boots it to recall
The strife, the tears? Once more a prison wall
Shuts the green hills and woodlands from my sight,
And joyous glance of waters to the light,
And thee, my Seymour!— thee!
                    I will not sink!
Thou, *thou* hast rent the heavy chain that bound thee!
And this shall be my strength — the joy to think
  That thou may'st wander with heaven's breath around thee,
And all the laughing sky! This thought shall yet
Shine o'er my heart a radiant amulet,
Guarding it from despair. Thy bonds are broken;
And unto me, I know, thy true love's token
Shall one day be deliverance, though the years
Lie dim between, o'erhung with mists of tears.

VII.

My friend! my friend! where art thou? Day by day,
Gliding like some dark mournful stream away,
My silent youth flows from me. Spring, the while,
  Comes and rains beauty on the kindling boughs
Round hall and hamlet; summer with her smile
  Fills the green forest; young hearts breathe their vows;
Brothers long parted meet; fair children rise
Round the glad board; hope laughs from loving eyes:
All this is in the world! — these joys lie sown,
The dew of every path! On *one* alone

Their freshness may not fall — the stricken deer
Dying of thirst with all the waters near.

VIII.

Ye are from dingle and fresh glade, ye flowers!
  By some kind hand to cheer my dungeon sent;
O'er you the oak shed down the summer showers,
  And the lark's nest was where your bright cups bent,
Quivering to breeze and raindrop, like the sheen
Of twilight stars. On you heaven's eye hath been,
Through the leaves pouring its dark sultry blue
Into your glowing hearts; the bee to you
Hath murmur'd, and the rill. My soul grows faint
With passionate yearning, as its quick dreams paint
Your haunts by dell and stream — the green, the free,
The full of all sweet sound — the shut from me!

IX.

There went a swift bird singing past my cell — —
  O Love and Freedom! ye are lovely things!
With you the peasant on the hills may dwell,
  And by the streams. But I — the blood of kings,
A proud unmingling river, through my veins
Flows in lone brightness, and its gifts are chains!
Kings! — I had silent visions of deep bliss,
Leaving their thrones far distant; and for this
I am cast under their triumphal car,
An insect to be crush'd! Oh! heaven is far —
Earth pitiless!

Dost thou forget me, Seymour? I am proved
So long, so sternly! Seymour, my beloved!

There are such tales of holy marvels done
By strong affection, of deliverance won
Through its prevailing power! Are these things told
'Till the young weep with rapture, and the old
Wonder, yet dare not doubt; and thou! oh, thou!
    Dost thou forget me in my hope's decay? —
Thou canst not! Through the silent night, even now,
    I, that need prayer so much, awake and pray
Still first for thee. O gentle, gentle friend!
How shall I bear this anguish to the end?

Aid! — comes there yet no aid? The voice of blood
Passes heaven's gate, even ere the crimson flood
Sinks through the greensward! Is there not a cry
From the wrung heart, of power, through agony,
To pierce the clouds? Hear, Mercy! — hear me! None
That bleed and weep beneath the smiling sun
Have heavier cause! Yet hear! — my soul grows dark! — —
Who hears the last shriek from the sinking bark
On the mid seas, and with the storm alone,
And bearing to the abyss, unseen, unknown,
Its freight of human hearts? Th' o'ermastering wave!
Who shall tell how it rush'd — and none to save!

Thou hast forsaken me! I feel, I know,
There would be rescue if this were not so.
Thou'rt at the chase, thou'rt at the festive board,
Thou'rt where the red wine free and high is pour'd,
Thou'rt where the dancers meet! A magic glass
Is set within my soul, and proud shapes pass,
Flushing it o'er with pomp from bower and hall:
I see one shadow, stateliest there of all —

Thine! What dost *thou* amidst the bright and fair,
Whispering light words, and mocking my despair?
It is not well of thee! My love was more
Than fiery song may breathe, deep thought explore;
And there thou smilest, while my heart is dying,
With all its blighted hopes around it lying:
Even thou, on whom they hung their last green leaf — —
Yet smile, smile on! too bright art thou for grief!

Death! What! is death a lock'd and treasured thing,
Guarded by swords of fire?* a hidden spring,
A fabled fruit, that I should thus endure,
As if the world within me held no cure?
Wherefore not spread free wings — — Heaven, heaven!
        control
These thoughts! — they rush — I look into my soul
As down a gulf, and tremble at the array
Of fierce forms crowding it! Give strength to pray!
So shall their dark host pass.

            The storm is still'd.
Father in Heaven! thou, only thou, canst sound
The heart's great deep, with floods of anguish fill'd,
  For human line too fearfully profound.
Therefore, forgive, my Father! if thy child,
Rock'd on its heaving darkness, hath grown wild,
And sinn'd in her despair! It well may be
That thou wouldst lead my spirit back to thee,
By the crush'd hope too long on this world pour'd —
The stricken love which hath perchance adored

* "And if you remember of old, I dare die. Consider what the world would conceive if I should be violently enforced to do it." — *Fragments of her Letters.*

A mortal in thy place! Now let me strive
With thy strong arm no more! Forgive, forgive!
Take me to peace!
     And peace at last is nigh.
A sign is on my brow, a token sent
Th' o'erwearied dust from home: no breeze flits by,
But calls me with a strange sweet whisper, blent
Of many mysteries.

     Hark! the warning tone
Deepens — its word is *Death!* Alone, alone,
And sad in youth, but chasten'd, I depart,
Bowing to heaven. Yet, yet my woman's heart
Shall wake a spirit and a power to bless,
Even in this hour's o'ershadowing fearfulness,
Thee, its first love! O tender still, and true!
Be it forgotten if mine anguish threw
Drops from its bitter fountain on thy name,
Though but a moment!

     Now, with fainting frame,
With soul just lingering on the flight begun,
To bind for thee its last dim thoughts in one,
I bless thee! Peace be on thy noble head,
Years of bright fame, when I am with the dead!
I bid this prayer survive me, and retain
Its might, again to bless thee, and again!
Thou hast been gather'd into my dark fate
Too much; too long, for my sake, desolate
Hath been thine exiled youth: but now take back,
From dying hands, thy freedom, and retrack
(After a few kind tears for her whose days
Went out in dreams of thee) the sunny ways

Of hope, and find thou happiness! Yet send
Even then, in silent hours, a thought, dear friend!
Down to my voiceless chamber; for thy love
Hath been to me all gifts of earth above,
Though bought with burning tears! It is the sting
Of death to leave that vainly-precious thing
In this cold world! What were it, then, if thou,
With thy fond eyes, wert gazing on me now?
Too keen a pang! Farewell! and yet once more,
Farewell! The passion of long years I pour
Into that word! Thou hear'st not — but the woe
And fervour of its tones may one day flow
To thy heart's holy place: there let them dwell.
We shall o'ersweep the grave to meet. Farewell!

THE SWITZER'S WIFE.

[Werner Stauffacher, one of the three confederates of the field of Grütli, had been alarmed by the envy with which the Austrian Bailiff, Landenberg, had noticed the appearance of wealth and comfort which distinguished his dwelling. It was not, however, until roused by the entreaties of his wife, a woman who seems to have been of a heroic spirit, that he was induced to deliberate with his friends upon the measures by which Switzerland was finally delivered.]

"Nor look nor tone revealeth aught
Save woman's quietness of thought;
And yet around her is a light
Of inward majesty and might."   M. J. J.

"Wer solch ein Herz an seinen Busen drückt,
Der kann für Herd und Hof mit Freuden fechten."
WILHELM TELL.

It was the time when children bound to meet
  Their father's homeward step from field or hill,

And when the herd's returning bells are sweet
   In the Swiss valleys, and the lakes grow still,
And the last note of that wild horn swells by
Which haunts the exile's heart with melody.

And lovely smiled full many an Alpine home,
   Touch'd with the crimson of the dying hour,
Which lit its low roof by the torrent's foam,
   And pierced its lattice through the vine-hung bower;
But one, the loveliest o'er the land that rose,
Then first look'd mournful in its green repose.

For Werner sat beneath the linden tree
   That sent its lulling whispers through his door,
Even as man sits, whose heart alone would be
   With some deep care, and thus can find no more
Th' accustom'd joy in all which evening brings,
Gathering a household with her quiet wings.

His wife stood hush'd before him — sad, yet mild
   In her beseeching mien! — he mark'd it not.
The silvery laughter of his bright-hair'd child
   Rang from the greensward round the shelter'd spot,
But seem'd unheard; until at last the boy
Raised from his heap'd up flowers a glance of joy,

And met his father's face. But then a change
   Pass'd swiftly o'er the brow of infant glee,
And a quick sense of something dimly strange
   Brought him from play to stand beside the knee
So often climb'd, and lift his loving eyes
That shone through clouds of sorrowful surprise.

THE SWITZER'S WIFE.

Then the proud bosom of the strong man shook;
   But tenderly his babe's fair mother laid
Her hand on his, and with a pleading look,
   Through tears half-quivering, o'er him bent and said,
"What grief, dear friend, hath made thy heart its prey —
'That thou shouldst turn thee from our love away?

"It is too sad to see thee thus, my friend!
   Mark'st thou the wonder on thy boy's fair brow,
Missing the smile from thine? Oh, cheer thee! bend
   To his soft arms: unseal thy thoughts e'en now!
Thou dost not kindly to withhold the share
Of tried affection in thy secret care."

He look'd up into that sweet earnest face,
   But sternly, mournfully: not yet the band
Was loosen'd from his soul; its inmost place
   Not yet unveil'd by love's o'ermastering hand.
"Speak low!" he cried, and pointed where on high
The white Alps glitter'd through the solemn sky:

"We must speak low amidst our ancient hills
   And their free torrents; for the days are come
When tyranny lies couch'd by forest rills,
   And meets the shepherd in his mountain-home.
Go, pour the wine of our own grapes in fear —
Keep silence by the hearth! its foes are near.

"The envy of th' oppressor's eye hath been
   Upon my heritage. I sit to-night
Under my household tree, if not serene,
   Yet with the faces best beloved in sight:
To-morrow eve may find me chain'd, and thee —
How can I bear the boy's young smiles to see?"

The bright blood left that youthful mother's cheek;
    Back on the linden stem she lean'd her form;
And her lip trembled as it strove to speak,
    Like a frail harp-string shaken by the storm.
'Twas but a moment, and the faintness pass'd,
And the free Alpine spirit woke at last.

And she, that ever through her home had moved
    With the meek thoughtfulness and quiet smile
Of woman, calmly loving and beloved,
    And timid in her happiness the while,
Stood brightly forth, and steadfastly, that hour —
Her clear glance kindling into sudden power.

Ay, pale she stood, but with an eye of light,
    And took her fair child to her holy breast,
And lifted her soft voice, that gather'd might
    As it found language: — "Are we thus oppress'd?
Then must we rise upon our mountain-sod,
And man must arm, and woman call on God!

"I know what thou wouldst do; — and be it done!
    Thy soul is darken'd with its fears for me.
Trust me to heaven, my husband! This, thy son,
    The babe whom I have borne thee, must be free!
And the sweet memory of our pleasant hearth
May well give strength — if aught be strong on earth.

"Thou hast been brooding o'er the silent dread
    Of my desponding tears; now lift once more,
My hunter of the hills! thy stately head,
    And let thine eagle glance my joy restore!
I can bear all, but seeing *thee* subdued —
Take to thee back thine own undaunted mood.

"Go forth beside the waters, and along
 The chamois paths, and through the forests go;
And tell, in burning words, thy tale of wrong
 To the brave hearts that midst the hamlets glow.
God shall be with thee, my beloved! Away!
Bless but thy child, and leave me — I can pray!"

He sprang up, like a warrior youth awaking
 To clarion sounds upon the ringing air;
He caught her to his heart, while proud tears breaking
 From his dark eyes fell o'er her braided hair;
And "Worthy art thou," was his joyous cry,
"That man for thee should gird himself to die!

"My bride, my wife, the mother of my child!
 Now shall thy name be armour to my heart:
And this our land, by chains no more defiled,
 Be taught of thee to choose the better part!
I go — thy spirit on my words shall dwell:
Thy gentle voice shall stir the Alps. Farewell!"

And thus they parted, by the quiet lake,
 In the clear starlight: he the strength to rouse
Of the free hills; she, thoughtful for his sake,
 To rock her child beneath the whispering boughs,
Singing its blue half-curtain'd eyes to sleep
With a low hymn, amidst the stillness deep.

PROPERZIA ROSSI.

[Properzia Rossi, a celebrated female sculptor of Bologna, possessed also of talents for poetry and music, died in consequence of an unrequited attachment. A painting, by Ducis, represents her showing her last work, a basso-relievo of Ariadne, to a Roman knight, the object of her affection, who regards it with indifference.]

> "Tell me no more, no more
> Of my soul's lofty gifts! Are they not vain
> To quench its haunting thirst for happiness?
> Have I not loved, and striven, and fail'd to bind
> One true heart unto me, whereon my own
> Might find a resting-place, a home for all
> Its burden of affections? I depart,
> Unknown, though Fame goes with me; I must leave
> The earth unknown. Yet it may be that death
> Shall give my name a power to win such tears
> As would have made life precious."

I.

One dream of passion and of beauty more!
And in its bright fulfilment let me pour
My soul away! Let earth retain a trace
Of that which lit my being, though its race
Might have been loftier far. Yet one more dream!
From my deep spirit one victorious gleam
Ere I depart! For thee alone, for thee!
May this last work, this farewell triumph be —
Thou, loved so vainly! I would leave enshrined
Something immortal of my heart and mind,
That yet may speak to thee when I am gone,
Shaking thine inmost bosom with a tone
Of lost affection, — something that may prove
What she hath been, whose melancholy love

On thee was lavish'd; silent pang and tear,
And fervent song that gush'd when none were near,
And dream by night, and weary thought by day,
Stealing the brightness from her life away —
While thou —— Awake! not yet within me die!
Under the burden and the agony
Of this vain tenderness — my spirit, wake!
Even for thy sorrowful affection's sake,
Live! in thy work breathe out! — that he may yet,
Feeling sad mastery there, perchance regret
Thine unrequited gift.

II.

It comes! the power
Within me born flows back — my fruitless dower
That could not win me love. Yet once again
I greet it proudly, with its rushing train
Of glorious images: they throng — they press —
A sudden joy lights up my loneliness —
I shall not perish all!
The bright work grows
Beneath my hand, unfolding, as a rose,
Leaf after leaf, to beauty — line by line,
Through the pale marble's veins. It grows! — and now
I fix my thought, heart, soul, to burn, to shine:
I give my own life's history to thy brow,
Forsaken Ariadne! — thou shalt wear
My form, my lineaments; but oh! more fair,
Touch'd into lovelier being by the glow
 Which in me dwells, as by the summer light
All things are glorified. From thee my woe
 Shall yet look beautiful to meet his sight,

When I am pass'd away. Thou art the mould,
Wherein I pour the fervent thoughts, th' untold,
The self-consuming! Speak to him of me,
Thou, the deserted by the lonely sea,
With the soft sadness of thine earnest eye —
Speak to him, lorn one! deeply, mournfully,
Of all my love and grief! Oh! could I throw
Into thy frame a voice — a sweet, and low,
And thrilling voice of song! when he came nigh,
To send the passion of its melody
Through his pierced bosom — on its tones to bear
My life's deep feeling, as the southern air
Wafts the faint myrtle's breath — to rise, to swell,
To sink away in accents of farewell,
Winning but one, *one* gush of tears, whose flow
Surely my parted spirit yet might know,
If love be strong as death!

III.

Now fair thou art,
Thou form, whose life is of my burning heart!
Yet all the vision that within me wrought,
I cannot make thee. Oh! I might have given
Birth to creations of far nobler thought;
I might have kindled, with the fire of heaven,
Things not of such as die! But I have been
Too much alone! A heart whereon to lean,
With all these deep affections that o'erflow
My aching soul, and find no shore below;
An eye to be my star; a voice to bring
Hope o'er my path like sounds that breathe of spring?
These are denied me — dreamt of still in vain.
Therefore my brief aspirings from the chain

Are ever but as some wild fitful song,
Rising triumphantly, to die ere long
In dirge-like echoes.

IV.

Yet the world will see
Little of this, my parting work! in thee.
  Thou shalt have fame! Oh, mockery! give the reed
From storms a shelter — give the drooping vine
Something round which its tendrils may entwine —
  Give the parch'd flower a rain-drop, and the meed
Of love's kind words to woman! Worthless fame!
That in *his* bosom wins not for my name
Th' abiding place it ask'd! Yet how my heart,
In its own fairy world of song and art,
Once beat for praise! Are those high longings o'er?
That which I have been can I be no more?
Never! oh, never more! though still thy sky
Be blue as then, my glorious Italy!
And though the music, whose rich breathings fill
Thine air with soul, be wandering past me still;
And though the mantle of thy sunlight streams
Unchanged on forms, instinct with poet-dreams.
Never! oh, never more! Where'er I move,
The shadow of this broken-hearted love
Is on me and around! Too well *they* know
  Whose life is all within, too soon and well,
When there the blight hath settled! But I go
  Under the silent wings of peace to dwell;
From the slow wasting, from the lonely pain,
The inward burning of those words — "*in vain*,"
  Sear'd on the heart — I go. 'Twill soon be past!
Sunshine and song, and bright Italian heaven,

And thou, oh! thou, on whom my spirit cast
Unvalued wealth — who know'st not what was given
In that devotedness — the sad, and deep,
And unrepaid — farewell! If I could weep
Once, only once, beloved one! on thy breast,
Pouring my heart forth ere I sink to rest!
But that were happiness! — and unto me
Earth's gift is *fame*. Yet I was form'd to be
So richly bless'd! With thee to watch the sky,
Speaking not, feeling but that thou wert nigh;
With thee to listen, while the tones of song
Swept even as part of our sweet air along —
To listen silently; with thee to gaze
On forms, the deified of olden days —
This had been joy enough; and hour by hour,
From its glad well-springs drinking life and power,
How had my spirit soar'd, and made its fame
A glory for thy brow! Dreams, dreams! — The fire
Burns faint within me. Yet I leave my name —
As a deep thrill may linger on the lyre
When its full chords are hush'd — awhile to live,
And one day haply in thy heart revive
Sad thoughts of me. I leave it, with a sound,
A spell o'er memory, mournfully profound;
I leave it, on my country's air to dwell —
Say proudly yet — *"'Twas hers who loved me well!"*

PAULINE.

> To die for what we love! Oh! there is power
> In the true heart, and pride, and joy, for this:
> It is to live without the vanish'd light
> That strength is needed.

> "Così trapassa al trapassar d'un giorno
> Della vita mortal il fiore e'l verde." — TASSO.

ALONG the starlit Seine went music swelling,
  Till the air thrill'd with its exulting mirth;
Proudly it floated, even as if no dwelling
  For cares or stricken hearts were found on earth;
And a glad sound the measure lightly beat,
A happy chime of many dancing feet.

For in a palace of the land that night,
  Lamps, and fresh roses, and green leaves were hung;
And from the painted walls, a stream of light
  On flying forms beneath soft splendour flung;
But loveliest far amidst the revel's pride
Was one — the lady from the Danube side.*

Pauline, the meekly bright! though now no more
  Her clear eye flash'd with youth's all-tameless glee,
Yet something holier than its dayspring wore,
  There in soft rest lay beautiful to see;
A charm with graver, tenderer, sweetness fraught —
The blending of deep love and matron thought.

---

* The Princess Pauline Schwartzenberg. The story of her fate is beautifully related in *L'Allemagne*, vol. III. p. 336.

Through the gay throng she moved, serenely fair,
    And such calm joy as fills a moonlight sky
Sat on her brow beneath its graceful hair,
    As her young daughter in the dance went by,
With the fleet step of one that yet hath known
Smiles and kind voices in this world alone.

Lurk'd there no secret boding in her breast?
    Did no faint whisper warn of evil nigh?
Such oft awake when most the heart seems blest
    Midst the light laughter of festivity.
Whence come those tones? Alas! enough we know
To mingle fear with all triumphal show!

Who spoke of evil when young feet were flying
    In fairy rings around the echoing hall —
Soft airs through braided locks in perfume sighing,
    Glad pulses beating unto music's call?
Silence! — the minstrels pause — and hark! a sound,
A strange quick rustling which their notes had drown'd!

And lo! a light upon the dancers breaking —
    Not such their clear and silvery lamps had shed!
From the gay dream of revelry awaking,
    One moment holds them still in breathless dread.
The wild fierce lustre grows: then bursts a cry —
Fire! through the hall and round it gathering — fly!

And forth they rush, as chased by sword and spear,
    To the green coverts of the garden bowers —
A gorgeous masque of pageantry and fear,
    Startling the birds and trampling down the flowers:
While from the dome behind, red sparkles driven
Pierce the dark stillness of the midnight heaven.

And where is she — Pauline! The hurrying throng
  Have swept her onward, as a stormy blast
Might sweep some faint o'erwearied bird along —
  Till now the threshold of that death is past,
And free she stands beneath the starry skies,
Calling her child — but no sweet voice replies.

"Bertha! where art thou? Speak! oh! speak, my own!"
  Alas! unconscious of her pangs the while,
The gentle girl, in fear's cold grasp alone,
  Powerless had sunk within the blazing pile;
A young bright form, deck'd gloriously for death,
With flowers all shrinking from the flame's fierce breath!

But oh! thy strength, deep love! There is no power
  To stay the mother from that rolling grave,
Though fast on high the fiery volumes tower,
  And forth like banners from each lattice wave:
Back, back she rushes through a host combined —
Mighty is anguish, with affection twined!

And what bold step may follow, midst the roar
  Of the red billows, o'er their prey that rise?
None! — Courage there stood still — and never more
  Did those fair forms emerge on human eyes!
Was one bright meeting theirs, one wild farewell?
And died they heart to heart? — Oh! who can tell?

Freshly and cloudlessly the morning broke
  On that sad palace, midst its pleasure shades;
Its painted roofs had sunk — yet black with smoke
  And lonely stood its marble colonnades:
But yester eve their shafts with wreaths were bound,
Now lay the scene one shrivell'd scroll around!

And bore the ruins no recording trace
  Of all that woman's heart had dared and done?
Yes! there were gems to mark its mortal place,
  That forth from dust and ashes dimly shone!
Those had the mother, on her gentle breast,
Worn round her child's fair image, there at rest.

And they were all! — the tender and the true
  Left this alone her sacrifice to prove,
Hallowing the spot where mirth once lightly flew,
  To deep lone chasten'd thoughts of grief and love.
Oh! we have need of patient faith below,
To clear away the mysteries of such woe!

JUANA.

[Juana, mother of the Emperor Charles V., upon the death of her husband, Philip the Handsome of Austria, who had treated her with uniform neglect, had his body laid upon a bed of state, in a magnificent dress; and being possessed with the idea that it would revive, watched it for a length of time, incessantly waiting for the moment of returning life.]

It is but dust thou look'st upon. This love,
This wild and passionate idolatry,
What doth it in the shadow of the grave?
Gather it back within thy lonely heart,
So must it ever end: too much we give
Unto the things that perish.

THE night-wind shook the tapestry round an ancient palace
    room,
And torches, as it rose and fell, waved through the gorgeous
    gloom,

And o'er a shadowy regal couch threw fitful gleams and red,
Where a woman with long raven hair sat watching by the dead.

Pale shone the features of the dead, yet glorious still to see,
Like a hunter or a chief struck down while his heart and step were free:
No shroud he wore, no robe of death, but there majestic lay,
Proudly and sadly glittering in royalty's array.

But she that with the dark hair watch'd by the cold slumberer's side,
On *her* wan cheek no beauty dwelt, and in her garb no pride;
Only her full impassion'd eyes as o'er that clay she bent,
A wildness and a tenderness in strange resplendence blent.

And as the swift thoughts cross'd her soul, like shadows of a cloud,
Amidst the silent room of death the dreamer spoke aloud;
She spoke to him that could not hear, and cried, "Thou yet wilt wake,
And learn my watchings and my tears, beloved one! for thy sake.

"They told me this was death, but well I knew it could not be;
Fairest and stateliest of the earth! who spoke of death for *thee?*
They would have wrapp'd the funeral shroud thy gallant form around,
But I forbade — and there thou art, a monarch, robed and crown'd!

"With all thy bright locks gleaming still, their coronal
    beneath,
And thy brow so proudly beautiful — who said that this was
    death?
Silence hath been upon thy lips, and stillness round thee
    long,
But the hopeful spirit in my breast is all undimm'd and
    strong.

"I know thou hast not loved me yet; I am not fair like
    thee,
The very glance of whose clear eye threw round a light of
    glee!
A frail and drooping form is mine — a cold unsmiling cheek —
Oh! I have but a woman's heart wherewith *thy* heart to seek.

"But when thou wakest, my prince, my lord! and hear'st
    how I have kept
A lonely vigil by thy side, and o'er thee pray'd and wept —
How in one long deep dream of thee my nights and days
    have past —
Surely that humble patient love *must* win back love at last!

And thou wilt smile — my own, my own, shall be the sunny
    smile,
Which brightly fell, and joyously, on all *but* me erewhile!
No more in vain affection's thirst my weary soul shall pine —
Oh! years of hope deferr'd were paid by one fond glance of
    thine!

"Thou'lt meet me with that radiant look when thou comest
    from the chase —
For me, for me, in festal halls it shall kindle o'er thy face!

Thou'lt reck no more though beauty's gift mine aspect may
    not bless;
In thy kind eyes this deep, deep love shall give me loveliness.

"But wake! my heart within me burns, yet once more to re-
    joice
In the sound to which it ever leap'd, the music of thy voice.
Awake! I sit in solitude, that thy first look and tone,
And the gladness of thine opening eyes, may all be mine
    alone."

In the still chambers of the dust, thus pour'd forth day by
    day,
The passion of that loving dream from a troubled soul found
    way,
Until the shadows of the grave had swept o'er every grace,
Left midst the awfulness of death on the princely form and
    face.

And slowly broke the fearful truth upon the watcher's breast,
And they bore away the royal dead with requiems to his
    rest,
With banners and with knightly plumes all waving in the
    wind —
But a woman's broken heart was left in its lone despair be-
    hind.

THE GRAVE OF A POETESS.*

I stood beside thy lowly grave;
　　Spring odours breathed around,
And music, in the river wave,
　　Pass'd with a lulling sound.

All happy things that love the sun
　　In the bright air glanced by,
And a glad murmur seem'd to run
　　Through the soft azure sky.

Fresh leaves were on the ivy bough
　　That fringed the ruins near;
Young voices were abroad — but thou
　　Their sweetness couldst not hear.

And mournful grew my heart for thee!
　　Thou in whose woman's mind
The ray that brightens earth and sea,
　　The light of song, was shrined.

* "Extrinsic interest has lately attached to the fine scenery of Woodstock, near Kilkenny, on account of its having been the last residence of the author of *Psyche*. Her grave is one of many in the churchyard of the village. The river runs smoothly by. The ruins of an ancient abbey, that have been partially converted into a church, reverently throw their mantle of tender shadow over it." — *Tales by the O'Hara Family.*

Mournful, that thou wert slumbering low,
  With a dread curtain drawn
Between thee and the golden glow
  Of this world's vernal dawn.

Parted from all the song and bloom
  Thou wouldst have loved so well,
To thee the sunshine round thy tomb
  Was but a broken spell.

The bird, the insect on the wing,
  In their bright reckless play,
Might feel the flush and life of spring —
  And thou wert pass'd away.

But then, e'en then, a nobler thought
  O'er my vain sadness came;
Th' immortal spirit woke, and wrought
  Within my thrilling frame.

Surely on lovelier things, I said,
  Thou must have look'd ere now,
Than all that round our pathway shed
  Odours and hues below.

The shadows of the tomb are here,
  Yet beautiful is earth!
What see'st thou, then, where no dim fear,
  No haunting dream hath birth?

Here a vain love to passing flowers
    Thou gavest; but where thou art,
The sway is not with changeful hours —
    There love and death must part.

Thou hast left sorrow in thy song,
    A voice not loud but deep!
The glorious bowers of earth among,
    How often didst thou weep?

Where couldst thou fix on mortal ground
    Thy tender thoughts and high? —
Now peace the woman's heart hath found,
    And joy the poet's eye.

LAYS OF MANY LANDS.

THE BIRD'S RELEASE.

[The Indians of Bengal and of the coast of Malabar bring cages filled with birds to the graves of their friends, over which they set the birds at liberty. This custom is alluded to in the description of Virginia's funeral. — See *Paul and Virginia*.]

Go forth! for she is gone!
With the golden light of her wavy hair,
She is gone to the fields of the viewless air;
    She hath left her dwelling lone!

Her voice hath pass'd away!
It hath pass'd away like a summer breeze,
When it leaves the hills for the far blue seas,
    Where we may not trace its way.

Go forth, and like her be free!
With thy radiant wing, and thy glancing eye,
Thou hast all the range of the sunny sky,
    And what is our grief to thee?

Is it aught e'en to her we mourn?
Doth she look on the tears by her kindred shed?
Doth she rest with the flowers o'er her gentle head,
    Or float, on the light wind borne?

We know not — but she is gone!
Her step from the dance, her voice from the song,
And the smile of her eye from the festal throng;
    She hath left her dwelling lone!

When the waves at sunset shine,
We may hear thy voice amidst thousands more,
In the scented woods of our glowing shore;
    But we shall not know 'tis thine!

Even so with the loved one flown!
Her smile in the starlight may wander by,
Her breath may be near in the wind's low sigh,
    Around us — but all unknown.

Go forth! we have loosed thy chain!
We may deck thy cage with the richest flowers
Which the bright day rears in our Eastern bowers;
    But thou wilt not be lured again.

Even thus may the summer pour
All fragrant things on the land's green breast,
And the glorious earth like a bride be dress'd,
    But it wins *her* back no more!

THE CAVERN OF THE THREE TELLS.

A SWISS TRADITION.

[The three founders of the Helvetic Confederacy are thought to sleep in a cavern near the Lake of Lucerne. The herdsmen call them the Three Tells; and say that they lie there in their antique garb, in quiet slumber; and when Switzerland is in her utmost need, they will awaken and regain the liberties of the land. — See *Quarterly Review*, No. 44.

The Grütli, where the confederates held their nightly meetings, is a meadow on the shore of the Lake of Lucerne, or Lake of the Forest Cantons, here called the Forest-Sea.]

Oh! enter not yon shadowy cave,
  Seek not the bright spars there,
Though the whispering pines that o'er it wave
  With freshness fill the air;
    For there the Patriot Three,
      In the garb of old array'd,
    By their native Forest-Sea
      On a rocky couch are laid.

The Patriot Three that met of yore
  Beneath the midnight sky,
And leagued their hearts on the Grütli shore
  In the name of liberty!
    Now silently they sleep
      Amidst the hills they freed;
    But their rest is only deep
      Till their country's hour of need.

They start not at the hunter's call,
  Nor the Lammer-geyer's cry,
Nor the rush of a sudden torrent's fall,
  Nor the Lauwine thundering by;

And the Alpine herdsman's lay,
    To a Switzer's heart so dear:
On the wild wind floats away,
    No more for them to hear.

But when the battle-horn is blown
    Till the Schreckhorn's peaks reply,
When the Jungfrau's cliffs send back the tone
    Through their eagles' lonely sky;
        When the spear-heads light the lakes,
            When trumpets loose the snows,
        When the rushing war-steed shakes
            The glacier's mute repose;

When Uri's beechen woods wave red
    In the burning hamlet's light —
Then from the cavern of the dead
    Shall the sleepers wake in might!
        With a leap, like Tell's proud leap
            When away the helm he flung,
        And boldly up the steep
            From the flashing billow sprung!*

They shall wake beside their Forest-Sea,
    In the ancient garb they wore
When they link'd the hands that made us free,
    On the Grütli's moonlight shore;
        And their voices shall be heard,
            And be answer'd with a shout,
        Till the echoing Alps are stirr'd,
            And the signal-fires blaze out.

* The point of rock on which Tell leaped from the boat of Gessler is marked by a chapel, and called the *Tellensprung*.

And the land shall see such deeds again
  As those of that proud day
When Winkelried, on Sempach's plain,
  Through the serried spears made way;
    And when the rocks came down
      On the dark Morgarten dell,
    And the crownèd casques,* o'erthrown,
      Before our fathers fell!

For the Kuhreigen's** notes must never sound
  In a land that wears the chain,
And the vines on freedom's holy ground
  Untrampled must remain;
    And the yellow harvests wave
      For no stranger's hand to reap,
    While within their silent cave
      The men of Grütli sleep!

SWISS SONG,
ON THE ANNIVERSARY OF AN ANCIENT BATTLE.

[The Swiss, even to our days, have continued to celebrate the anniversaries of their ancient battles with much solemnity; assembling in the open air on the fields where their ancestors fought, to hear thanksgivings offered up by the priests, and the names of all who shared in the glory of the day enumerated. They afterwards walk in procession to chapels, always erected in the vicinity of such scenes, where masses are sung for the souls of the departed. — See PLANTA's *History of the Helvetic Confederacy.*]

  Look on the white Alps round!
  If yet they gird a land

---

* Crowned Helmets, as a distinction of rank, are mentioned in Simond's *Switzerland*.
** The Kuhreigen — the celebrated *Rans des Vaches*.

Where Freedom's voice and step are found,
    Forget ye not the band, —
The faithful band, our sires, who fell
Here in the narrow battle-dell!

If yet, the wilds among,
    Our silent hearts may burn,
When the deep mountain-horn hath rung
    And home our steps may turn, —
Home! — home! — if still that name be dear,
Praise to the men who perish'd here!

Look on the white Alps round!
    Up to their shining snows
That day the stormy rolling sound,
    The sound of battle, rose!
Their caves prolong'd the trumpet's blast,
Their dark pines trembled as it pass'd!

They saw the princely crest,
    They saw the knightly spear,
The banner and the mail-clad breast,
    Borne down and trampled here!
They saw — and glorying there they stand,
Eternal records to the land!

Praise to the mountain-born,
    The brethren of the glen!
By them no steel array was worn,
    They stood as peasant-men!
They left the vineyard and the field,
To break an empire's lance and shield!

Look on the white Alps round!
  If yet, along their steeps,
  Our children's fearless feet may bound,
    Free as the chamois leaps:
Teach them in song to bless the band
Amidst whose mossy graves we stand!

If, by the wood-fire's blaze,
  When winter stars gleam cold,
  The glorious tales of elder days
    May proudly yet be told,
Forget not then the shepherd race,
Who made the hearth a holy place!

Look on the white Alps round!
  If yet the Sabbath-bell
  Comes o'er them with a gladdening sound,
    Think on the battle-dell!
For blood first bathed its flowery sod,
That chainless hearts might worship God!

THE MESSENGER BIRD.

[Some of the native Brazilians pay great veneration to a certain bird that sings mournfully in the night-time. They say it is a messenger which their deceased friends and relations have sent, and that it brings them news from the other world. — See PICART's *Ceremonies and Religious Customs.*]

Thou art come from the spirits' land, thou bird!
  Thou art come from the spirits' land:
  Through the dark pine grove let thy voice be heard,
    And tell of the shadowy band!

We know that the bowers are green and fair
    In the light of that summer shore;
And we know that the friends we have lost are there,
    They are there — and they weep no more!

And we know they have quench'd their fever's thirst
    From the fountain of youth ere now,*
For *there* must the stream in its freshness burst
    Which none may find below!

And we know that they will not be lured to earth
    From the land of deathless flowers,
By the feast, or the dance, or the song of mirth,
    Though their hearts were once with ours:

Though they sat with us by the night-fire's blaze,
    And bent with us the bow,
And heard the tales of our fathers' days,
    Which are told to others now!

But tell us, thou bird of the solemn strain!
    Can those who have loved forget?
We call — and they answer not again:
    Do they love — do they love us yet?

Doth the warrior think of his brother *there*,
    And the father of his child?
And the chief of those that were wont to share
    His wandering through the wild?

---

* An expedition was actually undertaken by Juan Ponce de Leon, in the 16th century, with a view of discovering a wonderful fountain, believed by the natives of Puerto Rico to spring in one of the Lucayo Isles, and to possess the virtue of restoring youth to all who bathed in its waters. — See ROBERTSON's *History of America*.

THE MESSENGER BIRD.

We call them far through the silent night,
    And they speak not from cave or hill;
We know, thou bird! that their land is bright,
    But say, do they love there still?*

---

* ANSWER TO "THE MESSENGER BIRD."
BY AN AMERICAN QUAKER LADY.

Yes! I came from the spirits' land,
    From the land that is bright and fair;
I came with a voice from the shadowy band,
    To tell that they love you there.

To say, if a wish or a vain regret
    Could live in Elysian bowers,
'Twould be for the friends they can ne'er forget,
    The beloved of their youthful hours.

To whisper the dear deserted band,
    Who smiled on their tarriance here,
That a faithful guard in the dreamless land
    Are the friends they have loved so dear.

'Tis true, in the silent night you call,
    And they answer you not again;
But the spirits of bliss are voiceless all —
    Sound only was made for pain.

That their land is bright and they weep no more,
    I have warbled from hill to hill;
But my plaintive strain should have told before,
    That they love, oh! they love you still.

They bid me say that unfading flowers
    You'll find in the path they trode;
And a welcome true to their deathless bowers,
    Pronounced by the voice of God.

1827.

CŒUR-DE-LION AT THE BIER OF HIS FATHER.

[The body of Henry the Second lay in state in the abbey-church of Fontevraud, where it was visited by Richard Cœur-de-Lion, who, on beholding it, was struck with horror and remorse, and bitterly reproached himself for that rebellious conduct which had been the means of bringing his father to an untimely grave.]

Torches were blazing clear,
    Hymns pealing deep and slow,
Where a king lay stately on his bier
    In the church of Fontevraud.
Banners of battle o'er him hung,
    And warriors slept beneath;
And light, as noon's broad light, was flung
    On the settled face of death.

On the settled face of death
    A strong and ruddy glare,
Though dimm'd at times by the censer's breath,
    Yet it fell still brightest there:
As if each deeply furrow'd trace
    Of earthly years to show.
Alas! that sceptred mortal's race
    Had surely closed in woe!

The marble floor was swept
    By many a long dark stole.
As the kneeling priests round him that slept
    Sang mass for the parted soul:
And solemn were the strains they pour'd
    Through the stillness of the night,
With the cross above, and the crown and sword,
    And the silent king in sight.

There was heard a heavy clang,
    As of steel-girt men the tread,
And the tombs and the hollow pavement rang
    With a sounding thrill of dread;
And the holy chant was hush'd awhile,
    As, by the torch's flame,
A gleam of arms up the sweeping aisle
    With a mail-clad leader came.

He came with haughty look,
    An eagle-glance and clear;
But his proud heart through its breastplate shook
    When he stood beside the bier!
He stood there still with a drooping brow,
    And clasp'd hands o'er it raised;
For his father lay before him low —
    It was Cœur-de-Lion gazed!

And silently he strove
    With the workings of his breast;
But there's more in late repentant love
    Than steel may keep suppress'd!
And his tears brake forth, at last, like rain, —
    Men held their breath in awe;
For his face was seen by his warrior train,
    And he reck'd not that they saw.

He look'd upon the dead —
    And sorrow seem'd to lie,
A weight of sorrow, even like lead,
    Pale on the fast-shut eye.
He stoop'd — and kiss'd the frozen cheek,
    And the heavy hand of clay;

Till bursting words — yet all too weak —
   Gave his soul's passion way.

"O father! is it vain,
   This late remorse and deep?
Speak to me, father! once again:
   I weep — behold, I weep!
Alas! my guilty pride and ire! —
   Were but this work undone,
I would give England's crown, my sire!
   To hear thee bless thy son.

"Speak to me! Mighty grief
   Ere now the dust hath stirr'd!
Hear me, but hear me! — father, chief,
   My king! I *must* be heard!
Hush'd, hush'd — how is it that I call,
   And that thou answerest not?
When was it thus? —— Woe, woe for all
   The love my soul forgot!

"Thy silver hairs I see,
   So still, so sadly bright!
And father, father! but for me,
   They had not been so white!
I bore thee down, high heart! at last:
   No longer couldst thou strive.
Oh! for one moment of the past,
   To kneel and say — 'forgive!'

"Thou wert the noblest king
   On royal throne e'er seen;
And thou didst wear in knightly ring,
   Of all, the stateliest mien;

And thou didst prove, where spears are proved,
  In war, the bravest heart:
Oh! ever the renown'd and loved
  Thou wert — and *there* thou art!

"Thou that my boyhood's guide
  Didst take fond joy to be! —
The times I've sported at thy side,
  And climb'd thy parent knee!
And there before the blessed shrine,
  My sire! I see thee lie, —
How will that sad still face of thine
  Look on me till I die!"

THE WILD HUNTSMAN.

[It is a popular belief in the Odenwald, that the passing of the Wild Huntsman announces the approach of war. He is supposed to issue with his train from the ruined castle of Rodenstein, and traverse the air to the opposite castle of Schnellerts. It is confidently asserted, that the sound of his phantom horses and hounds was heard by the Duke of Baden before the commencement of the last war in Germany.]

Thy rest was deep at the slumberer's hour,
  If thou didst not hear the blast
Of the savage horn from the mountain-tower,
  As the Wild Night-Huntsman pass'd,
And the roar of the stormy chase went by
Through the dark unquiet sky!

The stag sprang up from his mossy bed
  When he caught the piercing sounds,
And the oak-boughs crash'd to his antler'd head,
  As he flew from the viewless hounds;

And the falcon soar'd from her craggy height,
Away through the rushing night!

The banner shook on its ancient hold,
　And the pine in its desert place,
As the cloud and tempest onward roll'd
　With the din of the trampling race;
And the glens were fill'd with the laugh and shout,
And the bugle, ringing out!

From the chieftain's hand the wine-cup fell,
　At the castle's festive board,
And a sudden pause came o'er the swell
　Of the harp's triumphal chord;
And the Minnesinger's* thrilling lay
In the hall died fast away.

The convent's chanted rite was stay'd,
　And the hermit dropp'd his beads,
And a trembling ran through the forest-shade,
　At the neigh of the phantom steeds,
And the church-bells peal'd to the rocking blast
As the Wild Night-Huntsman pass'd.

The storm hath swept with the chase away,
　There is stillness in the sky;
But the mother looks on her son to-day
　With a troubled heart and eye,
And the maiden's brow hath a shade of care
Midst the gleam of her golden hair!

---

* Minnesinger, *love-singer* — the wandering minstrels of Germany were so called in the middle ages.

The Rhine flows bright; but its waves ere long
   Must hear a voice of war,
And a clash of spears our hills among,
   And a trumpet from afar;
And the brave on a bloody turf must lie —
For the Huntsman hath gone by!

THE SHADE OF THESEUS.

AN ANCIENT GREEK TRADITION.

Know ye not when our dead
   From sleep to battle sprung? —
When the Persian charger's tread
   On their covering greensward rung;
When the trampling march of foes
   Had crush'd our vines and flowers,
When jewel'd crests arose
   Through the holy laurel bowers;
      When banners caught the breeze,
         When helms in sunlight shone,
      When masts were on the seas,
      And spears on Marathon.

There was one, a leader crown'd,
   And arm'd for Greece that day;
But the falchions made no sound
   On his gleaming war-array.
In the battle's front he stood,
   With his tall and shadowy crest;
But the arrows drew no blood,
   Though their path was through his breast.

When banners caught the breeze,
　When helms in sunlight shone,
　When masts were on the seas,
　　And spears on Marathon.

His sword was seen to flash
　Where the boldest deeds were done;
But it smote without a clash —
　The stroke was heard by none!
His voice was not of those
　That swell'd the rolling blast,
And his steps fell hush'd like snows —
　'Twas the Shade of Theseus pass'd!
　　When banners caught the breeze,
　　　When helms in sunlight shone,
　　　When masts were on the seas,
　　　　And spears on Marathon.

Far sweeping through the foe,
　With a fiery charge he bore;
And the Mede left many a bow
　On the sounding ocean-shore.
And the foaming waves grew red,
　And the sails were crowded fast,
When the sons of Asia fled,
　As the Shade of Theseus pass'd!
　　When banners caught the breeze,
　　　When helms in sunlight shone,
　　　When masts were on the seas,
　　　　And spears on Marathon.

ANCIENT GREEK SONG OF EXILE.

Where is the summer with her golden sun? —
  That festal glory hath not pass'd from earth:
For me alone the laughing day is done!
  Where is the summer with her voice of mirth?
    — Far in my own bright land?

Where are the Fauns, whose flute-notes breathe and die
  On the green hills? — the founts, from sparry caves
Through the wild places bearing melody? —
  The reeds, low whispering o'er the river waves?
    — Far in my own bright land!

Where are the temples, through the dim wood shining,
  The virgin dances, and the choral strains?
Where the sweet sisters of my youth, entwining
  The spring's first roses for their sylvan fanes?
    — Far in my own bright land!

Where are the vineyards, with their joyous throngs,
  The red grapes pressing when the foliage fades?
The lyres, the wreaths, the lovely Dorian songs,
  And the pine forests, and the olive shades?
    — Far in my own bright land!

Where the deep haunted grots, the laurel bowers,
  The Dryad's footsteps, and the minstrel's dreams? —
Oh, that my life were as a southern flower's! —
  I might not languish then by these chill streams,
    Far from my own bright land!

THE SULIOTE MOTHER.

[It is related, in a French life of Ali Pasha, that several of the Suliote women, on the advance of the Turkish troops into the mountain fastnesses, assembled on a lofty summit, and, after chanting a wild song, precipitated themselves, with their children, into the chasm below, to avoid becoming the slaves of the enemy.]

   She stood upon the loftiest peak,
    Amidst the clear blue sky;
   A bitter smile was on her cheek,
    And a dark flash in her eye.

"Dost thou see them, boy? — through the dusky pines
Dost thou see where the foeman's armour shines?
Hast thou caught the gleam of the conqueror's crest?
My babe, that I cradled on my breast!
Wouldst thou spring from thy mother's arms with joy?
— That sight hath cost thee a father, boy!"

   For in the rocky strait beneath,
    Lay Suliote sire and son:
   They had heap'd high the piles of death
    Before the pass was won.

"They have cross'd the torrent, and on they come:
Woe for the mountain hearth and home!
There, where the hunter laid by his spear,
There, where the lyre hath been sweet to hear,
There, where I sang thee, fair babe! to sleep,
Naught but the blood-stain our trace shall keep!"

THE SULIOTE MOTHER.

And now the horn's loud blast was heard,
    And now the cymbal's clang,
Till even the upper air was stirr'd,
    As cliff and hollow rang.

"Hark! they bring music, my joyous child!
What saith the trumpet to Suli's wild?
Doth it light thine eye with so quick a fire,
As if at a glance of thine armèd sire?
Still! — be thou still! — there are brave men low:
Thou wouldst not smile couldst thou see him now!"

    But nearer came the clash of steel,
        And louder swell'd the horn,
    And farther yet the tambour's peal
        Through the dark pass was borne.

"Hear'st thou the sound of their savage mirth?
Boy! thou wert free when I gave thee birth, —
Free, and how cherish'd, my warrior's son!
He too hath bless'd thee, as I have done!
Ay, and unchain'd must his loved ones be —
Freedom, young Suliote! for thee and me!"

    And from the arrowy peak she sprung,
        And fast the fair child bore: —
    A veil upon the wind was flung,
        A cry — and all was o'er!

THE FAREWELL TO THE DEAD.

[The following piece is founded on a beautiful part of the Greek funeral service, in which relatives and friends are invited to embrace the deceased (whose face is uncovered) and to bid their final adieu. — See *Christian Researches in the Mediterranean.*]

> "'Tis hard to lay into the earth
> A countenance so benign! a form that walk'd
> But yesterday so stately o'er the earth!"   WILSON.

  Come near! Ere yet the dust
Soil the bright paleness of the settled brow,
Look on your brother; and embrace him now,
  In still and solemn trust!
Come near! — once more let kindred lips be press'd
On his cold cheek; then bear him to his rest!

  Look yet on this young face!
What shall the beauty, from amongst us gone,
Leave of its image, even where most it shone,
  Gladdening its hearth and race?
Dim grows the semblance on man's heart impress'd.
Come near, and bear the beautiful to rest!

  Ye weep, and it is well!
For tears befit earth's partings! Yesterday,
Song was upon the lips of this pale clay,
  And sunshine seem'd to dwell
Where'er he moved — the welcome and the bless'd.
Now gaze! and bear the silent unto rest!

  Look yet on him whose eye
Meets yours no more, in sadness or in mirth.
Was he not fair amidst the sons of earth,
  The beings born to die? —

But not where death has power may love be bless'd.
Come near! and bear ye the beloved to rest!

    How may the mother's heart
Dwell on her son, and dare to hope again?
The spring's rich promise hath been given in vain —
    The lovely must depart!
Is *he* not gone, our brightest and our best?
Come near! and bear the early-call'd to rest!

    Look on him! Is he laid
To slumber from the harvest or the chase? —
Too still and sad the smile upon his face;
    Yet that, even that must fade:
Death holds not long unchanged his fairest guest.
Come near! and bear the mortal to his rest!

    His voice of mirth hath ceased
Amidst the vineyards! there is left no place
For him whose dust receives your vain embrace,
    At the gay bridal-feast!
Earth must take earth to moulder on her breast.
Come near! weep o'er him! bear him to his rest.

    Yet mourn ye not as they
Whose spirits' light is quench'd! For him the past
Is seal'd: he may not fall, he may not cast
    His birthright's hope away!
All is not *here* of our beloved and bless'd.
Leave ye the sleeper with his God to rest!

SONGS OF THE AFFECTIONS.

A SPIRIT'S RETURN.

> "This is to be a mortal,
> And seek the things beyond mortality!" MANFRED.

Thy voice prevails — dear friend, my gentle friend!
This long-shut heart for thee shall be unseal'd;
And though thy soft eye mournfully will bend
Over the troubled stream, yet once reveal'd
Shall its freed waters flow; then rocks must close
For evermore, above their dark repose.

Come while the gorgeous mysteries of the sky
Fused in the crimson sea of sunset lie;
Come to the woods, where all strange wandering sound
Is mingled into harmony profound;
Where the leaves thrill with spirit, while the wind
Fills with a viewless being, unconfined,
The trembling reeds and fountains. Our own dell,
With its green dimness and Æolian breath,
Shall suit th' unveiling of dark records well —
Hear me in tenderness and silent faith!

Thou knew'st me not in life's fresh vernal morn —
I would thou hadst! — for then my heart on thine
Had pour'd a worthier love; now, all o'erworn
By its deep thirst for something too divine,

A SPIRIT'S RETURN.

It hath but fitful music to bestow,
Echoes of harp-strings broken long ago.

Yet even in youth companionless I stood,
As a lone forest-bird midst ocean's foam;
For me the silver cords of brotherhood
Were early loosed; the voices from my home
Pass'd one by one, and melody and mirth
Left me a dreamer by a silent hearth.

But, with the fulness of a heart that burn'd
For the deep sympathies of mind, I turn'd
From that unanswering spot, and fondly sought
In all wild scenes with thrilling murmurs fraught,
In every still small voice and sound of power,
And flute-note of the wind through cave and bower,
A perilous delight! — for then first woke
My life's lone passion, the mysterious quest
Of secret knowledge; and each tone that broke
From the wood-arches or the fountain's breast,
Making my quick soul vibrate as a lyre,
But minister'd to that strange inborn fire.

Midst the bright silence of the mountain dells,
In noontide-hours or golden summer-eves,
My thoughts have burst forth as a gale that swells
Into a rushing blast, and from the leaves
Shakes out response. O thou rich world unseen!
Thou curtain'd realm of spirits! — thus my cry
Hath troubled air and silence — dost thou lie
Spread all around, yet by some filmy screen
Shut from us ever? The resounding woods,
Do their depths teem with marvels? — and the floods,

And the pure fountains, leading secret veins
Of quenchless melody through rock and hill,
Have they bright dwellers? — are their lone domains
Peopled with beauty, which may never still
Our weary thirst of soul? Cold, weak and cold,
Is earth's vain language, piercing not one fold
Of our deep being! Oh, for gifts more high!
For a seer's glance to rend mortality!
For a charm'd rod, to call from each dark shrine
The oracles divine!

I woke from those high fantasies, to know
My kindred with the earth — I woke to love.
O gentle friend! to love in doubt and woe,
Shutting the heart the worshipp'd name above,
Is to love deeply; and *my* spirit's dower
Was a sad gift, a melancholy power
Of so adoring — with a buried care,
And with the o'erflowing of a voiceless prayer,
And with a deepening dream, that day by day,
In the still shadow of its lonely sway,
Folded me closer, till the world held naught
Save the *one* being to my centred thought.
There was no music but his voice to hear,
No joy but such as with *his* step drew near;
Light was but where he look'd — life where he moved:
Silently, fervently, thus, thus I loved.
Oh! but such love is fearful! — and I knew
Its gathering doom: the soul's prophetic sight
Even then unfolded in my breast, and threw
O'er all things round a full, strong, vivid light,
Too sorrowfully clear! — an under-tone
Was given to Nature's harp, for me alone

A SPIRIT'S RETURN.

Whispering of grief. Of grief? — be strong, awake!
Hath not thy love been victory, O my soul?
Hath not its conflict won a voice to shake
Death's fastnesses? — a magic to control
Worlds far removed? — from o'er the grave to thee
Love hath made answer; and *thy* tale should be
Sung like a lay of triumph! Now return
And take thy treasure from its bosom'd urn,
And lift it once to light!

      In fear, in pain,
I said I loved — but yet a heavenly strain
Of sweetness floated down the tearful stream,
A joy flash'd through the trouble of my dream!
I knew myself beloved! We breathed no vow,
No mingling visions might our fate allow,
As unto happy hearts; but still and deep,
Like a rich jewel gleaming in a grave,
Like golden sand in some dark river's wave,
So did my soul that costly knowledge keep,
So jealously! — a thing o'er which to shed,
When stars alone beheld the drooping head,
Lone tears! yet ofttimes burden'd with the excess
Of our strange nature's quivering happiness.

But, oh! sweet friend! we dream not of love's might
Till death has robed with soft and solemn light
The image we enshrine! Before *that* hour,
We have but glimpses of the o'ermastering power
Within us laid! — *then* doth the spirit-flame
With sword-like lightning rend its mortal frame;

The wings of that which pants to follow fast
Shake their clay-bars, as with a prison'd blast —
The sea is in our souls!

       He died — *he* died
On whom my lone devotedness was cast!
I might not keep one vigil by his side,
I, whose wrung heart watch'd with him to the last!
I might not once his fainting head sustain,
Nor bathe his parch'd lips in the hour of pain,
Nor say to him, "Farewell!" He pass'd away —
Oh! had *my* love been there, its conquering sway
Had won him back from death! But thus removed,
Borne o'er th' abyss no sounding line hath proved,
Join'd with the unknown, the viewless — he became
Unto my thoughts another, yet the same —
Changed — hallow'd — glorified! — and his low grave
Seem'd a bright mournful altar — mine, all mine:
Brother and friend soon left me *that* sole shrine,
The birthright of the faithful! — *their* world's wave
Soon swept them from its brink. Oh! deem thou not
That on the sad and consecrated spot
My soul grew weak! I tell thee that a power
There kindled heart and lip — a fiery shower
My words were made — a might was given to prayer,
And a strong grasp to passionate despair,
And a dread triumph! Know'st thou what I sought?
For what high boon my struggling spirit wrought?
— Communion with the dead! I sent a cry
Through the veil'd empires of eternity —
A voice to cleave them! By the mournful truth,
By the lost promise of my blighted youth

A SPIRIT'S RETURN.

By the strong chain a mighty love can bind
On the beloved, the spell of mind o'er mind;
By words, which in themselves are magic high,
Armed, and inspired, and wing'd with agony;
By tears, which comfort not, but burn, and seem
To bear the heart's blood in their passion-stream;
I summon'd, I adjured! — with quicken'd sense,
With the keen vigil of a life intense.
I watch'd, an answer from the winds to wring,
I listen'd, if perchance the stream might bring
Token from worlds afar; I taught *one* sound
Unto a thousand echoes — one profound
Imploring accent to the tomb, the sky —
One prayer to night — "Awake! appear! reply!"
Hast thou been told that from the viewless bourne
The dark way never hath allow'd return?
That all, which tears can move, with life is fled —
That earthly love is powerless on the dead?
Believe it not! — There is a large lone star
Now burning o'er yon western hill afar,
And under its clear light there lies a spot
Which well might utter forth — Believe it not!

I sat beneath that planet. I had wept
My woe to stillness; every night-wind slept;
A hush was on the hills; the very streams
Went by like clouds, or noiseless founts in dreams;
And the dark tree o'ershadowing me that hour,
Stood motionless, even as the gray church-tower
Whereon I gazed unconsciously. There came
A low sound, like the tremor of a flame,
Or like the light quick shiver of a wing,
Flitting through twilight woods, across the air;

And I look'd up! Oh! for strong words to bring
Conviction o'er thy thought! Before me there,
He, the departed, stood! Ay, face to face,
So near, and yet how far! His form, his mien,
Gave to remembrance back each burning trace
Within: — Yet something awfully serene,
Pure, sculpture-like, on the pale brow, that wore
Of the once beating heart no token more;
And stillness on the lip — and o'er the hair
A gleam, that trembled through the breathless air;
And an unfathom'd calm, that seem'd to lie
In the grave sweetness of th'illumined eye,
Told of the gulfs between our being set,
And, as that unsheath'd spirit-glance I met,
Made my soul faint: — with *fear?* Oh! *not* with fear
With the sick feeling that in *his* far sphere
My love could be as nothing! But he spoke —
How shall I tell thee of the startling thrill
In that low voice, whose breezy tones could fill
My bosom's infinite? O friend! I woke
Then first to heavenly life! Soft, solemn, clear,
Breathed the mysterious accents on mine ear,
Yet strangely seem'd as if the while they rose
From depths of distance, o'er the wide repose
Of slumbering waters wafted, or the dells
Of mountains, hollow with sweet echo-cells
But, as they murmur'd on, the mortal chill
Pass'd from me, like a mist before the morn;
And, to that glorious intercourse upborne
By slow degrees, a calm, divinely still,
Possess'd my frame. I sought that lighted eye —
From its intense and searching purity
I drank in *soul!* — I question'd of the dead —

Of the hush'd, starry shores their footsteps tread,
And I was answer'd. If remembrance there
With dreamy whispers fill the immortal air;
If thought, here piled from many a jewel-heap,
Be treasure in that pensive land to keep;
If love, o'ersweeping change, and blight, and blast,
Find *there* the music of his home at last:
I ask'd, and I was answer'd. Full and high
Was that communion with eternity —
Too rich for aught so fleeting! Like a knell
Swept o'er my sense its closing words, "Farewell!
On earth we meet no more!" And all was gone —
The pale, bright settled brow — the thrilling tone,
The still and shining eye! and never more
May twilight gloom or midnight hush restore
That radiant guest! One full-fraught hour of heaven,
To earthly passion's wild implorings given,
Was made my own — the ethereal fire hath shiver'd
The frugile censer in whose mould it quiver'd;
Brightly, consumingly! What now is left?
A faded world, of glory's hues bereft —
A void, a chain! I dwell midst throngs, apart,
In the cold silence of the stranger's heart;
A fix'd immortal shadow stands between
My spirit and life's fast-receding scene;
A gift hath sever'd me from human ties,
A power is gone from all earth's melodies,
Which never may return: their chords are broken,
The music of another land hath spoken —
No after-sound is sweet! This weary thirst!
And I have heard celestial fountains burst!
What *here* shall quench it?

Dost thou not rejoice,
When the spring sends forth an awakening voice
Through the young woods? Thou dost! And in that birth
Of early leaves, and flowers, and songs of mirth,
Thousands, like thee, find gladness! Couldst thou know
How every breeze then summons *me* to go!
How all the light of love and beauty shed
By those rich hours, but woos me to the dead!
The *only* beautiful that change no more!
The only loved! — the dwellers on the shore
Of spring fulfill'd! The dead! *whom* call we so?
They that breathe purer air, that feel, that know
Things wrapt from us! Away! within me pent,
That which is barr'd from its own element
Still droops or struggles! But the day *will* come —
Over the deep the free bird finds its home;
And the stream lingers midst the rocks, yet greets
The sea at last; and the wing'd flower-seed meets
A soil to rest in: shall not *I*, too, be,
My spirit-love! upborne to dwell with thee?
Yes! by the power whose conquering anguish stirr'd
The tomb, whose cry beyond the stars was heard,
Whose agony of triumph won thee back
Through the dim pass no mortal step may track,
Yet shall we meet! that glimpse of joy divine
Proved thee for ever and for ever mine!

THE CORONATION OF INEZ DE CASTRO.

"Tableau, ou l'Amour fait alliance avec la Tombe; union redoutable
de la mort et de la vie."— MADAME de STAEL.

There was music on the midnight —
  From a royal fane it roll'd;
And a mighty bell, each pause between,
  Sternly and slowly toll'd.
Strange was their mingling in the sky,
  It hush'd the listener's breath;
For the music spoke of triumph high,
  The lonely bell — of death!

There was hurrying through the midnight
  A sound of many feet;
But they fell with a muffled fearfulness
  Along the shadowy street:
And softer, fainter, grew their tread,
  As it near'd the minster gate,
Whence a broad and solemn light was shed
  From a scene of royal state.

Full glow'd the strong red radiance
  In the centre of the nave,
Where the folds of a purple canopy
  Swept down in many a wave,
Loading the marble pavement old
  With a weight of gorgeous gloom;
For something lay midst their fretted gold,
  Like a shadow of the tomb.

And within that rich pavilion,
  High on a glittering throne,
A woman's form sat silently,
  Midst the glare of light alone.
Her jewell'd robes fell strangely still —
  The drapery on her breast
Seem'd with no pulse beneath to thrill,
  So stonelike was its rest!

But a peal of lordly music
  Shook e'en the dust below,
When the burning gold of the diadem
  Was set on her pallid brow!
Then died away that haughty sound;
  And from the encircling band
Stepp'd prince and chief, midst the hush profound,
  With homage to her hand.

Why pass'd a faint, cold shuddering
  Over each martial frame,
As one by one, to touch that hand,
  Noble and leader came?
Was not the settled aspect fair?
  Did not a queenly grace,
Under the parted ebon hair,
  Sit on the pale still face?

Death! death! canst *thou* be lovely
  Unto the eye of life?
Is not each pulse of the quick high breast
  With thy cold mien at strife?
— It was a strange and fearful sight,
  The crown upon that head,

The glorious robes, and the blaze of light,
  All gather'd round the Dead!

And beside her stood in silence
  One with a brow as pale,
And white lips rigidly compress'd,
  Lest the strong heart should fail:
King Pedro, with a jealous eye,
  Watching the homage done
By the land's flower and chivalry
  To her, his martyr'd one.

But on the face he look'd not,
  Which once his star had been;
To every form his glance was turn'd,
  Save of the breathless queen:
Though something, won from the grave's embrace,
  Of her beauty still was there,
Its hues were all of that shadowy place,
  It was not for *him* to bear.

Alas! the crown, the sceptre,
  The treasures of the earth,
And the priceless love that pour'd those gifts,
  Alike of wasted worth!
The rites are closed: — bear back the dead
  Unto the chamber deep!
Lay down again the royal head,
  Dust with the dust to sleep!

There is music on the midnight —
  A requiem sad and slow,
As the mourners through the sounding aisle
  In dark procession go;

And the ring of state, and the starry crown,
    And all the rich array,
Are borne to the house of silence down,
    With her, that queen of clay!

And tearlessly and firmly
    King Pedro led the train;
But his face was wrapt in his folding robe,
    When they lower'd the dust again.
'Tis hush'd at last the tomb above —
    Hymns die, and steps depart:
Who call'd thee strong as Death, O Love?
    Mightier thou wast and art.

THE VAUDOIS WIFE.*

> "Clasp me a little longer, on the brink
>   Of fate! while I can feel thy dear caress;
> And when this heart hath ceased to beat, oh! think —
>   And let it mitigate thy woe's excess —
> That thou hast been to me all tenderness,
> And friend, to more than human friendship just.
> Oh! by that retrospect of happiness,
> And by the hopes of an immortal trust,
> God shall assuage thy pangs, when I am laid in dust."
>   GERTRUDE OF WYOMING.

Thy voice is in mine ear, beloved!
    Thy look is in my heart,
Thy bosom is my resting-place,
    And yet I must depart.

---

* The wife of a Vaudois leader, in one of the attacks made on the Protestant hamlets, received a mortal wound, and died in her husband's arms, exhorting him to courage and endurance.

THE VAUDOIS WIFE.

Earth on my soul is strong — too strong —
  Too precious is its chain,
All woven of thy love, dear friend,
  Yet vain — though mighty — vain!

Thou see'st mine eye grow dim, beloved!
  Thou see'st my life-blood flow —
Bow to the Chastener silently,
  And calmly let me go!
A little while between our hearts
  The shadowy gulf must lie,
Yet have we for their communing
  Still, still Eternity!

Alas! thy tears are on my cheek.
  My spirit they detain;
I know that from thine agony
  Is wrung that burning rain.
Best! kindest! weep not — make the pang,
  The bitter conflict less —
Oh! sad it is, and yet a joy,
  To feel thy love's excess!

But calm thee! let the thought of death
  A solemn peace restore!
The voice that must be silent soon
  Would speak to thee once more,
That thou may'st bear its blessing on
  Through years of after life —
A token of consoling love,
  Even from this hour of strife.

I bless thee for the noble heart,
    The tender and the true,
Where mine hath found the happiest rest
    That e'er fond woman's knew;
I bless thee, faithful friend and guide!
    For my own, my treasured share
In the mournful secrets of thy soul,
    In thy sorrow, in thy prayer.

I bless thee for kind looks and words
    Shower'd on my path like dew,
For all the love in those deep eyes,
    A gladness ever new!
For the voice which ne'er to mine replied
    But in kindly tones of cheer;
For every spring of happiness
    My soul hath tasted here!

I bless thee for the last rich boon
    Won from affection tried —
The right to gaze on death with thee,
    To perish by thy side!
And yet more for the glorious hope
    Even to *these* moments given —
Did not *thy* spirit ever lift
    The trust of *mine* to heaven?

Now be *thou* strong! Oh, knew we not
    Our path must lead to this?
A shadow and a trembling still
    Were mingled with our bliss!

We plighted our young hearts when storms
    Were dark upon the sky,
In full, deep knowledge of their task
    To suffer and to die!

Be strong! I leave the living voice
    Of this, my martyr'd blood,
With the thousand echoes of the hills,
    With the torrent's foaming flood, —
A spirit midst the caves to dwell,
    A token on the air,
To rouse the valiant from repose,
    The fainting from despair.

Hear it, and bear thou on, my love!
    Ay, joyously endure!
Our mountains must be altars yet,
    Inviolate and pure;
There must our God be worshipp'd still
    With the worship of the free:
Farewell! — there's but *one* pang in death,
    One only, — leaving thee!

THE GUERILLA LEADER'S VOW.

> "All my pretty ones!
> Did you say all?
> . . . .
> Let us make medicine of this great revenge,
> To cure this deadly grief!" MACBETH.

My battle-vow! — no minster walls
  Gave back the burning word,
Nor cross nor shrine the low deep tone
  Of smother'd vengeance heard:
But the ashes of a ruin'd home
  Thrill'd as it sternly rose,
With the mingling voice of blood that shook
  The midnight's dark repose.

I breathed it not o'er kingly tombs,
  But where my children lay,
And the startled vulture at my step
  Soar'd from their precious clay.
I stood amidst my dead alone —
  I kiss'd their lips — I pour'd,
In the strong silence of that hour,
  My spirit on my sword.

The roof-tree fallen, the smouldering floor,
  The blacken'd threshold-stone,
The bright hair torn, and soil'd with blood,
  Whose fountain was my own —
These, and the everlasting hills,
  Bore witness that wild night;
Before them rose th' avenger's soul
  In crush'd affection's might.

The stars, the searching stars of heaven,
  With keen looks would upbraid
If from my heart the fiery vow,
  Sear'd on it then, could fade.
They have no cause! Go, ask the streams
  That by my paths have swept,
The red waves that unstain'd were born —
  How hath my faith been kept?

And other eyes are on my soul,
  That never, never close,
The sad, sweet glances of the lost —
  They leave me no repose.
Haunting my night-watch midst the rocks,
  And by the torrent's foam,
Through the dark-rolling mists they shine,
  Full, full of love and home!

Alas! the mountain eagle's heart,
  When wrong'd, may yet find rest;
Scorning the place made desolate,
  He seeks another nest.
But I — your soft looks wake the thirst
  That wins no quenching rain;
Ye drive me back, my beautiful!
  To the stormy fight again.

BERNARDO DEL CARPIO.

[The celebrated Spanish champion, Bernardo del Carpio, having made many ineffectual efforts to procure the release of his father, the Count Saldana, who had been imprisoned by King Alfonso of Asturias, almost from the time of Bernardo's birth, at last took up arms in despair. The war which he maintained proved so destructive, that the men of the land gathered round the King, and united in demanding Saldana's liberty. Alfonso, accordingly, offered Bernardo immediate possession of his father's person in exchange for his castle of Carpio. Bernardo, without hesitation, gave up his stronghold, with all his captives; and being assured that his father was then on his way from prison, rode forth with the King to meet him. "And when he saw his father approaching, he exclaimed," says the ancient chronicle, "'Oh, God! is the Count of Saldana indeed coming?'— 'Look where he is,' replied the cruel King; 'and now go and greet him whom you have so long desired to see.'" The remainder of the story will be found related in the ballad. The chronicles and romances leave us nearly in the dark as to Bernardo's history after this event.]

The warrior bow'd his crested head, and tamed his heart of
 fire,
And sued the haughty king to free his long-imprison'd sire:
"I bring thee here my fortress keys, I bring my captive train,
I pledge thee faith, my liege, my lord! — oh, break my
 father's chain!"

'Rise, rise! even now thy father comes, a ransom'd man this
 day:
Mount thy good horse, and thou and I will meet him on his
 way.'
Then lightly rose that loyal son, and bounded on his steed,
And urged, as if with lance in rest, the charger's foamy
 speed.

And lo! from far, as on they press'd, there came a glittering
 band,
With one that midst them stately rode, as a leader in the
 land;

"Now haste, Bernardo, haste! for there, in very truth, is he,
The father whom thy faithful heart hath yearn'd so long to
    see."

His dark eye flash'd, his proud breast heaved, his cheek's
    blood came and went;
He reach'd that gray-hair'd chieftain's side, and there, dis-
    mounting, bent;
A lowly knee to earth he bent, his father's hand he took, —
What was there in its touch that all his fiery spirit shook?

That hand was cold — a frozen thing — it dropp'd from his
    like lead:
He look'd up to the face above — the face was of the dead!
A plume waved o'er the noble brow — the brow was fix'd and
    white;
He met at last his father's eyes — but in them was no sight!

Up from the ground he sprang, and gazed, but who could
    paint that gaze?
They hush'd their very hearts, that saw its horror and amaze;
They might have chain'd him, as before that stony form he
    stood,
For the power was stricken from his arm, and from his lip the
    blood.

"Father!" at length he murmur'd low, and wept like child-
    hood then —
Talk not of grief till thou hast seen the tears of warlike
    men! —
He thought on all his glorious hopes, and all his young
    renown, —
He flung the falchion from his side, and in the dust sat down.

Then covering with his steel-gloved hands his darkly mourn-
    ful brow,
"No more, there is no more," he said, "to lift the sword for
    now. —
My king is false, my hope betray'd, my father — oh! the
    worth,
The glory and the loveliness, are pass'd away from earth!

"I thought to stand where banners waved, my sire! beside
    thee yet —
I would that *there* our kindred blood on Spain's free soil had
    met!
Thou wouldst have known my spirit then — for thee my fields
    were won, —
And thou hast perish'd in thy chains, as though thou hadst no
    son!"

Then, starting from the ground once more, he seized the
    monarch's rein,
Amidst the pale and wilder'd looks of all the courtier train;
And with a fierce, o'ermastering grasp, the rearing war-
    horse led,
And sternly set them face to face — the king before the
    dead! —

"Came I not forth upon thy pledge, my father's hand to
    kiss? —
Be still, and gaze thou on, false king! and tell me what is
    this!
The voice, the glance, the heart I sought — give answer,
    where are they? —
If thou wouldst clear thy perjured soul, send life through this
    cold clay!

"Into these glassy eyes put light —— Be still! keep down
    thine ire, —
Bid these white lips a blessing speak — this earth is *not* my
    sire!
Give me back him for whom I strove, for whom my blood was
    shed, —
Thou canst not — and a king! His dust be mountains on thy
    head!"

He loosed the steed; his slack hand fell — upon the silent
    face
He cast one long, deep, troubled look — then turn'd from
    that sad place:
His hope was crush'd, his after-fate untold in martial
    strain, —
His banner led the spears no more amidst the hills of Spain.

THE DREAMING CHILD.

> "Alas! what kind of grief should thy years know?
> Thy brow and cheek are smooth as waters be
> When no breath troubles them."
>
>   BEAUMONT AND FLETCHER.

AND is there sadness in *thy* dreams, my boy?
What should the cloud be made of? Blessed child!
Thy spirit, borne upon a breeze of joy,
All day hath ranged through sunshine clear, yet mild:

And now thou tremblest! — wherefore? — in *thy* soul
There lies no past, no future. Thou hast heard

No sound of presage from the distance roll,
Thy heart bears traces of no arrowy word.

From thee no love hath gone; thy mind's young eye
Hath look'd not into death's, and thence become
A questioner of mute eternity,
A weary searcher for a viewless home:

Nor hath thy sense been quicken'd unto pain
By feverish watching for some step beloved:
Free are thy thoughts, an ever-changeful train,
Glancing like dewdrops, and as lightly moved.

Yet now, on billows of strange passion toss'd,
How art thou wilder'd in the cave of sleep!
My gentle child! midst what dim phantoms lost,
Thus in mysterious anguish dost thou weep?

Awake! they sadden me — those early tears,
First gushings of the strong, dark river's flow,
That *must* o'ersweep thy soul with coming years,
Th' unfathomable flood of human woe!

Awful to watch, even rolling through a dream,
Forcing wild spray-drops but from childhood's eyes!
Wake, wake! as yet *thy* life's transparent stream
Should wear the tinge of none but summer skies.

Come from the shadow of those realms unknown,
Where now thy thoughts dismay'd and darkling rove;
Come to the kindly region all thine own,
The home still bright for thee with guardian love.

Happy, fair child! that yet a mother's voice
Can win thee back from visionary strife! —
Oh, shall *my* soul, thus waken'd to rejoice,
Start from the dreamlike wilderness of life?

THE CHARMED PICTURE.

"Oh! that those lips had language! Life hath pass'd
With me but roughly since I saw thee last."
COWPER.

THINE eyes are charm'd — thine earnest eyes —
  Thou image of the dead!
A spell within their sweetness lies,
  A virtue thence is shed.

Oft in their meek blue light enshrined
  A blessing seems to be,
And sometimes there my wayward mind
  A still reproach can see:

And sometimes pity — soft and deep,
  And quivering through a tear;
Even as if love in heaven could weep
  For grief left drooping here.

And oh, my spirit needs that balm!
  Needs it midst fitful mirth!
And in the night-hour's haunted calm,
  And by the lonely hearth.

Look on me *thus*, when hollow praise
    Hath made the weary pine
For one true tone of other days,
    One glance of love like thine!

Look on me *thus*, when sudden glee
    Bears my quick heart along,
On wings that struggle to be free,
    As bursts of skylark song.

In vain, in vain! — too soon are felt
    The wounds they cannot flee:
Better in childlike tears to melt,
    Pouring my soul on thee!

Sweet face, that o'er my childhood shone!
    Whence is thy power of change,
Thus ever shadowing back my own,
    The rapid and the strange?

Whence are they charm'd — those earnest eyes?
    — I know the mystery well!
In mine own trembling bosom lies
    The spirit of the spell!

Of Memory, Conscience, Love, 'tis born —
    Oh! change no longer, thou!
For ever be the blessing worn
    On thy pure thoughtful brow!

THE MESSAGE TO THE DEAD.

Thou'rt passing hence, my brother!
  O my earliest friend, farewell!
Thou'rt leaving me, without thy voice,
  In a lonely home to dwell;
And from the hills, and from the hearth,
  And from the household tree,
With thee departs the lingering mirth,
  The brightness goes with thee.*

But thou, my friend, my brother!
  Thou'rt speeding to the shore
Where the dirgelike tone of parting words
  Shall smite the soul no more!
And thou wilt see our holy dead,
  The lost on earth and main:
Into the sheaf of kindred hearts,
  Thou wilt be bound again!

Tell, then, our friend of boyhood
  That yet his name is heard
On the blue mountains, whence his youth
  Pass'd like a swift, bright bird.

---

* "Messages from the living to the dead are not uncommon in the Highlands. The Gaels have such a ceaseless consciousness of immortality, that their departed friends are considered as merely absent for a time, and permitted to relieve the hours of separation by occasional intercourse with the objects of their earliest affections." — See the Notes to Mrs. Brunton's Works.

The light of his exulting brow,
    The vision of his glee,
Are on me still — oh! still I trust
    That smile again to see.

And tell our fair young sister,
    The rose cut down in spring,
That yet my gushing soul is fill'd
    With lays she loved to sing.
Her soft deep eyes look through my dreams,
    Tender and sadly sweet; —
Tell her my heart within me burns
    Once more that gaze to meet.

And tell our white-hair'd father,
    That in the paths he trode,
The child he loved, the last on earth,
    Yet walks and worships God.
Say, that his last fond blessing yet
    Rests on my soul like dew,
And by its hallowing might I trust
    Once more his face to view.

And tell our gentle mother,
    That on her grave I pour
The sorrows of my spirit forth,
    As on her breast of yore.
Happy thou art that soon, how soon,
    Our good and bright will see! —
O brother, brother! may I dwell,
    Ere long, with them and thee!

THE DESERTED HOUSE.

Gloom is upon thy lonely hearth,
O silent house! once fill'd with mirth;
Sorrow is in the breezy sound
Of thy tall poplars whispering round.

The shadow of departed hours
Hangs dim upon thine early flowers;
Ev'n in thy sunshine seems to brood
Something more deep than solitude.

Fair art thou, fair to a stranger's gaze,
Mine own sweet home of other days!
My children's birthplace! — yet for me
It is too much to look on thee.

Too much! for all about thee spread,
I feel the memory of the dead,
And almost linger for the feet
That never more my step shall meet.

The looks, the smiles, all vanish'd now,
Follow me where thy roses blow;
The echoes of kind household-words
Are with me midst thy singing-birds.

Till my heart dies, it dies away
In yearnings for what might not stay;
For love which ne'er deceived my trust,
For all which went with "dust to dust!"

What now is left me, but to raise
From thee, lorn spot! my spirit's gaze,
To lift through tears my straining eye
Up to my Father's house on high?

Oh! many are the mansions there,*
But not in one hath grief a share!
No haunting shade from things gone by
May there o'ersweep th' unchanging sky.

And *they* are there, whose long-loved mien
In earthly home no more is seen;
Whose places, where they smiling sate,
Are left unto us desolate.

We miss them when the board is spread;
We miss them when the prayer is said;
Upon our dreams their dying eyes
In still and mournful fondness rise.

But they are where these longings vain
Trouble no more the heart and brain;
The sadness of this aching love
Dims not our Father's house above.

Ye are at rest, and I in tears,**
Ye dwellers of immortal spheres!

---

* "In my father's house there are many mansions." —
                                                        John, chap. xiv.

* From an ancient Hebrew dirge:
"Mourn for the mourner, and not for the dead,
For he is at rest, and we in tears!"

Under the poplar boughs I stand,
And mourn the broken household band.

But, by your life of lowly faith,
And by your joyful hope in death,
Guide me, till on some brighter shore
The sever'd wreath is bound once more!

Holy ye were, and good, and true!
No change can cloud my thoughts of you;
Guide me, like you to live and die,
And reach my Father's house on high!

THE STRANGER'S HEART.

The stranger's heart! Oh, wound it not!
A yearning anguish is its lot;
In the green shadow of thy tree,
The stranger finds no rest with thee.

Thou think'st the vine's low rustling leaves
Glad music round thy household eaves;
To him that sound hath sorrow's tone —
The stranger's heart is with his own.

Thou think'st thy children's laughing play
A lovely sight at fall of day;
Then are the stranger's thoughts oppress'd —
His mother's voice comes o'er his breast.

Thou think'st it sweet when friend with friend
Beneath one roof in prayer may blend;
Then doth the stranger's eye grow dim —
Far, far are those who pray'd with him.

Thy hearth, thy home, thy vintage-land,
The voices of thy kindred band —
Oh! midst them all when bless'd thou art,
Deal gently with the stranger's heart!

THE FOUNTAIN OF OBLIVION.

"Implora pace!" *

One draught, kind fairy! from that fountain deep,
To lay the phantoms of a haunted breast;
And lone affections, which are griefs, to steep
In the cool honey-dews of dreamless rest;
And from the soul the lightning-marks to lave —
    One draught of that sweet wave!

Yet, mortal! pause! Within thy mind is laid
Wealth, gather'd long and slowly; thoughts divine
Heap that full treasure-house; and thou hast made
The gems of many a spirit's ocean thine; —
Shall the dark waters to oblivion bear
    A pyramid so fair?

---

* Quoted from a letter of Lord Byron's. He describes the impression produced upon him by some tombs at Bologna, bearing this simple inscription, and adds, "When I die, I could wish that some friend would see these words, and no other, placed above my grave, — '*Implora pace!*'"

THE FOUNTAIN OF OBLIVION.

Pour from the fount! and let the draught efface
All the vain lore by memory's pride amass'd,
So it but sweep along the torrent's trace,
And fill the hollow channels of the past;
And from the bosom's inmost folded leaf,
    Rase the one master-grief!

Yet pause once more! All, *all* thy soul hath known,
Loved, felt, rejoiced in, from its grasp must fade!
Is there no voice whose kind, awakening tone
A sense of spring-time in thy heart hath made?
No eye whose glance thy daydreams would recall?
    — Think — wouldst thou part with all?

Fill with forgetfulness! There are, there *are*
Voices whose music I have loved too well —
Eyes of deep gentleness; but they are far —
Never! oh never, in my home to dwell!
Take their soft looks from off my yearning soul —
    Fill high th' oblivious bowl!

Yet pause again! With memory wilt thou cast
The undying hope away, of memory born?
Hope of reunion, heart to heart at last,
No restless doubt between, no rankling thorn?
Wouldst thou erase all records of delight
    That make such visions bright?

Fill with forgetfulness, fill high! — Yet stay —
'Tis from the past we shadow forth the land!
Where smiles, long lost, again shall light our way,
And the soul's friends be wreath'd in one bright band.

Pour the sweet waters back on their own rill —
   I *must* remember still.

For their sake, for the dead — whose image naught
May dim within the temple of my breast —
For their love's sake, which now no earthly thought
May shake or trouble with its own unrest,
  Though the past haunt me as a spirit — yet
     I ask not to forget.

SCENES AND HYMNS OF LIFE.

PRAYER OF THE LONELY STUDENT

> "Soul of our souls! and safeguard of the world!
> Sustain — Thou only canst — the sick at heart;
> Restore their languid spirits, and recall
> Their lost affections unto thee and thine." — WORDSWORTH.

Night — holy night — the time
For mind's free breathings in a purer clime!
Night! — when in happier hour the unveiling sky
    Woke all my kindled soul
To meet its revelations, clear and high,
With the strong joy of immortality!
Now hath strange sadness wrapp'd me, strange and deep —
And my thoughts faint, and shadows o'er them roll,
E'en when I deem'd them seraph-plumed, to sweep
    Far beyond earth's control.

Wherefore is this? I see the stars returning,
Fire after fire in heaven's rich temple burning:
Fast shine they forth — my spirit-friends, my guides,
Bright rulers of my being's inmost tides;
They shine — but faintly, through a quivering haze:
Oh! is the dimness *mine* which clouds those rays?
They from whose glance my childhood drank delight!
A joy unquestioning — a love intense —
They that, unfolding to more thoughtful sight
The harmony of their magnificence,

Drew silently the worship of my youth
To the grave sweetness on the brow of truth;
Shall they shower blessing, with their beams divine,
Down to the watcher on the stormy sea,
And to the pilgrim toiling for his shrine
Through some wild pass of rocky Apennine,
  And to the wanderer lone
   On wastes of Afric thrown,
    And not to *me?*
  Am I a thing forsaken?
  And is the gladness taken
From the bright-pinion'd nature which hath soar'd
Through realms by royal eagle ne'er explored,
And, bathing there in streams of fiery light,
Found strength to gaze upon the Infinite?

And now an alien! Wherefore must this be?
  How shall I rend the chain?
  How drink rich life again
From those pure urns of radiance, welling free?
— Father of Spirits! let me turn to thee!

Oh! if too much exulting in her dower,
 My soul, not yet to lowly thought subdued,
Hath stood without thee on her hill of power —
 A fearful and a dazzling solitude!
And therefore from that haughty summit's crown
To dim desertion is by thee cast down;
Behold! thy child submissively hath bow'd —
  Shine on him through the cloud!

Let the now darken'd earth and curtain'd heaven
Back to his vision with thy face be given!

PRAYER OF THE LONELY STUDENT.

   Bear him on high once more,
   But in thy strength to soar,
And wrapt and still'd by that o'ershadowing might,
Forth on the empyreal blaze to look with chasten'd sight.

Or if it be that, like the ark's lone dove
My thoughts go forth, and find no resting-place,
No sheltering home of sympathy and love
In the responsive bosoms of my race,
And back return, a darkness and a weight,
Till my unanswer'd heart grows desolate —
Yet, yet sustain me, Holiest! — I am vow'd
   To solemn service high;
And shall the spirit, for thy tasks endow'd,
Sink on the threshold of the sanctuary,
Fainting beneath the burden of the day,
   Because no human tone
   Unto the altar-stone
Of that pure spousal fane inviolate,
Where it should make eternal truth its mate,
May cheer the sacred, solitary way?

Oh! be the whisper of thy voice within
Enough to strengthen! Be the hope to win
A more deep-seeing homage for thy name,
Far, far beyond the burning dream of fame!
Make me thine only! — Let me add but one
To those refulgent steps all undefiled,
   Which glorious minds have piled
Through bright self-offering, earnest, childlike, lone,
   For mounting to thy throne!
   And let my soul, upborne
   On wings of inner morn,

Find, in illumined secrecy, the sense
Of that bless'd work, its own high recompense.

    The dimness melts away
    That on your glory lay,
O ye majestic watchers of the skies!
    Through the dissolving veil,
    Which made each aspect pale,
Your gladdening fires once more I recognise;
    And once again a shower
    Of hope, and joy, and power,
Streams on my soul from your immortal eyes.
And if that splendour to my sober'd sight
Come tremulous, with more of pensive light —
Something, though beautiful, yet deeply fraught
With more that pierces through each fold of thought
    Than I was wont to trace
    On heaven's unshadow'd face —
Be it e'en so! — be mine, though set apart
Unto a radiant ministry, yet still
A lowly, fearful, self-distrusting heart,
Bow'd before thee, O Mightiest! whose bless'd will
All the pure stars rejoicingly fulfil.*

  * Written after hearing the Introductory Lecture on Astronomy delivered in Trinity College, Dublin, by Sir William Hamilton, royal astronomer of Ireland, on the 8th November 1832.

EASTER-DAY IN A MOUNTAIN CHURCHYARD.

There is a wakening on the mighty hills,
A kindling with the spirit of the morn!
Bright gleams are scatter'd from the thousand rills,
And a soft visionary hue is born
    On the young foliage, worn
By all the embosom'd woods — a silvery green,
Made up of spring and dew, harmoniously serene.

And lo! where, floating through a glory, sings
The lark, alone amidst a crystal sky!
Lo! where the darkness of his buoyant wings,
Against a soft and rosy cloud on high,
    Trembles with melody!
While the far-echoing solitudes rejoice
To the rich laugh of music in that voice.

But purer light than of the early sun
Is on you cast, O mountains of the earth!
And for your dwellers nobler joy is won
Than the sweet echoes of the skylark's mirth,
    By this glad morning's birth!
And gifts more precious by its breath are shed
Than music on the breeze, dew on the violet's head.

Gifts for the *soul*, from whose illumined eye
O'er nature's face the colouring glory flows;
Gifts from the fount of immortality,
Which, fill'd with balm, unknown to human woes,
    Lay hush'd in dark repose,

Till thou, bright dayspring! madest its waves our own,
By thine unsealing of the burial stone.

Sing, then, with all your choral strains, ye hills!
And let a full victorious tone be given,
By rock and cavern, to the wind which fills
Your urn-like depths with sound! The tomb is riven,
    The radiant gate of heaven
Unfolded — and the stern, dark shadow cast
By death's o'ersweeping wing, from the earth's bosom past.

And you, ye graves! upon whose turf I stand,
Girt with the slumber of the hamlet's dead,
Time, with a soft and reconciling hand,
The covering mantle of bright moss hath spread
    O'er every narrow bed:
But not by time, and not by nature sown
Was the celestial seed, whence round you peace hath grown.

Christ hath arisen! Oh, not one cherish'd head
Hath, midst the flowery sods, been pillow'd here
Without a hope — (howe'er the heart hath bled
In its vain yearnings o'er the unconscious bier) —
    A hope, upspringing clear
From those majestic tidings of the morn,
Which lit the living way to all of woman born.

Thou hast wept mournfully, O human love!
E'en on this greensward: night hath heard thy cry,
Heart-stricken one! thy precious dust above —
Night, and the hills, which sent forth no reply
    Unto thine agony!

EASTER-DAY IN A MOUNTAIN CHURCHYARD.

But He who wept like thee, thy Lord, thy guide,
Christ hath arisen, O love! thy tears shall all be dried.

Dark must have been the gushing of those tears,
Heavy the unsleeping phantom of the tomb
On thine impassion'd soul, in elder years,
When, burden'd with the mystery of its doom,
    Mortality's thick gloom
Hung o'er the sunny world, and with the breath
Of the triumphant rose came blending thoughts of death.

By thee, sad Love! and by thy sister, Fear,
Then was the ideal robe of beauty wrought
To vail that haunting shadow, still too near,
Still ruling secretly the conqueror's thought,
    And where the board was fraught
With wine and myrtles in the summer bower,
Felt, e'en when disavow'd, a presence and a power.

But that dark night is closed: and o'er the dead,
Here, where the gleamy primrose-tufts have blown,
And where the mountain-heath a couch has spread,
And, settling oft on some gray, letter'd stone,
    The redbreast warbles lone;
And the wild-bee's deep drowsy murmurs pass,
Like a low thrill of harp-strings, through the grass:

Here, midst the chambers of the Christian's sleep,
We o'er death's gulf may look with trusting eye;
For Hope sits, dovelike, on the gloomy deep,
And the green hills wherein these valleys lie
    Seem all one sanctuary
Of holiest thought — nor needs their fresh, bright sod,
Urn, wreath, or shrine, for tombs all dedicate to God.

Christ hath arisen! O mountain-peaks! attest —
Witness, resounding glen and torrent-wave!
The immortal courage in the human breast
Sprung from that victory — tell how oft the brave
    To camp midst rock and cave,
Nerved by those words, their struggling faith have borne,
Planting the cross on high above the clouds of morn!

The Alps have heard sweet hymnings for to-day —
Ay, and wild sounds of sterner, deeper tone
Have thrill'd their pines, when those that knelt to pray
Rose up to arm! The pure, high snows have known
    A colouring not their own,
But from true hearts, which, by that crimson stain,
Gave token of a trust that call'd no suffering vain.

Those days are past — the mountains wear no more
The solemn splendour of the martyr's blood;
And may that awful record, as of yore,
Never again be known to field or flood!
    E'en though the faithful stood,
A noble army, in the exulting sight
Of earth and heaven, which bless'd their battle for the right!

But many a martyrdom by hearts unshaken
Is yet borne silently in homes obscure;
And many a bitter cup is meekly taken;
And, for the strength whereby the just and pure
    Thus steadfastly endure,
Glory to Him whose victory won that dower!
Him from whose rising stream'd that robe of spirit-power.

Glory to Him! Hope to the suffering breast!
Light to the nations! He hath roll'd away

The mists which, gathering into deathlike rest,
Between the soul and heaven's calm ether lay —
    His love hath made it day
With those that sat in darkness. Earth and sea!
Lift up glad strains for man by truth divine made free!

A POET'S DYING HYMN.

> "Be mute who will, who can,
> Yet I will praise thee with impassion'd voice!
> Me didst thou constitute a priest of thine
> In such a temple as we now behold,
> Rear'd for thy presence; therefore am I bound
> To worship, here and every where." — WORDSWORTH.

THE blue, deep, glorious heavens! — I lift mine eye,
  And bless thee, O my God! that I have met
And own'd thine image in the majesty
  Of their calm temple still! — that, never yet,
There hath thy face been shrouded from my sight
By noontide blaze, or sweeping storm of night:
    I bless thee, O my God!

That now still clearer, from their pure expanse,
  I see the mercy of thine aspect shine,
Touching death's features with a lovely glance
  Of light, serenely, solemnly divine,
And lending to each holy star a ray
As of kind eyes, that woo my soul away:
    I bless thee, O my God!

That I have heard thy voice nor been afraid,
  In the earth's garden — midst the mountains old,

And the low thrillings of the forest-shade,
   And the wild sound of waters uncontroll'd —
And upon many a desert plain and shore —
No solitude — for there I felt *thee* more:
       I bless thee, O my God!

And if thy spirit on thy child hath shed
   The gift, the vision of the unseal'd eye,
To pierce the mist o'er life's deep meanings spread,
   To reach the hidden fountain-urns that lie
Far in man's heart — if I have kept it free
And pure, a consecration unto thee:
       I bless thee, O my God!

If my soul's utterance hath by thee been fraught
   With an awakening power — if thou hast made
Like the wing'd seed the breathings of my thought,
   And by the swift winds bid them be convey'd
To lands of other lays, and there become
Native as early melodies of home:
       I bless thee, O my God!

Not for the brightness of a mortal wreath,
   Not for a place midst kingly minstrels dead,
But that, perchance, a faint gale of thy breath,
   A still small whisper, in my song hath led
One struggling spirit upwards to thy throne,
Or but one hope, one prayer, — for this alone
       I bless thee, O my God!

That I have loved — that I have known the love
   Which troubles in the soul the tearful springs,
Yet, with a colouring halo from above,
   Tinges and glorifies all earthly things,

A POET'S DYING HYMN.

Whate'er its anguish or its woe may be,
Still weaving links for intercourse with thee:
   I bless thee, O my God!

That by the passion of its deep distress,
   And by the o'erflowing of its mighty prayer,
And by the yearning of its tenderness,
   Too full for words upon their stream to bear,
I have been drawn still closer to thy shrine,
Well-spring of love, the unfathom'd, the divine,
   I bless thee, O my God!

That hope hath ne'er my heart or song forsaken,
   High hope, which even from mystery, doubt, or dread,
Calmly, rejoicingly, the things hath taken
   Whereby its torchlight for the race was fed:
That passing storms have only fann'd the fire
Which pierced them still with its triumphal spire,
   I bless thee, O my God!

Now art thou calling me in every gale,
   Each sound and token of the dying day;
Thou leav'st me not — though early life grows pale,
   I am not darkly sinking to decay;
But, hour by hour, my soul's dissolving shroud
Melts off to radiance, as a silvery cloud,
   I bless thee, O my God!

And if this earth, with all its choral streams,
   And crowning woods, and soft or solemn skies,
And mountain sanctuaries for poet's dreams,
   Be lovely still in my departing eyes —

'Tis not that fondly I would linger here,
But that thy foot-prints on its dust appear:
    I bless thee, O my God!

And that the tender shadowing I behold,
  The tracery veining every leaf and flower,
Of glories cast in more consummate mould,
  No longer vassals to the changeful hour;
That life's last roses to my thoughts can bring
Rich visions of imperishable spring:
    I bless thee, O my God!

Yes! the young, vernal voices in the skies
  Woo me not back, but, wandering past mine ear,
Seem heralds of th' eternal melodies,
  The spirit-music, imperturb'd and clear —
The full of soul, yet passionate no more:
Let *me*, too, joining those pure strains, adore!
    I bless thee, O my God!

Now aid, sustain me still. To thee I come —
  Make thou my dwelling where thy children are!
And for the hope of that immortal home,
  And for thy Son, the bright and morning star,
The sufferer and the victor-king of death,
I bless thee with my glad song's dying breath!
    I bless thee, O my God!

HYMN OF THE VAUDOIS MOUNTAINEERS IN TIMES OF PERSECUTION.

"Thanks be to God for the mountains!"
HOWITT's "Book of the Seasons."

For the strength of the hills we bless thee,
  Our God, our fathers' God!
Thou hast made thy children mighty,
  By the touch of the mountain-sod.
Thou hast fix'd our ark of refuge
  Where the spoiler's foot ne'er trod;
For the strength of the hills we bless thee,
  Our God, our fathers' God!

We are watchers of a beacon
  Whose light must never die;
We are guardians of an altar
  Midst the silence of the sky;
The rocks yield founts of courage,
  Struck forth as by thy rod;
For the strength of the hills we bless thee,
  Our God, our fathers' God!

For the dark, resounding caverns,
  Where thy still, small voice is heard;
For the strong pines of the forests,
  That by thy breath are stirr'd;
For the storms, on whose free pinions
  Thy spirit walks abroad;
For the strength of the hills we bless thee,
  Our God, our fathers' God!

The royal eagle darteth
  On his quarry from the heights,
And the stag that knows no master,
  Seeks there his wild delights;
But we, for *thy* communion,
  Have sought the mountain-sod;
For the strength of the hills we bless thee,
  Our God, our fathers' God!

The banner of the chieftain
  Far, far below us waves;
The war-horse of the spearman
  Cannot reach our lofty caves:
Thy dark clouds wrap the threshold
  Of freedom's last abode;
For the strength of the hills we bless thee,
  Our God, our fathers' God!

For the shadow of thy presence,
  Round our camp of rock outspread;
For the stern defiles of battle,
  Bearing record of our dead;
For the snows and for the torrents,
  For the free heart's burial-sod;
For the strength of the hills we bless thee,
  Our God, our fathers' God!

PRAYER AT SEA AFTER VICTORY.

*"The land shall never rue,
So England to herself do prove but true."* — SHAKSPEARE.

Through evening's bright repose
A voice of prayer arose,
   When the sea-fight was done:
The sons of England knelt,
With hearts that now could melt,
For on the wave her battle had been won.

Round their tall ship, the main
Heaved with a dark red stain,
   Caught not from sunset's cloud;
While with the tide swept past
Pennon and shiver'd mast,
Which to the Ocean Queen that day had bow'd.

But free and fair on high,
A native of the sky,
   Her streamer met the breeze;
It flow'd o'er fearless men,
Though, hush'd and child-like then,
Before their God they gather'd on the seas.

Oh! did not thoughts of home
O'er each bold spirit come,
   As from the land sweet gales?
In every word of prayer
Had not some hearth a share,
Some bower, inviolate midst England's vales?

Yes! bright, green spots that lay
In beauty far away,
   Hearing no billow's roar,
Safer from touch of spoil,
For that day's fiery toil,
Rose on high hearts, that now with love gush'd o'er.

A solemn scene and dread!
The victors and the dead,
   The breathless burning sky!
And, passing with the race
Of waves that keep no trace,
The wild, brief signs of human victory!

A stern, yet holy scene!
Billows, where strife hath been,
   Sinking to awful sleep;
And words, that breathe the sense
Of God's omnipotence,
Making a minster of that silent deep.

Borne through such hours afar,
Thy flag hath been a star,
   Where eagle's wings near flew:
England! the unprofaned,
Thou of the earth unstain'd,
Oh! to the banner and the shrine be true!

MISCELLANEOUS POEMS.

THE VOICE OF SPRING.

I come, I come! ye have call'd me long —
I come o'er the mountains with light and song!
Ye may trace my step o'er the wakening earth
By the winds which tell of the violet's birth,
By the primrose-stars in the shadowy grass,
By the green leaves opening as I pass.

I have breathed on the South, and the chestnut flowers
By thousands have burst from the forest-bowers,
And the ancient graves and the fallen fanes
Are veil'd with wreaths on Italian plains; —
But it is not for me, in my hour of bloom,
To speak of the ruin or the tomb!

I have look'd on the hills of the stormy North,
And the larch has hung all his tassels forth,
The fisher is out on the sunny sea,
And the reindeer bounds o'er the pastures free,
And the pine has a fringe of softer green,
And the moss looks bright where my foot hath been.

I have sent through the wood-paths a glowing sigh,
And call'd out each voice of the deep blue sky;
From the night-bird's lay through the starry time,
In the groves of the soft Hesperian clime,

To the swan's wild note by the Iceland lakes,
When the dark fir-branch into verdure breaks.

From the streams and founts I have loosed the chain,
They are sweeping on to the silvery main,
They are flashing down from the mountain brows,
They are flinging spray o'er the forest boughs,
They are bursting fresh from their sparry caves,
And the earth resounds with the joy of waves!

Come forth, O ye children of gladness! come!
Where the violets lie may be now your home.
Ye of the rose-lip and dew-bright eye,
And the bounding footstep, to meet me fly!
With the lyre, and the wreath, and the joyous lay,
Come forth to the sunshine — I may not stay.

Away from the dwellings of care-worn men,
The waters are sparkling in grove and glen!
Away from the chamber and sullen hearth,
The young leaves are dancing in breezy mirth!
Their light stems thrill to the wild-wood strains,
And youth is abroad in my green domains.

But ye! — ye are changed since ye met me last!
There is something bright from your features pass'd!
There is that come over your brow and eye
Which speaks of a world where the flowers must die!
— Ye smile! but your smile hath a dimness yet:
Oh! what have you look'd on since last we met?

Ye are changed, ye are changed! — and I see not here
All whom I saw in the vanish'd year!

There were graceful heads, with their ringlets bright,
Which toss'd in the breeze with a play of light;
There were eyes in whose glistening laughter lay
No faint remembrance of dull decay!

There were steps that flew o'er the cowslip's head,
As if for a banquet all earth were spread;
There were voices that rang through the sapphire sky,
And had not a sound of mortality!
Are they gone? is their mirth from the mountains pass'd?
Ye have look'd on death since ye met me last!

I know whence the shadow comes o'er you now —
Ye have strewn the dust on the sunny brow!
Ye have given the lovely to earth's embrace —
She has taken the fairest of beauty's race,
With their laughing eyes and their festal crown:
They are gone from amongst you in silence down!

They are gone from amongst you, the young and fair,
Ye have lost the gleam of their shining hair!
But I know of a land where there falls no blight —
I shall find them there, with their eyes of light!
Where Death midst the blooms of the morn may dwell,
I tarry no longer — farewell, farewell!

The summer is coming, on soft winds borne —
Ye may press the grape, ye may bind the corn!
For me, I depart to a brighter shore —
Ye are mark'd by care, ye are mine no more;
I go where the loved who have left you dwell,
And the flowers are not Death's. Fare ye well, farewell!

THE TREASURES OF THE DEEP.*

What hidest thou in thy treasure caves and cells,
   Thou hollow-sounding and mysterious main? —
Pale glistening pearls, and rainbow-colour'd shells
   Bright things which gleam unreck'd of, and in vain.
Keep, keep thy riches, melancholy sea!
      We ask not such from thee.

Yet more, the depths have more! What wealth untold,
   Far down, and shining through their stillness lies!
Thou hast the starry gems, the burning gold,
   Won from ten thousand royal Argosies. —
Sweep o'er thy spoils, thou wild and wrathful main!
      Earth claims not *these* again.

Yet more, the depths have more! Thy waves have roll'd
   Above the cities of a world gone by!
Sand hath fill'd up the palaces of old,
   Sea-weed o'ergrown the halls of revelry. —
Dash o'er them, ocean! in thy scornful play:
      Man yields them to decay.

Yet more! the billows and the depths have more!
   High hearts and brave are gather'd to thy breast!
They hear not now the booming waters roar,
   The battle-thunders will not break their rest. —
Keep thy red gold and gems, thou stormy grave!
      Give back the true and brave!

* Originally introduced in the "Forest Sanctuary."

Give back the lost and lovely! — those for whom
  The place was kept at board and hearth so long,
The prayer went up through midnight's breathless gloom,
  And the vain yearning woke midst festal song!
Hold fast thy buried isles, thy towers o'erthrown —
      But all is not thine own.

To thee the love of woman hath gone down,
  Dark flow thy tides o'er manhood's noble head,
O'er youth's bright locks, and beauty's flowery crown:
  Yet must thou hear a voice — Restore the dead!
Earth shall reclaim her precious things from thee! —
      Restore the dead, thou sea!

THE HOMES OF ENGLAND.

*"Where's the coward that would not dare.
  To fight for such a land?"* MARMION.

The stately homes of England!
  How beautiful they stand,
Amidst their tall ancestral trees,
  O'er all the pleasant land!
The deer across their greensward bound,
  Through shade and sunny gleam;
And the swan glides past them with the sound
  Of some rejoicing stream.

The merry homes of England!
  Around their hearths by night,
What gladsome looks of household love
  Meet in the ruddy light!

There woman's voice flows forth in song,
  Or childhood's tale is told,
Or lips move tunefully along
  Some glorious page of old.

The blessed homes of England!
  How softly on their bowers
Is laid the holy quietness
  That breathes from Sabbath hours!
Solemn, yet sweet, the church-bell's chime
  Floats through their woods at morn;
All other sounds, in that still time,
  Of breeze and leaf are born.

The cottage homes of England!
  By thousands on her plains,
They are smiling o'er the silvery brooks,
  And round the hamlet fanes.
Through glowing orchards forth they peep,
  Each from its nook of leaves;
And fearless there the lowly sleep,
  As the bird beneath their eaves.

The free, fair homes of England!
  Long, long, in hut and hall,
May hearts of native proof be rear'd
  To guard each hallow'd wall!
And green for ever be the groves,
  And bright the flowery sod,
Where first the child's glad spirit loves
  Its country and its God!

THE GRAVES OF A HOUSEHOLD.

They grew in beauty side by side,
   They fill'd one home with glee; —
Their graves are sever'd far and wide,
   By mount, and stream, and sea.

The same fond mother bent at night
   O'er each fair sleeping brow:
She had each folded flower in sight —
   Where are those dreamers now?

One, midst the forest of the West,
   By a dark stream is laid —
The Indian knows his place of rest,
   Far in the cedar-shade.

The sea, the blue lone sea, hath one —
   He lies where pearls lie deep;
He was the loved of all, yet none
   O'er his low bed may weep.

One sleeps where southern vines are drest
   Above the noble slain:
He wrapt his colours round his breast
   On a blood-red field of Spain.

And one — o'er *her* the myrtle showers
   Its leaves by soft winds fann'd;
She faded 'midst Italian flowers —
   The last of that bright band.

And parted thus they rest, who play'd
    Beneath the same green tree;
Whose voices mingled as they pray'd
    Around one parent knee!

They that with smiles lit up the hall,
    And cheer'd with song the hearth! —
Alas, for love! if *thou* wert all,
    And naught beyond, O Earth!

CASABIANCA.*

The boy stood on the burning deck
    Whence all but he had fled;
The flame that lit the battle's wreck
    Shone round him o'er the dead.

Yet beautiful and bright he stood,
    As born to rule the storm —
A creature of heroic blood,
    A proud, though child-like form.

The flames roll'd on — he would not go
    Without his father's word;
That father, faint in death below,
    His voice no longer heard.

---

* Young Casabianca, a boy about thirteen years old, son to the Admiral of the Orient, remained at his post (in the Battle of the Nile) after the ship had taken fire, and all the guns had been abandoned; and perished in the explosion of the vessel, when the flames had reached the powder.

He call'd aloud: — "Say, father! say
 If yet my task is done!"
He knew not that the chieftain lay
 Unconscious of his son.

"Speak, father!" once again he cried,
 "If I may yet be gone!"
And but the booming shots replied,
 And fast the flames roll'd on.

Upon his brow he felt their breath,
 And in his waving hair,
And look'd from that lone post of death
 In still yet brave despair;

And shouted but once more aloud,
 "My father! must I stay?"
While o'er him fast, through sail and shroud,
 The wreathing fires made way.

They wrapt the ship in splendour wild,
 They caught the flag on high,
And stream'd above the gallant child
 Like banners in the sky.

There came a burst of thunder-sound —
 The boy — oh! where was he?
Ask of the winds that far around
 With fragments strew'd the sea! —

With mast, and helm, and pennon fair,
 That well had borne their part;
But the noblest thing which perish'd there
 Was that young faithful heart!

THE LANDING OF THE PILGRIM FATHERS IN NEW ENGLAND.

> "Look now abroad! Another race has fill'd
> Those populous borders — wide the wood recedes,
> And towns shoot up, and fertile realms are till'd;
> The land is full of harvest and green meads." — BRYANT.

The breaking waves dash'd high
  On a stern and rock-bound coast,
And the woods against a stormy sky
  Their giant branches toss'd;

And the heavy night hung dark
  The hills and waters o'er,
When a band of exiles moor'd their bark
  On the wild New England shore.

Not as the conqueror comes,
  They, the true-hearted, came;
Not with the roll of the stirring drums,
  And the trumpet that sings of fame;

Not as the flying come,
  In silence and in fear; —
They shook the depths of the desert gloom
  With their hymns of lofty cheer.

Amidst the storm they sang,
  And the stars heard and the sea;
And the sounding aisles of the dim woods rang
  To the anthem of the free!

The ocean eagle soar'd
  From his nest by the white wave's foam;
And the rocking pines of the forest roar'd —
  This was their welcome home!

There were men with hoary hair
  Amidst that pilgrim band; —
Why had *they* come to wither there,
  Away from their childhood's land?

There was woman's fearless eye,
  Lit by her deep love's truth;
There was manhood's brow serenely high,
  And the fiery heart of youth.

What sought they thus afar? —
  Bright jewels of the mine?
The wealth of seas, the spoils of war? —
  They sought a faith's pure shrine!

Ay, call it holy ground,
  The soil where first they trode.
They have left unstain'd what there they found —
  Freedom to worship God.

THE CHILD'S FIRST GRIEF.

"Ou! call my brother back to me!
  I cannot play alone;
The summer comes with flower and bee —
  Where is my brother gone?

"The butterfly is glancing bright
  Across the sunbeam's track;
I care not now to chase its flight —
  Oh! call my brother back!

"The flowers run wild — the flowers we sow'd
  Around our garden tree;
Our vine is drooping with its load —
  Oh! call him back to me!"

"He would not hear thy voice, fair child!
  He may not come to thee;
The face that once like spring-time smiled,
  On earth no more thou'lt see.

"A rose's brief, bright life of joy,
  Such unto him was given:
Go — thou must play alone, my boy!
  Thy brother is in heaven."

"And has he left his birds and flowers;
  And must I call in vain?
And through the long, long summer hours,
  Will he not come again?

"And by the brook and in the glade
  Are all our wanderings o'er?
Oh! while my brother with me play'd,
  Would I had loved him more!"

THE HOUR OF DEATH.

"Il est dans la Nature d'aimer à se livrer à l'idée même qu'on redoute." — CORINNE.

Leaves have their time to fall,
And flowers to wither at the north wind's breath,
   And stars to set — but all,
Thou hast *all* seasons for thine own, O Death!

   Day is for mortal care,
Eve, for glad meetings round the joyous hearth,
   Night, for the dreams of sleep, the voice of prayer —
But all for thee, thou mightiest of the earth.

   The banquet hath its hour —
Its feverish hour, of mirth, and song, and wine;
   There comes a day for grief's o'erwhelming power,
A time for softer tears — but all are thine.

   Youth and the opening rose
May look like things too glorious for decay,
   And smile at thee — but thou art not of those
That wait the ripen'd bloom to seize their prey.

   Leaves have their time to fall,
And flowers to wither at the north wind's breath,
   And stars to set — but all,
Thou hast *all* seasons for thine own, O Death!

   We know when moons shall wane,
When summer birds from far shall cross the sea,
   When autumn's hue shall tinge the golden grain —
But who shall teach us when to look for thee!

Is it when spring's first gale
Comes forth to whisper where the violets lie?
Is it when roses in our paths grow pale? —
They have *one* season — *all* are ours to die!

Thou art where billows foam,
Thou art where music melts upon the air;
Thou art around us in our peaceful home,
And the world calls us forth — and thou art there.

Thou art where friend meets friend,
Beneath the shadow of the elm to rest —
Thou art where foe meets foe, and trumpets rend
The skies, and swords beat down the princely crest.

Leaves have their time to fall,
And flowers to wither at the north wind's breath,
And stars to set — but all —
Thou hast *all* seasons for thine own, O Death!

BOOKS AND FLOWERS.

"La vue d'une fleur caresse mon imagination, et flatte mes sens à un point inexprimable. Sous le tranquille abri du toit paternel j'étais nourrie dès l'enfance avec des fleurs et des livres; dans l'étroite enceinte d'une prison, au milieu des fers imposés par la tyrannie, j'oublie l'injustice des hommes, leurs sottises et mes maux, avec des livres et des fleurs."

Come! let me make a sunny realm around thee
Of thought and beauty! Here are books and flowers,
With spells to loose the fetter which hath bound thee —
The ravel'd coil of this world's feverish hours.

BOOKS AND FLOWERS.

The soul of song is in these deathless pages,
    Even as the odour in the flower enshrined;
Here the crown'd spirits of departed ages
    Have left the silent melodies of mind.

Their thoughts, that strove with time, and change, and anguish,
    For some high place where faith her wing might rest,
Are burning here — a flame that may not languish —
    Still pointing upward to that bright hill's crest!

Their grief, the veil'd infinity exploring
    For treasures lost, is here; — their boundless love,
Its mighty streams of gentleness outpouring
    On all things round, and clasping all above.

And the bright beings, their own heart's creations,
    Bright, yet all human, here are breathing still;
Conflicts, and agonies, and exultations
    Are here, and victories of prevailing will!

Listen! oh, listen! let their high words cheer thee!
    Their swan-like music ringing through all woes;
Let my voice bring their holy influence near thee —
    The Elysian air of their divine repose!

Or would'st thou turn to earth? *Not* earth all furrow'd
    By the old traces of man's toil and care,
But the green peaceful world that never sorrow'd,
    The world of leaves, and dews, and summer air!

Look on these flowers! as o'er an altar shedding,
    O'er Milton's page, soft light from colour'd urns!
They are the links, man's heart to nature wedding,
    When to her breast the prodigal returns.

They are from lone wild places, forest dingles,
  Fresh banks of many a low-voiced hidden stream,
Where the sweet star of eve looks down and mingles
  Faint lustre with the water-lily's gleam.

They are from where the soft winds play in gladness,
  Covering the turf with flowery blossom-showers;
— Too richly dower'd, O friend! are we for sadness —
  Look on an empire — mind and nature — ours!

THE WORLD IN THE OPEN AIR.

Come, while in freshness and dew it lies,
To the world that is under the free blue skies!
Leave ye man's home, and forget his care —
There breathes no sigh on the dayspring's air.

Come to the woods, in whose mossy dells
A light, all made for the poet dwells —
A light, colour'd softly by tender leaves,
Whence the primrose a mellower glow receives.

The stock-dove is there in the beechen tree,
And the lulling tone of the honey-bee;
And the voice of cool waters midst feathery fern,
Shedding sweet sounds from some hidden urn.

There is life, there is youth, there is tameless mirth,
Where the streams, with the lilies they wear, have birth;
There is peace where the alders are whispering low:
Come from man's dwellings with all their woe!

THE WORLD IN THE OPEN AIR.

Yes! we will come — we will leave behind
The homes and the sorrows of human kind.
It is well to rove where the river leads
Its bright blue vein along sunny meads:

It is well through the rich wild woods to go,
And to pierce the haunts of the fawn and doe;
And to hear the gushing of gentle springs,
When the heart has been fretted by worldly stings;

And to watch the colours that flit and pass,
With insect-wings, through the wavy grass;
And the silvery gleams o'er the ash-tree's bark,
Borne in with a breeze through the foliage dark.

Joyous and far shall our wanderings be,
As the flight of birds o'er the glittering sea:
To the woods, to the dingles where violets blow,
We will bear no memory of earthly woe.

But if, by the forest-brook, we meet
A line like the pathway of former feet;
If, midst the hills, in some lonely spot,
We reach the gray ruins of tower or cot; —

If the cell, where a hermit of old hath pray'd,
Lift up its cross through the solemn shade;
Or if some nook, where the wild flowers wave,
Bear token sad of a mortal grave, —

Doubt not but *there* will our steps be stay'd,
There our quick spirits awhile delay'd;
There will thought fix our impatient eyes,
And win back our hearts to their sympathies.

Mrs. Hemans

For what though the mountains and skies be fair,
Steep'd in soft hues of the summer air?
'Tis the soul of man, by its hopes and dreams,
That lights up all nature with living gleams.

Where it hath suffer'd and nobly striven,
Where it hath pour'd forth its vows to heaven;
Where to repose it hath brightly pass'd,
O'er this green earth there is glory cast.

And by that soul, midst groves and rills,
And flocks that feed on a thousand hills,
Birds of the forest, and flowers of the sod,
We, only *we*, may be link'd to God!

THE DIAL OF FLOWERS.*

'Twas a lovely thought to mark the hours,
 As they floated in light away,
By the opening and the folding flowers,
 That laugh to the summer's day.

Thus had each moment its own rich hue,
 And its graceful cup and bell,
In whose colour'd vase might sleep the dew,
 Like a pearl in an ocean-shell.

---

* This dial was, I believe, formed by Linnæus, and marked the hours by the opening and closing, at regular intervals, of the flowers arranged in it.

To such sweet signs might the time have flow'd
    In a golden current on,
Ere from the garden, man's first abode,
    The glorious guests were gone.

So might the days have been brightly told —
    Those days of song and dreams —
When shepherds gather'd their flocks of old
    By the blue Arcadian streams.

So in those isles of delight, that rest
    Far off in a breezeless main,
Which many a bark, with a weary quest,
    Has sought, but still in vain.

Yet is not life, in its real flight,
    Mark'd thus — even thus — on earth,
By the closing of one hope's delight,
    And another's gentle birth?

Oh! let us live, so that flower by flower,
    Shutting in turn, may leave
A lingerer still for the sunset hour,
    A charm for the shaded eve.

THE DREAMER.

"There is no such thing as forgetting, possible to the mind; a thousand accidents may, and will, interpose a veil between our present consciousness and the secret inscription on the mind; but alike, whether veiled or unveiled, the inscription remains for ever."
ENGLISH OPIUM-EATER.

"Thou hast been call'd, O sleep! the friend of woe,
But 'tis the happy who have call'd thee so." SOUTHEY.

PEACE to thy dreams! thou art slumbering now —
The moonlight's calm is upon thy brow;
All the deep love that o'erflows thy breast
Lies midst the hush of thy heart at rest —
Like the scent of a flower in its folded bell,
When eve through the woodlands hath sigh'd farewell.

Peace! The sad memories that through the day
With a weight on thy lonely bosom lay,
The sudden thoughts of the changed and dead,
That bow'd thee as winds bow the willow's head,
The yearnings for faces and voices gone —
All are forgotten! Sleep on, sleep on!

Are they forgotten? It is not so!
Slumber divides not the heart from its woe.
E'en now o'er thine aspect swift changes pass,
Like lights and shades over wavy grass:
Tremblest thou, Dreamer? O love and grief!
Ye have storms that shake e'en the closed-up leaf!

On thy parted lips there's a quivering thrill,
As on a lyre ere its chords are still;

On the long silk lashes that fringe thine eye,
There's a large tear gathering heavily —
A rain from the clouds of thy spirit press'd:
Sorrowful Dreamer! this is not rest!

It is Thought at work amidst buried hours —
It is Love keeping vigil o'er perish'd flowers.
— Oh, we bear within us mysterious things!
Of Memory and Anguish, unfathom'd springs;
And Passion — those gulfs of the heart to fill
With bitter waves, which it ne'er may still.

Well might we pause ere we gave them sway,
Flinging the peace of our couch away!
Well might we look on our souls in fear —
They find no fount of oblivion here!
They forget not, the mantle of sleep beneath —
How know we if under the wings of death?

THE STREAMS.

> "The power, the beauty, and the majesty,
> That had their haunts in dale or piny mountain,
> Or forest by slow stream, or pebbly spring,
> Or chasms and watery depths; all those have vanish'd!
> They live no longer in the faith of heaven,
> But still the heart doth need a language!"
>   COLERIDGE'S "Wallenstein.

Ye have been holy, O founts and floods
Ye of the ancient and solemn woods,
Ye that are born of the valleys deep,
With the water-flowers on your breast asleep,
And ye that gush from the sounding caves —
      Hallow'd have been your waves.

Hallow'd by man, in his dreams of old,
Unto beings not of this mortal mould —
Viewless, and deathless, and wondrous powers,
Whose voice he heard in his lonely hours,
And sought with its fancied sound to still
    The heart earth could not fill.

Therefore the flowers of bright summers gone,
O'er your sweet waters, ye streams! were thrown;
Thousands of gifts to the sunny sea
Have ye swept along, in your wanderings free,
And thrill'd to the murmur of many a vow —
    Where all is silent now!

Nor seems it strange that the heart hath been
So link'd in love to your margins green;
That still, though ruin'd, your early shrines
In beauty gleam through the southern vines,
And the ivied chapels of colder skies
    On your wild banks arise.

For the loveliest scenes of the glowing earth
Are those, bright streams! where your springs have birth;
Whether their cavern'd murmur fills,
With a tone of plaint, the hollow hills,
Or the glad sweet laugh of their healthful flow
    Is heard midst the hamlets low.

Or whether ye gladden the desert sands
With a joyous music to pilgrim bands,
And a flash from under some ancient rock,
Where a shepherd king might have watch'd his flock,
Where a few lone palm-trees lift their heads,
    And a green acacia spreads.

Or whether, in bright old lands renown'd,
The laurels thrill to your first-born sound,
And the shadow, flung from the Grecian pine,
Sweeps with the breeze o'er your gleaming line,
And the tall reeds whisper to your waves,
    Beside heroic graves.

Voices and lights of the lonely place!
By the freshest fern your path we trace;
By the brightest cups on the emerald moss,
Whose fairy goblets the turf emboss;
By the rainbow-glancing of insect wings,
    In a thousand mazy rings.

There sucks the bee, for the richest flowers
Are all your own through the summer hours;
There the proud stag his fair image knows,
Traced on your glass beneath alder-boughs;
And the halcyon's breast, like the skies array'd,
    Gleams through the willow shade.

But the wild sweet tales that with elves and fays
Peopled your banks in the olden days,
And the memory left by departed love
To your antique founts in glen and grove,
And the glory born of the poet's dreams —
    These are your charms, bright streams!

Now is the time of your flowery rites
Gone by with its dances and young delights:
From your marble urns ye have burst away,
From your chapel-cells to the laughing day;
Low lie your altars with moss o'ergrown,
    And the woods again are lone.

Yet holy still be your living springs,
Haunts of all gentle and gladsome things!
Holy, to converse with nature's lore,
That gives the worn spirit its youth once more,
And to silent thoughts of the love divine,
    Making the heart a shrine!

THE CHILD'S RETURN FROM THE WOODLANDS.
SUGGESTED BY A PICTURE OF SIR THOMAS LAWRENCE'S.

> "All good and guiltless as thou art,
> Some transient griefs will touch thy heart —
> Griefs that along thy alter'd face
> Will breathe a more subduing grace,
> Than even those looks of joy that lie
> On the soft cheek of infancy."   WILSON.

Hast thou been in the woods with the honey-bee?
Hast thou been with the lamb in the pastures free?
With the hare through the copses and dingles wild?
With the butterfly over the heath, fair child?
Yes! the light fall of thy bounding feet
Hath not startled the wren from her mossy seat:
Yet hast thou ranged the green forest-dells,
And brought back a treasure of buds and bells.

Thou know'st not the sweetness, by antique song
Breathed o'er the names of that flowery throng:
The woodbine, the primrose, the violet dim,
The lily that gleams by the fountain's brim;
These are old words, that have made each grove
A dreaming haunt for romance and love —
Each sunny bank, where faint odours lie,
A place for the gushings of poesy.

Thou know'st not the light wherewith fairy lore
Sprinkles the turf and the daisies o'er:
Enough for thee are the dews that sleep
Like hidden gems in the flower-urns deep;
Enough the rich crimson spots that dwell
Midst the gold of the cowslip's perfumed cell;
And the scent by the blossoming sweetbriers shed,
And the beauty that bows the wood-hyacinth's head.

O happy child! in thy fawn-like glee,
What is remembrance or thought to thee?
Fill thy bright locks with those gifts of spring,
O'er thy green pathway their colours fling;
Bind them in chaplet and wild festoon —
What if to droop and to perish soon?
Nature hath mines of such wealth — and thou
Never will prize its delights as now!

For a day is coming to quell the tone
That rings in thy laughter, thou joyous one!
And to dim thy brow with a touch of care,
Under the gloss of its clustering hair;
And to tame the flash of thy cloudless eyes
Into the stillness of autumn skies;
And to teach thee that grief hath her needful part
Midst the hidden things of each human heart.

Yet shall we mourn, gentle child! for this?
Life hath enough of yet holier bliss!
Such be thy portion! — the bliss to look,
With a reverent spirit, through nature's book;
By fount, by forest, by river's line,
To track the paths of a love divine;

To read its deep meanings — to see and hear
God in earth's garden — and not to fear!

THE WRECK.

All night the booming minute-gun
    Had peal'd along the deep,
And mournfully the rising sun
    Look'd o'er the tide-worn steep.
A bark from India's coral strand,
    Before the raging blast,
Had vail'd her topsails to the sand,
    And bow'd her noble mast.

The queenly ship! — brave hearts had striven,
    And true ones died with her!
We saw her mighty cable riven,
    Like floating gossamer.
We saw her proud flag struck that morn —
    A star once o'er the seas, —
Her anchor gone, her deck uptorn,
    And sadder things than these!

We saw her treasures cast away,
    The rocks with pearls were sown;
And, strangely sad, the ruby's ray
    Flash'd out o'er fretted stone.
And gold was strewn the wet sands o'er,
    Like ashes by a breeze;
And gorgeous robes — but oh! that shore
    Had sadder things than these!

We saw the strong man still and low,
  A crush'd reed thrown aside;
Yet, by that rigid lip and brow,
  Not without strife he died.
And near him on the sea-weed lay —
  Till then we had not wept —
But well our gushing hearts might say,
  That there a *mother* slept!

For her pale arms a babe had press'd
  With such a wreathing grasp,
Billows had dash'd o'er that fond breast,
  Yet not undone the clasp.
Her very tresses had been flung
  To wrap the fair child's form,
Where still their wet long streamers hung
  All tangled by the storm.

And beautiful, midst that wild scene,
  Gleam'd up the boy's dead face,
Like slumber's, trustingly serene,
  In melancholy grace.
Deep in her bosom lay his head,
  With half-shut violet-eye —
He had known little of her dread,
  Naught of her agony!

O human love! whose yearning heart,
  Through all things vainly true,
So stamps upon thy mortal part
  Its passionate adieu —
Surely thou hast another lot:
  There is some home for thee,

Where thou shalt rest, remembering not
The moaning of the sea!

ELYSIUM.

["In the Elysium of the ancients we find none but heroes and persons who had either been fortunate or distinguished on earth; the children, and apparently the slaves and lower classes — that is to say, Poverty, Misfortune, and Innocence — were banished to the infernal Regions." — CHATEAUBRIAND, *Génie du Christianisme.*]

Fair wert thou in the dreams
Of elder time, thou land of glorious flowers
And summer winds and low-toned silvery streams,
Dim with the shadows of thy laurel bowers,
　　Where, as they pass'd, bright hours
Left no faint sense of parting, such as clings
To earthly love, and joy in loveliest things!

　　Fair wert thou, with the light
On thy blue hills and sleepy waters cast
From purple skies ne'er deep'ning into night,
Yet soft, as if each moment were their last
　　Of glory, fading fast
Along the mountains! — but *thy* golden day
Was not as those that warn us of decay.

　　And ever, through thy shades,
A swell of deep Æolian sound went by
From fountain-voices in their secret glades,
And low reed-whispers, making sweet reply
　　To summer's breezy sigh,
And young leaves trembling to the wind's light breath,
Which ne'er had touch'd them with a hue of death!

And the transparent sky
Rang as a dome, all thrilling to the strain
Of harps that midst the woods made harmony,
Solemn and sweet; yet troubling not the brain
  With dreams and yearnings vain,
And dim remembrances, that still draw birth
From the bewildering music of the earth.

  And who, with silent tread,
Moved o'er the plains of waving asphodel?
Call'd from the dim procession of the dead,
Who midst the shadowy amaranth-bowers might dwell,
  And listen to the swell
Of those majestic hymn-notes, and inhale
The spirit wandering in the immortal gale?

  They of the sword, whose praise,
With the bright wine, at nations' feasts went round!
They of the lyre, whose unforgotten lays
Forth on the winds had sent their mighty sound,
  And in all regions found
Their echoes midst the mountains! — and become
In man's deep heart as voices of his home!

  They of the daring thought!
Daring and powerful, yet to dust allied —
Whose flight through stars, and seas, and depths, had sought
The soul's far birthplace — but without a guide!
  Sages and seers, who died,
And left the world their high mysterious dreams,
Born midst the olive woods by Grecian streams.

  But the most *loved* are they
Of whom fame speaks not with her clarion voice

In regal halls! The shades o'erhang their way;
The vale, with its deep fountains, is their choice,
    And gentle hearts rejoice
Around their steps; till silently they die,
As a stream shrinks from summer's burning eye.

    And these — of whose abode,
Midst her green valleys, earth retain'd no trace,
Save a flower springing from their burial-sod,
A shade of sadness on some kindred face,
    A dim and vacant place
In some sweet home; — thou hadst no wreaths for *these*,
Thou sunny land! with all thy deathless trees!

    The peasant at his door
Might sink to die when vintage-feasts were spread,
And songs on every wind! From *thy* bright shore
No lovelier vision floated round his head —
    Thou wert for nobler dead!
He heard the bounding steps which round him fell,
And sigh'd to bid the festal sun farewell!

    The slave, whose very tears
Were a forbidden luxury, and whose breast
Kept the mute woes and burning thoughts of years,
As embers in a burial-urn compress'd;
    He might not be thy guest!
No gentle breathings from thy distant sky
Came o'er *his* path, and whisper'd "Liberty!"

    Calm, on its leaf-strewn bier,
Unlike a gift of Nature to Decay,
Too rose-like still, too beautiful, too dear,

ELYSIUM.

The child at rest before the mother lay,
    E'en so to pass away,
With its bright smile! — Elysium! what wert *thou*
To her, who wept o'er that young slumb'rer's brow?

    Thou hadst no home, green land!
For the fair creature from her bosom gone,
With life's fresh flowers just opening in its hand,
And all the lovely thoughts and dreams unknown,
    Which in its clear eye shone
Like spring's first wakening! but that light was past —
Where went the dewdrop swept before the blast?

    Not where *thy* soft winds play'd,
Not where thy waters lay in glassy sleep!
Fade with thy bowers, thou Land of Visions, fade!
From thee no voice came o'er the gloomy deep,
    And bade man cease to weep!
Fade, with the amaranth plain, the myrtle grove,
Which could not yield one hope to sorrowing love!*

---

* The form of this poem was a good deal altered by Mrs. Hemans some years after its first publication, and, though done so perhaps to advantage, one verse was omitted. As originally written, the two following stanzas concluded the piece : —

    For the most loved are they
Of whom Fame speaks not with her clarion voice
In regal halls! The shades o'erhang their way;
The vale, with its deep fountains, is their choice,
    And gentle hearts rejoice
Around their steps; till silently they die,
As a stream shrinks from summer's burning eye.

    And the world knows not then,
Not then, nor ever, what pure thoughts are fled!
Yet these are they, who on the souls of men
Come back, when night her folding veil hath spread,
    The long-remember'd dead!
But not with thee might aught save glory dwell —
Fade, fade away, thou shore of asphodel!

ENGLAND'S DEAD.

Son of the Ocean Isle!
 Where sleep your mighty dead!
Show me what high and stately pile
 Is rear'd o'er Glory's bed.

Go, stranger! track the deep —
 Free, free the white sail spread!
Wave may not foam, nor wild wind sweep,
 Where rest not England's dead.

On Egypt's burning plains,
 By the pyramid o'ersway'd,
With fearful power the noonday reigns,
 And the palm-trees yield no shade; —

But let the angry sun
 From heaven look fiercely red,
Unfelt by those whose task is done! —
 There slumber England's dead.

The hurricane hath might
 Along the Indian shore,
And far by Ganges' banks at night
 Is heard the tiger's roar; —

But let the sound roll on!
 It hath no tone of dread
For those that from their toils are gone, —
 There slumber England's dead.

ENGLAND'S DEAD.

Loud rush the torrent-floods
The Western wild among,
And free, in green Columbia's woods,
The hunter's bow is strung; —

But let the floods rush on!
Let the arrow's flight be sped!
Why should *they* reck whose task is done? —
There slumber England's dead!

The mountain storms rise high
In the snowy Pyrenees,
And toss the pine-boughs through the sky
Like rose-leaves on the breeze; —

But let the storm rage on!
Let the fresh wreaths be shed!
For the Roncesvalles' field is won, —
There slumber England's dead.

On the frozen deep's repose
'Tis a dark and dreadful hour,
When round the ship the ice-fields close,
And the northern night-clouds lower; —

But let the ice drift on!
Let the cold-blue desert spread!
Their course with mast and flag is done, —
Even there sleep England's dead.

The warlike of the isles,
The men of field and wave!
Are not the rocks their funeral piles,
The seas and shores their grave?

　　　　Go, stranger! track the deep —
　　　　Free, free the white sail spread!
　　Wave may not foam, nor wild wind sweep,
　　　　Where rest not England's dead.

THE GRAVES OF MARTYRS.

The kings of old have shrine and tomb
In many a minster's haughty gloom;
And green, along the ocean side,
The mounds arise where heroes died;
But show me, on thy flowery breast,
Earth! where thy *nameless* martyrs rest!

The thousands that, uncheer'd by praise,
Have made one offering of their days;
For Truth, for Heaven, for Freedom's sake,
Resign'd the bitter cup to take;
And silently, in fearless faith,
Bowing their noble souls to death.

Where sleep they, Earth? By no proud stone
Their narrow couch of rest is known;
The still sad glory of their name
Hallows no fountain unto Fame;
No — not a tree the record bears
Of their deep thoughts and lonely prayers.

Yet haply all around lie strew'd
The ashes of that multitude:

It may be that each day we tread
Where thus devoted hearts have bled;
And the young flowers our children sow,
Take root in holy dust below.

Oh, that the many-rustling leaves,
Which round our homes the summer weaves,
Or that the streams, in whose glad voice
Our own familiar paths rejoice,
Might whisper through the starry sky,
To tell where those blest slumberers lie!

Would not our inmost hearts be still'd,
With knowledge of their presence fill'd,
And by its breathings taught to prize
The meekness of self-sacrifice?
— But the old woods and sounding waves
Are silent of those hidden graves.

Yet what if no light footstep there
In pilgrim-love and awe repair,
So let it be! Like him, whose clay
Deep buried by his Maker lay,
They sleep in secret, — but their sod,
Unknown to man, is mark'd of God!

THE LYRE'S LAMENT.

"A large lyre hung in an opening of the rock, and gave forth its melancholy music to the wind — but no human being was to be seen."
SALATHIEL.

A DEEP-TONED lyre hung murmuring
   To the wild wind of the sea;
"O melancholy wind," it sigh'd,
   "What would thy breath with me?

"Thou canst not wake the spirit
   That in me slumbering lies,
Thou strikest not forth th' electric fire
   Of buried melodies.

"Wind of the dark sea-waters!
   Thou dost but sweep my strings
Into wild gusts of mournfulness,
   With the rushing of thy wings.

"But the spell — the gift — the lightning —
   Within my frame conceal'd,
Must I moulder on the rock away
   With their triumphs unreveal'd?

"I have power, high power, for freedom
   To wake the burning soul!
I have sounds that through the ancient hills
   Like a torrent's voice might roll.

"I have pealing notes of victory
   That might welcome kings from war,

I have rich, deep tones to send the wail
    For a hero's death afar.

"I have chords to lift the pæan
    From the temple to the sky,
Full as the forest-unisons
    When sweeping winds are high.

"And love — for love's lone sorrow
    I have accents that might swell
Through the summer air with the rose's breath,
    Or the violet's faint farewell:

"Soft — spiritual — mournful —
    Sighs in each note enshrined —
But who shall call that sweetness forth?
    Thou can'st not, ocean-wind!

"I pass without my glory,
    Forgotten I decay —
Where is the touch to give me life?
    — Wild, fitful wind, away!"

So sigh'd the broken music
    That in gladness had no part —
How like art thou, neglected Lyre!
    To many a human heart!

THE LYRE AND FLOWER.

A LYRE its plaintive sweetness pour'd
    Forth on the wild wind's track;
The stormy wanderer jarr'd the chord,
    But gave no music back. —

    O child of song!
      Bear hence to heaven thy fire:
What hopest thou from the reckless throng?
    Be not like that lost lyre!
      Not like that lyre!

A flower its leaves and odours cast
  On a swift-rolling wave;
Th' unheeding torrent darkly pass'd,
  And back no treasure gave. —
    O heart of love!
      Waste not thy precious dower:
Turn to thine only home above!
    Be not like that lost flower!
      Not like that flower!

THE RUIN.

"Oh! 'tis the heart that magnifies this life,
Making a truth and beauty of its own."
                WORDSWORTH.

"Birth has gladden'd it: death has sanctified it."
                GUESSES AT TRUTH.

No dower of storied song is thine,
  O desolate abode!
Forth from thy gates no glittering line
  Of lance and spear hath flow'd.
Banners of knighthood have not flung
  Proud drapery o'er thy walls,
Nor bugle-notes to battle rung
  Through thy resounding halls.

Nor have rich bowers of *pleasaunce* here
  By courtly hands been dress'd,
For princes, from the chase of deer,
  Under green leaves to rest:
Only some rose, yet lingering bright
  Beside thy casements lone,
Tells where the spirit of delight
  Hath dwelt, and now is gone.

Yet minstrel-tale of harp and sword,
  And sovereign beauty's lot,
House of quench'd light and silent board!
  For me thou needest not.
It is enough to know that *here*,
  Where thoughtfully I stand,
Sorrow and love, and hope and fear,
  Have link'd one kindred band.

Thou bindest me with mighty spells!
  — A solemnising breath,
A presence all around thee dwells
  Of human life and death.
I need but pluck yon garden flower
  From where the wild weeds rise,
To wake, with strange and sudden power,
  A thousand sympathies.

Thou hast heard many sounds, thou hearth!
  Deserted now by all!
Voices at eve here met in mirth
  Which eve may ne'er recall.
Youth's buoyant step, and woman's tone,
  And childhood's laughing glee,

And song and prayer, have all been known,
    Hearth of the dead! to thee.

Thou hast heard blessings fondly pour'd
    Upon the infant head,
As if in every fervent word
    The living soul were shed;
Thou hast seen partings, such as bear
    The bloom from life away —
Alas! for love in changeful air,
    Where naught beloved can stay!

Here, by the restless bed of pain,
    The vigil hath been kept,
Till sunrise, bright with hope in vain,
    Burst forth on eyes that wept;
Here hath been felt the hush, the gloom,
    The breathless influence, shed
Through the dim dwelling, from the room
    Wherein reposed the dead.

The seat left void, the missing face,
    Have here been mark'd and mourn'd,
And time hath fill'd the vacant place,
    And gladness hath return'd;
Till from the narrowing household chain
    The links dropp'd one by one!
And homewards hither, o'er the main,
    Came the spring-birds alone.

Is there not cause, then — cause for thought,
    Fix'd eye and lingering tread,
Where, with their thousand mysteries fraught,
    Even lowliest hearts have bled?

Where, in its ever-haunting thirst
  For draughts of purer day,
Man's soul, with fitful strength, hath burst
  The clouds that wrapt its way?

Holy to human nature seems
  The long-forsaken spot —
To deep affections, tender dreams,
  Hopes of a brighter lot!
Therefore in silent reverence here,
  Hearth of the dead! I stand,
Where joy and sorrow, smile and tear,
  Have link'd one household band.

A SONG OF THE ROSE.

*"Cosi fior diverrai che non soggiace
All' acqua, al gelo, al vento ed allo scherno
D' una stagion volubile e fugace;
E a piu fido Cultor posto in governo,
Unir potrai nello tranquilla pace,
Ad eterna Bellezza odore eterno."* METASTASIO.

  Rose! what dost thou here?
    Bridal, royal rose!
  How, midst grief and fear,
    Canst thou thus disclose
That fervid hue of love, which to thy heart-leaf glows?

  Rose! too much array'd
    For triumphal hours,
  Look'st thou through the shade
    Of these mortal bowers,
Not to disturb my soul, thou crown'd one of all flowers!

As an eagle soaring
  Through a sunny sky,
As a clarion pouring
  Notes of victory,
So dost *thou* kindle thoughts, for earthly life too high.

Thoughts of rapture, flushing
  Youthful poet's cheek;
Thoughts of glory, rushing
  Forth in song to break,
But finding the spring-tide of rapid song too weak.

Yet, O festal rose!
  I have seen thee lying
In thy bright repose
  Pillow'd with the dying,
Thy crimson by the lip whence life's quick blood was flying.

Summer, hope, and love
  O'er that bed of pain,
Met in thee, yet wove
  Too, too frail a chain
In its embracing links the lovely to detain.

Smilest thou, gorgeous flower?
  Oh! within the spells
Of thy beauty's power,
  Something dimly dwells,
At variance with a world of sorrows and farewells.

All the soul forth flowing
  In that rich perfume,
All the proud life glowing
  In that radiant bloom —
Have they no place but *here*, beneath th'o'ershadowing tomb?

THE SUNBEAM.

Crown'st thou but the daughters
  Of our tearful race?
Heaven's own purest waters
  Well might wear the trace
Of thy consummate form, melting to softer grace.

Will that clime enfold thee
  With immortal air?
Shall we not behold thee
  Bright and deathless there?
In spirit-lustre clothed, transcendantly more fair!

Yes! my fancy sees thee
  In that light disclose,
And its dream thus frees thee
  From the mist of woes,
Darkening thine earthly bowers, O bridal royal rose!

THE SUNBEAM.

Thou art no lingerer in monarch's hall —
A joy thou art, and a wealth to all!
A bearer of hope unto land and sea —
Sunbeam! what gift hath the world like thee?

Thou art walking the billows, and ocean smiles;
Thou hast touch'd with glory his thousand isles;
Thou hast lit up the ships and the feathery foam,
And gladden'd the sailor like words from home.

To the solemn depths of the forest-shades,
Thou art streaming on through their green arcades;

And the quivering leaves that have caught thy glow
Like fire-flies glance to the pools below.

I look'd on the mountains — a vapour lay
Folding their heights in its dark array:
Thou brakest forth, and the mist became
A crown and a mantle of living flame.

I look'd on the peasant's lowly cot —
Something of sadness had wrapt the spot;
But a gleam of *thee* on its lattice fell,
And it laugh'd into beauty at that bright spell.

To the earth's wild places a guest thou art,
Flushing the waste like the rose's heart;
And thou scornest not from thy pomp to shed
A tender smile on the ruin's head.

Thou tak'st through the dim church-aisle thy way,
And its pillars from twilight flash forth to day,
And its high, pale tombs, with their trophies old,
Are bathed in a flood as of molten gold.

And thou turnest not from the humblest grave,
Where a flower to the sighing winds may wave;
Thou scatter'st its gloom like the dreams of rest,
Thou sleepest in love on its grassy breast.

Sunbeam of summer! oh, what is like thee?
Hope of the wilderness, joy of the sea! —
One thing is like thee to mortals given,
The faith touching all things with hues of heaven!

TRIUMPHANT MUSIC.

"Tacete, tacete, O suoni trionfanti!
Risvegliate in vano 'l cor che non puo liberarsi."

Wherefore and whither bear'st thou up my spirit,
  On eagle wings, through every plume that thrill?
It hath no crown of victory to inherit —
  Be still, triumphant harmony! be still!

Thine are no sounds for earth, thus proudly swelling
  Into rich floods of joy. It is but pain
To mount so high, yet find on high no dwelling,
  To sink so fast, so heavily again!

No sounds for earth? Yes, to young chieftain dying
  On his own battle-field, at set of sun,
With his freed country's banner o'er him flying,
  Well mightst thou speak of fame's high guerdon won.

No sounds for earth? Yes, for the martyr, leading
  Unto victorious death serenely on;
For patriot by his rescued altars bleeding,
  Thou hast a voice in each majestic tone.

But speak not thus to one whose heart is beating
  Against life's narrow bound, in conflict vain!
For power, for joy, high hope, and rapturous greeting,
  Thou wakest lone thirst — be hush'd, exulting strain!

Be hush'd, or breathe of grief! — of exile yearnings
  Under the willows of the stranger-shore;

Breathe of the soul's untold and restless burnings
  For looks, tones, footsteps, that return no more.

Breathe of deep love — a lonely vigil keeping
  Through the night-hours, o'er wasted wealth to pine;
Rich thoughts and sad, like faded rose-leaves, heaping
  In the shut heart, at once a tomb and shrine.

Or pass as if thy spirit-notes came sighing
  From worlds beneath some blue Elysian sky;
Breathe of repose, the pure, the bright, th' undying —
  Of joy no more — bewildering harmony!

THE CROSS IN THE WILDERNESS.

Silent and mournful sat an Indian chief,
  In the red sunset, by a grassy tomb;
His eyes, that might not weep, were dark with grief,
  And his arms folded in majestic gloom;
And his bow lay unstrung, beneath the mound
Which sanctified the gorgeous waste around.

For a pale cross above its greensward rose,
  Telling the cedars and the pines that there
Man's heart and hope had struggled with his woes,
  And lifted from the dust a voice of prayer.
Now all was hush'd — and eve's last splendour shone
With a rich sadness on th' attesting stone.

There came a lonely traveller o'er the wild,
  And he, too, paused in reverence by that grave,

Asking the tale of its memorial, piled
  Between the forest and the lake's bright wave;
Till, as a wind might stir a wither'd oak,
On the deep dream of age his accents broke.

And the gray chieftain, slowly rising, said —
  "I listen'd for the words, which, years ago,
Pass'd o'er these waters. Though the voice is fled
  Which made them as a singing fountain's flow,
Yet, when I sit in their long-faded track,
Sometimes the forest's murmur gives them back.

"Ask'st thou of him whose house is lone beneath?
  I was an eagle in my youthful pride,
When o'er the seas he came, with summer's breath,
  To dwell amidst us, on the lake's green side.
Many the times of flowers have been since then —
Many, but bringing naught like *him* again!

"Not with the hunter's bow and spear he came,
  O'er the blue hills to chase the flying roe;
Not the dark glory of the woods to tame,
  Laying their cedars, like the corn-stalks, low;
But to spread tidings of all holy things,
Gladdening our souls, as with the morning's wings.

"Doth not yon cypress whisper how we met,
  I and my brethren that from earth are gone,
Under its boughs to hear his voice, which yet
  Seems through their gloom to send a silvery tone?
He told of One the grave's dark bonds who broke,
And our hearts burn'd within us as he spoke.

"He told of far and sunny lands, which lie
   Beyond the dust wherein our fathers dwell:
Bright must they be! for *there* are none that die,
   And none that weep, and none that say 'Farewell!'
He came to guide us thither; but away
The Happy call'd him, and he might not stay.

"We saw him slowly fade — athirst, perchance,
   For the fresh waters of that lovely clime;
Yet was there still a sunbeam in his glance,
   And on his gleaming hair no touch of time —
Therefore we hoped: but now the lake looks dim,
For the green summer comes — and finds not him!

"We gather'd round him in the dewy hour
   Of one still morn, beneath his chosen tree;
From his clear voice, at first, the words of power
   Came low, like moanings of a distant sea;
But swell'd and shook the wilderness ere long,
As if the spirit of the breeze grew strong.

"And then once more they trembled on his tongue,
   And his white eyelids flutter'd, and his head
Fell back, and mist upon his forehead hung — —
   Know'st thou not how we pass to join the dead?
It is enough! he sank upon my breast —
Our friend that loved us, he was gone to rest!

"We buried him where he was wont to pray,
   By the calm lake, e'en here, at eventide;
We rear'd this cross in token where he lay,
   For on the cross, he said, his Lord had died!

Now hath he surely reach'd, o'er mount and wave,
That flowery land whose green turf hides no grave.

"But I am sad! I mourn the clear light taken
  Back from my people, o'er whose place it shone,
The pathway to the better shore forsaken,
  And the true words forgotten, save by one,
Who hears them faintly sounding from the past,
Mingled with death-songs in each fitful blast."

Then spoke the wanderer forth with kindling eye:
  "Son of the wilderness! despair thou not,
Though the bright hour may seem to thee gone by,
  And the cloud settled o'er thy nation's lot!
Heaven darkly works — yet, where the seed hath been,
There shall the fruitage, glowing yet, be seen.

"Hope on, hope ever! — by the sudden springing
  Of green leaves which the winter hid so long;
And by the bursts of free, triumphant singing,
  After cold silent months the woods among;
And by the rending of the frozen chains,
Which bound the glorious rivers on their plains.

"Deem not the words of light that here were spoken,
  But as a lovely song, to leave no trace;
Yet shall the gloom which wraps thy hills be broken,
  And the full dayspring rise upon thy race!
And fading mists the better path disclose,
And the wide desert blossom as the rose."

So by the cross they parted, in the wild,
  Each fraught with musings for life's after day,

Mrs. Hemans.

Memories to visit *one*, the forest's child,
 By many a blue stream in its lonely way;
And upon *one*, midst busy throngs to press
Deep thoughts and sad, yet full of holiness.

OUR DAILY PATHS.

*"Naught shall prevail against us, or disturb
Our cheerful faith that all which we behold
Is full of blessings."* WORDSWORTH.

There's beauty all around our paths, if but our watchful eyes
Can trace it midst familiar things, and through their lowly guise;
We may find it where a hedgerow showers its blossoms o'er our way,
Or a cottage window sparkles forth in the last red light of day.

We may find it where a spring shines clear beneath an aged tree,
With the foxglove o'er the water's glass, borne downwards by the bee;
Or where a swift and sunny gleam on the birchen stems is thrown,
As a soft wind playing parts the leaves, in copses green and lone.

We may find it in the winter boughs, as they cross the cold blue sky,
While soft on icy pool and stream their pencil'd shadows lie.

When we look upon their tracery, by the fairy frost-work
    bound,
Whence the flitting redbreast shakes a shower of crystals to
    the ground.

Yes! beauty dwells in all our paths — but sorrow too is there:
How oft some cloud within us dims the bright, still summer
    air!
When we carry our sick hearts abroad amidst the joyous
    things,
That through the leafy places glance on many-colour'd wings,

With shadows from the past we fill the happy woodland
    shades,
And a mournful memory of the dead is with us in the glades;
And our dream-like fancies lend the wind an echo's plaintive
    tone
Of voices, and of melodies, and of silvery laughter gone.

But are we free to do even thus — to wander as we will,
Bearing sad visions through the grove, and o'er the breezy
    hill?
No! in our daily paths lie cares, that ofttimes bind us fast,
While from their narrow round we see the golden day fleet
    past.

They hold us from the woodlark's haunts, and violet dingles,
    back,
And from all the lovely sounds and gleams in the shining
    river's track;
They bar us from our heritage of spring-time, hope, and
    mirth,
And weigh our burden'd spirits down with the cumbering dust
    of earth.

Yet should this be? Too much, too soon, despondingly we
 yield!
A better lesson we are taught by the lilies of the field!
A sweeter by the birds of heaven — which tell us, in their
 flight,
Of One that through the desert air for ever guides them right.

Shall not this knowledge calm our hearts, and bid vain conflicts cease?
Ay, when they commune with themselves in holy hours of
 peace
And feel that by the lights and clouds through which our
 pathway lies,
By the beauty and the grief alike, we are training for the
 skies!

LAST RITES.

By the mighty minster's bell,
Tolling with a sudden swell;
By the colours half-mast high,
O'er the sea hung mournfully;
    Know, a prince hath died!

By the drum's dull muffled sound,
By the arms that sweep the ground,
By the volleying muskets' tone,
Speak ye of a soldier gone
    In his manhood's pride.

LAST RITES.

By the chanted psalm that fills
Reverently the ancient hills,*
Learn, that from his harvests done,
Peasants bear a brother on
    To his last repose.

By the pall of snowy white
Through the yew-trees gleaming bright;
By the garland on the bier,
Weep! a maiden claims thy tear —
    Broken is the rose!

Which is the tenderest rite of all? —
Buried virgin's coronal,
Requiem o'er the monarch's head,
Farewell gun for warrior dead,
    Herdsman's funeral hymn?

Tells not each of human woe?
Each of hope and strength brought low?
Number each with holy things,
If one chastening thought it brings
    Ere life's day grow dim!

---

* A custom still retained at rural funerals in some parts of England and Wales.

SONGS FOR SUMMER HOURS.

AND I TOO IN ARCADIA.

[A celebrated picture of Poussin represents a band of shepherd-youths and maidens suddenly checked in their wanderings, and affected with various emotions, by the sight of a tomb which bears this inscription — "*Et in Arcadia ego.*"]

They have wander'd in their glee
With the butterfly and bee;
They have climb'd o'er heathery swells,
They have wound through forest dells;
Mountain-moss hath felt their tread,
Woodland streams their way have led;
Flowers, in deepest shadowy nooks,
Nurslings of the loneliest brooks,
Unto them have yielded up
Fragrant bell and starry cup:
Chaplets are on every brow —
What hath staid the wanderers now?
Lo! a gray and rustic tomb,
Bower'd amidst the rich wood-gloom;
Whence these words their stricken spirits melt,
— "I too, Shepherds! in Arcadia dwelt."

There is many a summer sound
That pale sepulchre around;
Through the shade young birds are glancing,
Insect-wings in sun-streaks dancing;

Glimpses of blue festal skies
Pouring in when soft winds rise;
Violets o'er the turf below
Shedding out their warmest glow;
Yet a spirit not its own
O'er the greenwood now is thrown!
Something of an under-note
Through its music seems to float,
Something of a stillness gray
Creeps across the laughing day:
Something dimly from those old words felt,
— "I too, Shepherds! in Arcadia dwelt."

Was some gentle kindred maid
In that grave with dirges laid?
Some fair creature, with the tone
Of whose voice a joy is gone,
Leaving melody and mirth
Poorer on this alter'd earth?
Is it thus? that so they stand,
Dropping flowers from every hand —
Flowers, and lyres, and gather'd store
Of red wild-fruit prized no more?
— No! from that bright band of morn
Not one link hath yet been torn:
'Tis the shadow of the tomb
Falling o'er the summer-bloom —
O'er the flush of love and life
Passing with a sudden strife;
'Tis the low prophetic breath
Murmuring from that house of death,
Whose faint whisper thus their hearts can melt,
— "I too, Shepherds! in Arcadia dwelt."

THE WANDERING WIND.

The Wind, the wandering Wind
  Of the golden summer eves —
Whence is the thrilling magic
  Of its tones among the leaves?
Oh! is it from the waters,
  Or from the long tall grass?
Or is it from the hollow rocks
  Through which its breathings pass?

Or is it from the voices
  Of all in one combined,
That it wins the tone of mastery?
  The Wind, the wandering Wind!
No, no! the strange, sweet accents
  That with it come and go,
They are not from the osiers,
  Nor the fir-trees whispering low;

They are not of the waters,
  Nor of the cavern'd hill:
'Tis the human love within us
  That gives them power to thrill.
They touch the links of memory
  Around our spirits twined,
And we start, and weep, and tremble,
  To the Wind, the wandering Wind!

YE ARE NOT MISS'D, FAIR FLOWERS!

Ye are not miss'd, fair flowers, that late were spreading
  The summer's glow by fount and breezy grot;
There falls the dew, its fairy favours shedding —
  The leaves dance on, the young birds miss you not.

Still plays the sparkle o'er the rippling water,
  O lily! whence thy cup of pearl is gone;
The bright wave mourns not for its loveliest daughter,
  There is no sorrow in the wind's low tone.

And thou, meek hyacinth! afar is roving
  The bee that oft thy trembling bells hath kiss'd.
Cradled ye were, fair flowers! 'midst all things loving,
  A joy to all — yet, yet, ye are not miss'd!

Ye, that were born to lend the sunbeam gladness,
  And the winds fragrance, wandering where they list,
Oh! it were breathing words too deep in sadness,
  To say earth's *human* flowers not more are miss'd.

THE WILLOW SONG.

Willow! in thy breezy moan,
I can hear a deeper tone;
Through thy leaves come whispering low
Faint, sweet sounds of long ago.
    Willow, sighing willow!

Many a mournful tale of old
Heart-sick love to thee hath told,

Gathering from thy golden bough
Leaves to cool his burning brow.
    Willow! sighing willow!

Many a swan-like song to thee
Hath been sung, thou gentle tree!
Many a lute its last lament
Down thy moonlight stream hath sent.
    Willow! sighing willow!

Therefore, wave and murmur on!
Sigh for sweet affections gone,
And for tuneful voices fled,
And for love, whose heart hath bled,
    Ever, willow! willow!

LEAVE ME NOT YET.

Leave me not yet! through rosy skies from far,
  But now the song-birds to their nests return;
The quivering image of the first pale star
  On the dim lake scarce yet begins to burn:
    Leave me not yet!

Not yet! oh, hark! low tones from hidden streams,
  Piercing the shivery leaves, even now arise;
Their voices mingle not with daylight dreams,
  They are of vesper's hymns and harmonies:
    Leave me not yet!

My thoughts are like those gentle sounds, dear love!
  By day shut up in their own still recess;
They wait for dews on earth, for stars above,
  Then to breathe out their soul of tenderness:
    Leave me not yet?

THE ORANGE BOUGH.

Oh! bring me one sweet orange-bough,
To fan my cheek, to cool my brow;
One bough, with pearly blossoms drest,
And bind it, mother! on my breast!

Go, seek the grove along the shore,
Whose odours I must breathe no more;
The grove where every scented tree
Thrills to the deep voice of the sea.

Oh! Love's fond sighs, and fervent prayer,
And wild farewell, are lingering there:
Each leaf's light whisper hath a tone
My faint heart, even in death, would own.

Then bear me thence one bough, to shed
Life's parting sweetness round my head;
And bind it, mother! on my breast
When I am laid in lonely rest.

THE STREAM SET FREE.

Flow on, rejoice, make music,
  Bright living stream set free!
The troubled haunts of care and strife
  Were not for thee!

The woodland is thy country,
  Thou art all its own again;
The wild birds are thy kindred race,
  That fear no chain.

Flow on, rejoice, make music
  Unto the glistening leaves!
Thou, the beloved of balmy winds
  And golden eaves!

Once more the holy starlight
  Sleeps calm upon thy breast,
Whose brightness bears no token more
  Of man's unrest.

Flow, and let freeborn music
  Flow with thy wavy line,
While the stock-dove's lingering, loving voice
  Comes blent with thine.

And the green reeds quivering o'er thee,
  Strings of the forest-lyre,
All fill'd with answering spirit-sounds,
  In joy respire.

Yet, midst thy song's glad changes,
  Oh! keep one pitying tone
For gentle hearts, that bear to thee
  Their sadness lone.

One sound, of all the deepest,
  To bring, like healing dew,
A sense that nature ne'er forsakes
  The meek and true.

Then, then, rejoice, make music,
  Thou stream, thou glad and free!
The shadows of all glorious flowers
  Be set in thee!

THE SUMMER'S CALL

Come away! The sunny hours
Woo thee far to founts and bowers!
O'er the very waters now,
  In their play,
Flowers are shedding beauty's glow —
  Come away!
Where the lily's tender gleam
Quivers on the glancing stream,
  Come away!

All the air is fill'd with sound,
Soft, and sultry, and profound;
Murmurs through the shadowy grass
  Lightly stray;
Faint winds whisper as they pass
  Come away!
Where the bee's deep music swells
From the trembling foxglove bells,
  Come away!

In the skies the sapphire blue
Now hath won its richest hue;
In the woods the breath of song
  Night and day
Floats with leafy scents along —
  Come away!
Where the boughs with dewy gloom
Darken each thick bed of bloom,
  Come away!

In the deep heart of the rose
Now the crimson love-hue glows;

Now the glow-worm's lamp by night
    Sheds a ray,
Dreamy, starry, greenly bright —
    Come away!
Where the fairy cup-moss lies,
With the wild-wood strawberries,
    Come away!

Now each tree by summer crown'd,
Sheds its own rich twilight round;
Glancing there from sun to shade,
    Bright wings play;
There the deer its couch hath made —
    Come away!
Where the smooth leaves of the lime
Glisten in their honey-time,
    Come away — away!

OH! SKYLARK, FOR THY WING.

Oh! Skylark, for thy wing!
    Thou bird of joy and light,
That I might soar and sing
    At heaven's empyreal height!
With the heathery hills beneath me,
    Whence the streams in glory spring,
And the pearly clouds to wreathe me,
    O Skylark! on thy wing!

Free, free, from earth-born fear,
    I would range the blessed skies,

Through the blue divinely clear,
  Where the low mists cannot rise!
And a thousand joyous measures
  From my chainless heart should spring,
Like the bright rain's vernal treasures,
  As I wander'd on thy wing.

But oh! the silver cords
  That around the heart are spun,
From gentle tones and words,
  And kind eyes that make our sun!
To some low, sweet nest returning,
  How soon my love would bring
There, *there* the dews of morning,
  O Skylark! on thy wing!

MISCELLANEOUS POEMS.

THE TWO MONUMENTS.*

*"Oh! bless'd are they who live and die like 'him,'
Loved with such love, and with such sorrow mourn'd!"*
                                            WORDSWORTH.

BANNERS hung drooping from on high
  In a dim cathedral's nave,
Making a gorgeous canopy
  O'er a noble, noble grave!

And a marble warrior's form beneath,
  With helm and crest array'd,
As on his battle-bed of death,
  Lay in their crimson shade.

Triumph yet linger'd in his eye,
  Ere by the dark night seal'd;
And his head was pillow'd haughtily
  On standard and on shield.

And shadowing that proud trophy-pile,
  With the glory of his wing,
An eagle sat — yet seem'd the while
  Panting through heaven to spring.

---

* Suggested by a passage in Captain Sherer's "Notes and Reflections during a Ramble in Germany."

THE TWO MONUMENTS.

He sat upon a shiver'd lance,
   There by the sculptor bound;
But in the light of his lifted glance
   Was *that* which scorn'd the ground.

And a burning flood of gem-like hues,
   From a storied window pour'd,
There fell, there centred, to suffuse
   The conqueror and his sword.

A flood of hues — but *one* rich dye
   O'er all supremely spread,
With a purple robe of royalty
   Mantling the mighty dead.

Meet was that robe for *him* whose name
   Was a trumpet-note in war,
His pathway still the march of fame,
   His eye the battle-star.

But faintly, tenderly was thrown,
   From the colour'd light, one ray,
Where a low and pale memorial-stone
   By the couch of glory lay.

Few were the fond words chisell'd *there*,
   Mourning for parted worth;
But the very heart of love and prayer
   Had given their sweetness forth.

They spoke of one whose life had been
   As a hidden streamlet's course,
Bearing on health and joy unseen
   From its clear mountain-source:

Whose young, pure memory, lying deep
  Midst rock, and wood, and hill,
Dwelt in the homes where poor men sleep,*
  A soft light, meek and still:

Whose gentle voice, too early call'd
  Unto Music's land away,
Had won for God the earth's, enthrall'd
  By words of silvery sway.

These were *his* victories — yet, enroll'd
  In no high song of fame,
The pastor of the mountain-fold
  Left but to heaven his name.

To heaven, and to the peasant's hearth,
  A blessed household-sound;
And finding lowly love on earth,
  Enough, enough, he found!

Bright and more bright before me gleam'd
  That sainted image still,
Till one sweet moonlight memory seem'd
  The regal fane to fill.

Oh! how my silent spirit turn'd
  From those proud trophies nigh!
How my full heart within me burn'd
  Like *Him* to live and die!

---

* "Love had he seen in huts where poor men lie."   WORDSWORTH.

A THOUGHT OF PARADISE.

> "We receive but what we give,
> And in our life alone does nature live;
> Ours is her wedding-garment, ours her shroud;
> And, would we aught behold of higher worth
> Than that inanimate, cold world allow'd
> To the poor, loveless, ever-anxious crowd,
> Ah! from the soul itself must issue forth
> A light, a glory, a fair luminous cloud,
>   Enveloping the earth;
> And from the soul itself must there be sent
> A sweet and potent voice of its own birth,
> Of all sweet sounds the life and element." — COLERIDGE.

GREEN spot of holy ground!
If thou couldst yet be found,
Far in deep woods, with all thy starry flowers;
If not one sullying breath
Of time, or change, or death,
Had touch'd the vernal glory of thy bowers;

Might our tired pilgrim-feet,
Worn by the desert's heat,
On the bright freshness of thy turf repose?
Might our eyes wander there
Through heaven's transparent air,
And rest on colours of the immortal rose?

Say, would thy balmy skies
And fountain-melodies

Our heritage of lost delight restore?
　　Could thy soft honey-dews
　　Through all our veins diffuse
The early, child-like, trustful sleep once more?

　　And might we, in the shade
　　By thy tall cedars made,
With angel-voices high communion hold?
　　Would their sweet, solemn tone
　　Give back the music gone,
Our Being's harmony, so jarr'd of old?

　　Oh no! — thy sunny hours
　　Might come with blossom-showers,
All thy young leaves to spirit-lyres might thrill;
　　But *we* — should we not bring
　　Into thy realms of spring
The shadows of our souls to haunt us still?

　　What could *thy* flowers and airs
　　Do for our earth-born cares?
Would the world's chain melt off and leave us free?
　　No! — past each living stream,
　　Still would some fever-dream
Track the lorn wanderers, meet no more for thee!

　　Should we not shrink with fear
　　If angel-steps were near,
Feeling our burden'd souls within us die?
　　How might our passions brook
　　The still and searching look,
The starlike glance of seraph purity?

  Thy golden-fruited grove
  Was not for pining love;
Vain sadness would but dim thy crystal skies!
  Oh! *thou* wert but a part
  Of what man's exiled heart
Hath lost — the dower of *inborn* Paradise!

COMMUNINGS WITH THOUGHT.

"Could we but keep our spirits to that height,
We might be happy; but this clay will sink
Its spark immortal." — BYRON.

  RETURN, my thoughts — come home!
Ye wild and wing'd! what do ye o'er the deep?
And wherefore thus the abyss of time o'ersweep,
  As birds the ocean-foam?

  Swifter than shooting-star,
Swifter than lances of the northern-light,
Upspringing through the purple heaven of night,
  Hath been your course afar!

  Through the bright battle-clime,
Where laurel boughs make dim the Grecian streams,
And reeds are whispering of heroic themes,
  By temples of old time:

  Through the north's ancient halls,
Where banners thrill'd of yore — where harp-strings rung;
But grass waves now o'er those that fought and sung,
  Hearth-light hath left their walls!

Through forests old and dim,
Where o'er the leaves dread magic seems to brood;
And sometimes on the haunted solitude
   Rises the pilgrim's hymn:

   Or where some fountain lies,
With lotus-cups through orient spice-woods gleaming!
There have ye been, ye wanderers! idly dreaming
   Of man's lost paradise!

   Return, my thoughts — return!
Cares wait your presence in life's daily track,
And voices, not of music, call you back —
   Harsh voices, cold and stern!

   Oh, no! return ye not!
Still farther, loftier, let your soarings be!
Go, bring me strength from journeyings bright and free,
   O'er many a haunted spot.

   Go! seek the martyr's grave,
Midst the old mountains, and the deserts vast;
Or, through the ruin'd cities of the past,
   Follow the wise and brave!

   Go! visit cell and shrine,
Where woman hath endured! — thro' wrong, thro' scorn,
Uncheer'd by fame, yet silently upborne
   By promptings more divine!

   Go, shoot the gulf of death!
Track the pure spirit where no chain can bind,

Where the heart's boundless love its rest may find,
  Where the storm sends no breath!

  Higher, and yet more high!
Shake off the cumbering chain which earth would lay
On your victorious wings — mount, mount! Your way
  Is through eternity!

TO THE BLUE ANEMONE.

Flower of starry clearness bright!
Quivering urn of colour'd light!
Hast thou drawn thy cup's rich dye
From the intenseness of the sky?
From a long, long fervent gaze
Through the year's first golden days,
Up that blue and silent deep,
Where, like things of sculptured sleep,
Alabaster clouds repose,
With the sunshine on their snows?
Thither was thy heart's love turning,
Like a censer ever burning
Till the purple heavens in thee
Set their smile, Anemone?

Or can those warm tints be caught
Each from some quick glow of thought?
So much of bright *soul* there seems
In thy bendings and thy gleams,

So much thy sweet life resembles
That which feels, and weeps, and trembles,
I could deem thee spirit-fill'd,
As a reed by music thrill'd,
When thy being I behold
To each loving breath unfold,
Or, like woman's willowy form,
Shrink before the gathering storm!
I could ask a *voice* from thee,
Delicate Anemone!

Flower! thou seem'st not born to die
With thy radiant purity,
But to melt in air away,
Mingling with the soft Spring-day,
When the crystal heavens are still,
And faint azure veils each hill,
And the lime-leaf doth not move,
Save to songs that stir the grove,
And earth all glorified is seen,
As imaged in some lake serene;
— Then thy vanishing should be,
Pure and meek Anemone!

Flower! the laurel still may shed
Brightness round the victor's head;
And the rose in beauty's hair
Still its festal glory wear;
And the willow-leaves drop o'er
Brows which love sustains no more:
But by living rays refined,
Thou, the trembler of the wind,

TO THE BLUE ANEMONE.

Thou the spiritual flower,
Sentient of each breeze and shower,
Thou, rejoicing in the skies,
And transpierced with all their dyes;
Breathing vase, with light o'erflowing,
Gem-like to thy centre glowing,
Thou the poet's type shalt be,
Flower of soul, Anemone!

SONNETS.

THE RETURN TO POETRY.

Once more the eternal melodies from far
Woo me like songs of home: once more discerning,
Through fitful clouds, the pure majestic star
Above the poet's world serenely burning,
'Thither my soul, fresh-wing'd by love, is turning,
As o'er the waves the wood-bird seeks her nest,
For those green heights of dewy stillness yearning,
Whence glorious minds o'erlook this earth's unrest.
Now be the Spirit of heaven's truth my guide
'Through the bright land! — that no brief gladness, found
In passing bloom, rich odour, or sweet sound,
May lure my footsteps from their aim aside:
Their true, high quest — to seek, if ne'er to gain,
The inmost, purest shrine of that august domain.

DESIGN AND PERFORMANCE.

They float before my soul, the fair designs
Which I would body forth to life and power,
Like clouds, that with their wavering hues and lines
Portray majestic buildings: — dome and tower,

Bright spire, that through the rainbow and the shower
Points to th' unchanging stars; and high arcade,
Far-sweeping to some glorious altar, made
For holiest rites. Meanwhile the waning hour
Melts from me, and by fervent dreams o'erwrought,
I sink. O friend! O link'd with each high thought!
Aid me, of those rich visions to detain
All I may grasp; until thou see'st fulfill'd,
While time and strength allow, my hope to build
For lowly hearts devout, but *one* enduring fane!

MEMORIAL OF A CONVERSATION.

YES! all things tell us of a birthright lost —
A brightness from our nature pass'd away!
Wanderers we seem that from an alien coast
Would turn to where their Father's mansion lay;
And but by some lone flower, that midst decay
Smiles mournfully, or by some sculptured stone,
Revealing dimly, with gray moss o'ergrown,
The faint, worn impress of its glory's day,
Can trace their once free heritage, though dreams,
Fraught with its picture, oft in startling gleams
Flash o'er their souls. But One, oh! *One* alone,
For us the ruin'd fabric may rebuild,
And bid the wilderness again be fill'd
With Eden-flowers — One mighty to atone!

A THOUGHT AT SUNSET.

STILL that last look is solemn! though thy rays,
O sun! to-morrow will give back, we know,
The joy to nature's heart. Yet through the glow
Of clouds that mantle thy decline, our gaze
Tracks thee with love half-fearful: and in days
When earth too much adored thee, what a swell
Of mournful passion, deepening mighty lays,
Told how the dying bade thy light farewell,
O sun of Greece! O glorious, festal sun!
Lost, lost! — for them thy golden hours were done,
And darkness lay before them! Happier far
Are we, not thus to thy bright wheels enchain'd,
Not thus for thy last parting unsustain'd —
Heirs of a purer day, with its unsetting star.

A HAPPY HOUR.

OH! what a joy to feel that, in my breast,
The founts of childhood's vernal fancies lay
Still pure, though heavily and long repress'd
By early-blighted leaves, which o'er their way
Dark summer-storms had heaped. But free, glad play
Once more was given them: to the sunshine's glow,
And the sweet wood-song's penetrating flow,
And to the wandering primrose-breath of May,

And the rich hawthorn-odours, forth they sprung.
Oh! not less freshly bright, that now a thought
Of spiritual presence o'er them hung,
And of immortal life! a germ, unwrought
In childhood's soul to power — now strong, serene,
And full of love and light, colouring the whole blest scene.

A PRAYER.

Father in heaven! from whom the simplest flower,
On the high Alps or fiery desert thrown,
Draws not sweet odour or young life alone,
But the deep virtue of an inborn power,
To cheer the wanderer in his fainting hour
With thoughts of Thee — to strengthen, to infuse
Faith, love, and courage, by the tender hues
That speak thy presence! oh, with such a dower
Grace thou my song! — the precious gift bestow
From thy pure Spirit's treasury divine,
To wake one tear of purifying flow,
To soften one wrung heart for thee and thine;
So shall the life breathed through the lowly strain
Be as the meek wild-flower's — if transient, yet not vain.

PRAYER CONTINUED.

*"What in me is dark,
Illumine; what is low, raise and support." — MILTON.*

Far are the wings of intellect astray
That strive not, Father! to thy heavenly seat;
They rove, but mount not, and the tempests beat
Still on their plumes. O Source of mental day!
Chase from before my spirit's track the array
Of mists and shadows, raised by earthly care,
In troubled hosts that cross the purer air,
And veil the opening of the starry way,
Which brightens on to thee! Oh, guide thou right
My thought's weak pinion; clear my inward sight,
The eternal springs of beauty to discern,
Welling beside thy throne; unseal mine ear,
Nature's true oracles in joy to hear;
Keep my soul wakeful still to listen and to learn.

HOPE OF FUTURE COMMUNION WITH NATURE.

If e'er again my spirit be allow'd
Converse with Nature in her chambers deep,
Where lone, and mantled with the rolling cloud,
She broods o'er new-born waters, as they leap

SONNETS.

In sword-like flashes down the heathery steep
From caves of mystery; — if I roam once more
Where dark pines quiver to the torrent's roar,
And voiceful oaks respond; — may I not reap
A more ennobling joy, a loftier power,
Than e'er was shed on life's more vernal hour
From such communion? Yes! I then shall know
That not in vain have sorrow, love, and thought
Their long, still work of preparation wrought,
For that more perfect sense of God reveal'd below.

DESPONDENCY AND ASPIRATION.

> "Pàr correr miglior acqua alza le vele,
> Omai la navicella del mio Ingenio." — DANTE.

My soul was mantled with dark shadows, born
    Of lonely Fear, disquieted in vain;
Its phantoms hung around the star of morn,
    A cloud-like, weeping train:
'Thro' the long day they dimm'd the autumn gold
On all the glistening leaves, and wildly roll'd,
    When the last farewell flush of light was glowing
        Across the sunset sky,
    O'er its rich isles of vaporous glory throwing
        One melancholy dye.

    And when the solemn night
    Came rushing with her might
Of stormy oracles from caves unknown,
    Then with each fitful blast
    Prophetic murmurs pass'd,
Wakening or answering some deep Sybil-tone
Far buried in my breast, yet prompt to rise
With every gusty wail that o'er the wind-harp flies.

"Fold, fold thy wings," they cried, "and strive no more —
Faint spirit! strive no more: for thee too strong
    Are outward ill and wrong,
And inward wasting fires! Thou canst not soar

  Free on a starry way,
  Beyond their blighting sway,
At heaven's high gate serenely to adore!
How shouldst *thou* hope earth's fetters to unbind?
O passionate, yet weak! O trembler to the wind!

"Never shall aught but broken music flow
From joy of thine, deep love, or tearful woe —
Such homeless notes as through the forest sigh,
  From the reeds' hollow shaken,
  When sudden breezes waken
   Their vague, wild symphony.
No power is theirs, and no abiding-place
In human hearts; their sweetness leaves no trace —
  Born only so to die!

"Never shall aught but perfume, faint and vain,
 On the fleet pinion of the changeful hour,
  From thy bruised life again
   A moment's essence breathe;
 Thy life, whose trampled flower
  Into the blessed wreath
Of household-charities no longer bound,
Lies pale and withering on the barren ground.

"So fade, fade on! Thy gift of love shall cling
 A coiling sadness round thy heart and brain —
A silent, fruitless, yet undying thing,
  All sensitive to pain!
And still the shadow of vain dreams shall fall
O'er thy mind's world, a daily darkening pall.
Fold, then, thy wounded wing, and sink subdued
In cold and unrepining quietude!"

Mrs. Hemans.

Then my soul yielded: spells of numbing breath
Crept o'er it heavy with a dew of death —
Its powers, like leaves before the night-rain, closing;
  And, as by conflict of wild sea-waves toss'd
  On the chill bosom of some desert coast,
Mutely and hopelessly I lay reposing.

    When silently it seem'd
    As if a soft mist gleam'd
Before my passive sight, and, slowly curling,
    To many a shape and hue
    Of vision'd beauty grew,
Like a wrought banner, fold by fold unfurling.
Oh! the rich scenes that o'er mine inward eye
    Unrolling then swept by
With dreamy motion! Silvery seas were there,
  Lit by large dazzling stars, and arch'd by skies
  Of southern midnight's most transparent dyes;
And gemm'd with many an island, wildly fair,
Which floated past me into orient day,
Still gathering lustre on th' illumin'd way,
'Till its high groves of wondrous flowering-trees
    Colour'd the silvery seas.

And then a glorious mountain-chain uprose,
    Height above spiry height!
A soaring solitude of woods and snows,
    All steep'd in golden light!
While as it pass'd, those regal peaks unveiling,
  I heard, methought, a waving of dread wings,
And mighty sounds, as if the vision hailing,
  From lyres that quiver'd through ten thousand strings —

Or as if waters, forth to music leaping
   From many a cave, the Alpine Echo's hall,
On their bold way victoriously were sweeping,
   Link'd in majestic anthems — while through all
      That billowy swell and fall,
Voices, like ringing crystal, fill'd the air
   With inarticulate melody, that stirr'd
My being's core; then, moulding into word
Their piercing sweetness, bade me rise, and bear
In that great choral strain my trembling part,
Of tones by love and faith struck from a human heart.

Return no more, vain bodings of the night!
   A happier oracle within my soul
Hath swell'd to power; a clear, unwavering light
   Mounts through the battling clouds that round me roll;
      And to a new control
Nature's full harp gives forth rejoicing tones,
   Wherein my glad sense owns
The accordant rush of elemental sound
To one consummate harmony profound —
      One grand Creation-Hymn,
      Whose notes the seraphim
Lift to the glorious height of music wing'd and crown'd.

   Shall not those notes find echoes in my lyre,
Faithful though faint? Shall not my spirit's fire,
If slowly, yet unswervingly, ascend
      Now to its fount and end?
   Shall not my earthly love, all purified,
      Shine forth a heavenward guide.

An augel of bright power — and strongly bear
My being upward into holier air,
Where fiery passion-clouds have no abode,
And the sky's temple-arch o'erflows with God!

    The radiant hope new-born
    Expands like rising morn
In my life's life: and as a ripening rose
The crimson shadow of its glory throws
More vivid, hour by hour, on some pure stream;
    So from that hope are spreading
    Rich hues, o'er nature shedding
Each day a clearer, spiritual gleam.

Let not those rays fade from me! — once enjoy'd,
    Father of Spirits! let them not depart —
Leaving the chill'd earth, without form and void,
    Darken'd by mine own heart!
Lift, aid, sustain me! Thou, by whom alone
    All lovely gifts and pure
    In the soul's grasp endure;
Thou, to the steps of whose eternal throne
All knowledge flows — a sea for evermore
Breaking its crested waves on that sole shore —
Oh, consecrate my life! that I may sing
Of thee with joy that hath a living spring,
In a full heart of music! Let my lays
Through the resounding mountains waft thy praise,
And with that theme the wood's green cloisters fill,
And make their quivering, leafy dimness thrill
To the rich breeze of song! Oh! let me wake
    The deep religion, which hath dwelt from yore

DESPONDENCY AND ASPIRATION.

Silently brooding by lone cliff and lake,
    And wildest river-shore!
And let me summon all the voices dwelling
Where eagles build, and cavern'd rills are welling,
And where the cataract's organ-peal is swelling,
    In that one spirit gather'd to adore!

Forgive, O Father! if presumptuous though
    Too daringly in aspiration rise!
Let not thy child all vainly have been taught
    By weakness, and by wanderings, and by sighs
Of sad confession! Lowly be my heart,
    And on its penitential altar spread
The offerings worthless, till thy grace impart
    The fire from heaven, whose touch alone can shed
Life, radiance, virtue! — let that vital spark
Pierce my whole being, wilder'd else and dark!

Thine are all holy things — oh, make *me* thine!
So shall I, too, be pure — a living shrine
Unto that Spirit which goes forth from thee,
    Strong and divinely free,
Bearing thy gifts of wisdom on its flight,
And brooding o'er them with a dove-like wing,
Till thought, word, song, to thee in worship spring,
Immortally endow'd for liberty and light.

[This exquisite poem was composed during the Author's last illness; and the following account of her situation at the time, from the pen of her sister, cannot fail to be read with a deep and painful interest. It is another forcible, visible illustration of "the ruling passion strong in death." Happy, as in her case, when the direction of the mind is towards all that is high, pure, and excellent!

"A shuddering thrill pervaded her whole frame, and she felt, as she often afterwards declared, a presentiment that from that moment her hours were numbered. The same evening she was attacked by a fit of ague; and this insidious and harassing complaint continued its visitations for several weeks, reducing her poor, wasted form to the most lamentable state of debility, and at length retiring only to make way for a train of symptoms still more fatal and distressing. Yet, while the work of decay was going on thus surely and progressively upon the earthly tabernacle, the bright flame within continued to burn with a pure and holy light, and, at times, even to flash forth with more than wonted brightness. The lyric of 'Despondency and Aspiration,' which may be considered as her noblest and highest effort, and in which, from a feeling that it might be her last work, she felt anxious to concentrate all her powers, was written during the few intervals accorded her from acute suffering or powerless languor."]

THE END.

www.ingramcontent.com/pod-product-compliance
Lightning Source LLC
Chambersburg PA
CBHW030312240426
43673CB00040B/1140